BULLET PROOF

LANCE CORPORAL MATT CROUCHER grew up in the Midlands and joined the Royal Marines aged 16, passing through the legendary 30-week training programme and into 40 Commando despite a series of injuries. He served two tours with the Marines in Iraq before transferring into the Royal Marines Reserves and returning to Iraq as a private security contractor with the United Nations. He re-joined 40 Commando for the ultimate challenge of a tour of duty in war-torn Afghanistan in September 2007.

D0473970

MATT CROUCHER GC
BULLET PROOF

with Robert Jobson

arrow books

Published in the United Kingdom by Arrow Books in 2010

3 5 7 9 10 8 6 4 2

First published in the United Kingdom in 2009 by Century

Arrow Books
The Random House Group Limited
20 Vauxhall Bridge Road, London, SW1V 2SA

Addresses for companies within The Random House Group Limited can be found at:
www.randomhouse.co.uk/offices.htm

The Random House Group Limited Reg. No. 954009

www.rbooks.co.uk

A CIP catalogue record for this book
is available from the British Library

ISBN 9780099543084

The Random House Group Limited supports The Forest Stewardship
Council (FSC), the leading international forest certification organisation.
All our titles that are printed on Greenpeace approved FSC certified paper
carry the FSC logo. Our paper procurement policy can be found at
www.rbooks.co.uk/environment

Typeset by SX Composing DTP, Rayleigh, Essex
Printed and bound in Great Britain by
CPI Bookmarque, Croydon, CR0 4TD

CONTENTS

The legacy of heroes is the memory of a great name and the inheritance of a great example.
——*Benjamin Disraeli*

This book is dedicated to the memory of all those in 40 Commando Group who didn't make it back

Acknowledgements

I thought long and hard about writing this book. I decided in the end to do it because I wanted to tell people about what it is really like on the front line. This is a story that needs to be told, not because of what I have achieved personally, but because of what every serviceman and servicewoman has endured in the line of duty. The front line is a harsh place and this book is for everyone who has been there.

I could not have written this book without the dedication, support, friendship and patience of Robert Jobson, who aided me every step of the way. I must also thank my publisher Tim Andrews and the rest of the editorial team at Random House. Also my brilliant agent Humfrey Hunter for helping make this project a reality. And to Matt Nixson for his help and friendship.

Thanks to Steve, my business partner at Pinnacle Risk Management.

Of course I could not have done any of this without the love, understanding and support of my mum, Margaret, and my dad, Richard, my sister, Claire, and the rest of my wonderful family. I love you all dearly.

Last but certainly not least, this book is written with the men of the Royal Marines in mind. Their dedication and professionalism have no equal. I would particularly like to thank the lads I fought alongside: Shorty, Foxy, Gaz, Ads, Dave, Scottie. Well played, lads.

MATT CROUCHER GC

Land Forces
Orders of Battle

OPERATION TELIC

GOC 1st Armoured Division – Major General Robin Brims
(succeeded by Major General Peter Wall)
1st Armoured Division Headquarters and Signal Regiment
1st The Queen's Dragoon Guards
Joint Chemical, Biological, Radiation and Nuclear Regiment
1st Battalion, The Duke of Wellington's Regiment (West Riding)
28 Regiment Royal Engineers
1 General Support Regiment, Royal Logistic Corps
2 Close Support Regiment, Royal Logistic Corps
2nd Battalion, Royal Electrical and Mechanical Engineers
1 Close Support Medical Regiment
5 General Support Medical Regiment
1 Regiment Royal Military Police
A (Royal Wiltshire Yeomanry) Squadron and W (Westminster
Dragoons) Squadron, Royal Yeomanry
Elements of 5 (STA) Royal Regiment of Artillery
Elements of 33 (EOD) Regiment Royal Engineers

Elements of 32 Regiment Royal Artillery – Phoenix Unmanned
  Aerial Vehicles
Elements of 30 Signal Regiment
Elements of 14 Signal Regiment
3 Commando Brigade – Brigadier Jim Dutton
Headquarters 3 Commando Brigade
59 Independent (Commando) Squadron Royal Engineers
131 Independent (Commando) Squadron Royal Engineers
  (Volunteer)
9 (Commando) Assault Squadron
531 (Commando) Assault Squadron
29 (Commando) Regiment Royal Artillery – 18 105 mm howitzers
40 Commando, Royal Marines
42 Commando, Royal Marines
7 Armoured Brigade – Brigadier Graham Binns
7 Armoured Brigade Headquarters and Signal Squadron
32 (Armoured) Regiment Royal Engineers
3rd Regiment Royal Horse Artillery – 32 AS-90 155 mm howitzers
Royal Scots Dragoon Guards (Carabiniers and Greys)
  battlegroup, including elements of 1st Battalion Irish Guards –
  42 Challenger 2s, 28 Warrior Tracked Armoured Vehicles
  (Warriors)
2nd Royal Tank Regiment battlegroup, including elements of 1st
  Battalion The Light Infantry – 42 Challenger 2s, 28 Warriors
The Black Watch (Royal Highland Regiment) battlegroup,
  including elements of The Royal Scots Dragoon Guards and
  2nd Royal Tank Regiment – 28 Challenger 2s, 42 Warriors
1st Battalion Royal Regiment of Fusiliers battlegroup, including
  elements of Queen's Royal Lancers – 14 Challenger 2s, 42
  Warriors
16 Air Assault Brigade – Brigadier 'Jacko' Page
16 Air Assault Brigade Headquarters
216 Parachute Squadron Royal Signals
Pathfinder Platoon
1st Battalion, The Parachute Regiment

3rd Battalion, The Parachute Regiment
7th Parachute Regiment Royal Horse Artillery
9 Parachute Squadron Royal Engineers
23 (Air Assault) Engineer Regiment
D Squadron, Household Cavalry Regiment
7 Air Assault Battalion Royal Electrical and Mechanical Engineers
13 Air Assault Support Regiment Royal Logistics Corps
16 Close Support Medical Regiment
156 Provost Company Royal Military Police
1st Battalion, Royal Irish Regiment (27th [Inniskillings], 83rd,
     87th and Ulster Defence Regiment)

OPERATION HERRICK VII

HQ 52 Infantry Brigade
The Household Cavalry Regiment – 1 squadron
40 Commando, Royal Marines
1st Battalion, Coldstream Guards
2nd Battalion, The Yorkshire Regiment (14th/15th, 19th and
     33rd/76th Foot) (Green Howards)
1st Battalion, The Royal Gurkha Rifles
4th Regiment Royal Artillery
32nd Regiment Royal Artillery – 1 battery of UAVs
39th Regiment Royal Artillery – 1 troop of MLRS
36 Regiment, Royal Engineers
27 Transport Regiment, Royal Logistic Corps
5 General Support Medical Regiment
1st Battalion, Royal Electrical and Mechanical Engineers

3 Commando Brigade Structure

The Royal Marines of 3 Commando Brigade are one of the elite units in the British armed forces, along with the SAS, SBS, SFSG and 16 Air Assault Brigade. The Marines consist of three Commando units: **40 Commando**, based at Norton Manor Barracks in Taunton, Somerset; **42 Commando**, situated at Bickleigh Barracks, Plymouth, Devon; and **45 Commando**, based at Condor Barracks, Arbroath, Angus, Scotland.

Commando Unit Structure
1 Command Company:
Main HQ
Tactical HQ
Reconnaissance Troop
Signals Troop
Mortar Troop
Anti-Tank (AT) Troop
Medium Machine Gun Troop

1 Logistic Company:
A Echelon 1 (A Ech1)
A Echelon 2 (A Ech2)

FRT
RAP
B Echelon (B Ech)

2 Close Combat Companies (Alpha and Charlie Companies):
Company Headquarters (Coy HQ)
3 x Close Combat Troops
(Troop HQ, 3 Rifle Sections, Manoeuvre Support Section)

2 Stand Off Companies (Bravo and Delta Companies):
Company Headquarters (Coy HQ)
Heavy Machine Gun Troop
AT (Anti-Tank) Troop
1 Close Combat Troop

40 Commando
Service History

1942 Dieppe Raid
1943–45 Italian Campaign (World War II) Termoli, Lake Comacchio
1945 Liberation of Yugoslavia
1945–48 Palestine
1950–52 Malayan Emergency
1956 Suez Crisis
1957/58, 1959 Cyprus
1962–66 Borneo (six tours)
Nov 1967 Evacuation of Aden
Northern Ireland:
  Jun 1972–Oct 1972 Belfast
  Jun 1973–Oct 1973 Belfast
  Feb 1975–Jun 1975 Belfast
  Aug 1976–Dec 1976 South Armagh
  Mar 1979–Mar 1980 Ballykelly
  Jan 1983–Jun 1983 South Armagh
  Feb 1988–Jul 1988 South Armagh

Nov 1993–Apr 1994   West Belfast
Dec 1995–May 1996 East Tyrone
Apr 2000–Dec 2000 Belfast, Portadown
1982 Falklands War, Operation Corporate
Jun–Dec 1984   Cyprus
1991   Northern Iraq: Op Haven (humanitarian assistance to Kurds)
1998 Kinshasa: Non-combatant evacuation operation (NEO)

Recent Deployments
Iraq: Op Telic
2003 TELIC I
2004 TELIC IV
Afghanistan: Op Herrick
2007/8 HERRICK IV

List of Fallen Royal Marines in Afghanistan and Iraq

Afghanistan
Birch, Marc, Corporal, 26
Curry, Thomas, Marine, 21
Davies, Damian, Marine, 27
Deering, Robert, Corporal, 33
Dunstan, Neil David, Marine, 32
Elms, Liam, Corporal, 26
Evans, Tony, Marine, 20
Fellows, Steven, Lance Corporal, 26
Ford, Mathew, Lance Corporal, 30
Gostick, Dale, Marine, 22
Holland, Jonathan 'Dutchy', Marine, 23
Jones, Michael, Lance Corporal, 26
Laski, Michael 'Mick', Marine, 21
Lucas, Alexander, Marine, 24
Mackie, Jason, Marine, 21
Mackin, Travis, Marine, 22
Manuel, John Henry, Sergeant, 38
Marsh, David, Marine, 22
McKibben, Robert Joseph, Marine, 32

Mulvihill, Damian, Corporal, 32
Reddy, Benjamin, Marine, 22
Richards, Robert Martin, Lance Corporal, 24
Smith, Darren, Marine, 27
Sparks, Georgie, Marine, 19
Summers, Scott, Marine, 23
Thornton, John, Lieutenant, 23
Watson, Richard J., Marine, 42
Whatley, Benjamin, Lance Corporal, 20
Wigley, Jonathan, Marine, 21
Windall, Joseph David, Private, 22
Winter, Danny, Corporal, 28
Wright, Gary, Marine, 22

Iraq
Ballard, Steve, Major, 33
Cecil, John, Colour Sgt, 35
Collins, Paul, Marine, 21
Guy, Philip, Captain, 29
Hylton, Jason, Marine, 33
Maddison, Christopher, Marine, 24
Nowak, Ben, Corporal, 27
Plank, Ian, 31, Corporal (Special Boat Service)
Stratford, Mark, 39, Warrant Officer Class 2
Ward, Jason, Major, 34

* As of 01.06.09

BULLETPROOF

PROLOGUE

9 February 2008
Southern Sangin, Afghanistan

An icy chill runs down my spine. I have got seconds, if that. I know it – so do the lads in my unit.

I am the lead man of the team on callsign Spartacus Two Zero. They're just five yards behind me inside the Taliban compound – a sprawling, spacious series of dusty, sand-coloured walls and stables – in the dead of night.

I did not feel it at first. I must have inadvertently brushed the hidden tripwire in the black silence. There was something against my shins, just below knee-height. It is only then that I see the four-metre wire through the green haze of my NVGs (Night-Vision Goggles). It was a tripwire connected to a grenade booby trap, positioned to kill or maim intruders in the compound. The pineapple-shaped grenade, probably Russian-made and dating back to the Russian occupation, is taped to a stick behind a tree two feet away. In a split second, I hear a distinct ping as the fly-off lever ejects. The force of it coming out knocks it to the floor. It is now armed. Where the hell is it? There is no time, I must warn the others.

'Tripwire! . . . Grenade!' I scream. There is no cover around us and we are all in serious trouble.

There's no point in any of us pissing about now. Our covert reconnaissance mission is blown. Every Taliban fighter for miles around knows we're here and the ragheads will be crawling out of their ratholes to drop us within seconds.

I frantically scan the ground below me with my NVGs. Vision is poor, the light level too low. Time is running out. Through the green haze I see it. There it is, right at my feet now. I cannot see what type of grenade it is and cannot determine how long the fuse will take before it blows. It could be anything from three to five seconds. A second has already gone. I'm browners for sure; so are the lads unless I act now. There is no time to think. Instinct kicks in. What's the point of me taking cover? I'm a goner. I must shield the other lads from the explosion. There's no use all of us catching it. I tripped the wire. I am the closest. It might as well be me.

Adrenalin is pumping now, my hackles are up. In a few seconds I'll be ripped to pieces. Think, for Christ sake, think! If I don't do something right now all four of us will be riddled with shrapnel, sliced apart, and all of us fighting for our lives. If by some bloody miracle I survive the blast I'll probably suffer severe injuries afterwards anyway. If not, some Arab brandishing his AK-47 will probably drop me when he finds all four of us on the back foot. We are at least 300 metres away from supporting troops, totally exposed.

I flip my day sack from my shoulder and onto the grenade, dropping down with it, my back facing the grenade, and curling into the foetal position.

Cold sweat drips into my eyes. My NVG are misting up now. The hairs on the back of my neck are up too, tingling. I'm not a great believer, but I'll say my prayers now. I never really have been a practising Christian since Mum and Dad took me to church when I was a child. I'll be a bloody mess after this that's for sure. God help me.

Another second ticks in my head. Still no explosion, what's taking it so long?

Now my heart is thumping so hard inside, beating like a drum. I can hear myself breathing too. Deep, gasping breaths. No other sounds, just my breath. It's eerie. I know my number's up – so let's have it. Bring it on! I grit my teeth and wait. This is going to hurt.

It's bonkers what goes through your mind when you're about to die. All that crap about your life flashing before you is just that, bollocks. One thing's certain – I don't want my tackle blown off. Not that it'll be any use to me after this blows.

I silently hope and pray that my day sack will take the majority of the force and not me. At least I might keep my torso intact. I might survive if I can do that. If I'd been on my own, I may have legged it and hoped to get outside the five-metre killing zone and into cover before it went up.

What have I got inside the sack? A large lithium battery, extra ammo and my patrol medical kit; that should make me a human firework if I'm lucky. But it is not in me to run. The shrapnel would probably slice me to ribbons anyway.

Another second – or is it two?

What a stupid way to die. This is pointless. I've gone through similar scenarios a hundred times in my head. I've dodged bullets, RPGs (Rocket-Propelled Grenades) and mortars. Some of the lads joked I was a bullet magnet or dodger after all my scrapes. I've gone in with the best of them, right in the thick of it – now this, a bloody stupid Taliban booby trap and it's curtains.

Another second. I think that is four now isn't it or is it five? God, it's taking forever to blow!

My breathing is faster now, heavier. My heart is pounding so hard it feels like it's going jump clean out of my body. When it blows I'll be engulfed by the blast. My body is starting to shake involuntarily. What bastards! This is positively taking the piss. Blow, come on! Blow!

That's another second – that's definitely five, I think.

I saw Ads hit the deck as soon as I shouted the alarm. Dave's managed to get behind a wall, but Scottie's still trying to get flat down directly behind me only a couple of metres away. My head is pounding. I hope I've saved their bacon at least. I busted my guts to get my green lid. I earned it. Getting it was all that mattered since I was a lad. It's in my blood – the blood that is about to be splattered all over the dusty floor and compound walls around me.

Six seconds now. Blow for Christ's sake, blow!

In basic training they teach you to lie with your feet facing the grenade in a pencil shape, making as small a target as possible so that your vital organs are shielded from the blast. You'll still trash your legs though.

There's still nothing. That must be seven.

I grit my teeth, biting so hard I swear I've cracked them. What if it's not a grenade? I'm going to look a right dickhead. I'll get the piss ripped out of me big time for compromising the whole op.

It must be seven seconds. Still nothing. Why?

I never said my goodbyes. I left Mum and Dad a note. Just said I loved them.

Why is this thing not going off? It should have exploded by now.

It's strange waiting to die. Seconds seem like hours.

BOOM!

It's one of the loudest, most earthshaking noises I've ever heard!

The blast washes over me, engulfing me in a flash of white light and orange sparks. It feels like I've been kicked hard in the back, harder than anyone can imagine. I am blown off the ground and thrown to the side by a couple of metres.

Then there is nothing. I feel nothing.

There is just dead silence – blackness, and a high-pitched ringing in my ears.

ONE

Five years earlier
al-Faw peninsula, Iraq
20 March 2003
H hour

It was deafeningly loud inside, but no one said a thing.

When you are about to go to war you suddenly run out of things to say, even though all your oppos are in the same boat.

It is pitch-black inside with up to 40 of us jammed in like sardines in a tin. We're all camo'd up, tooled up and good to go. Inside it's a cauldron, simmering with unease. My heart is in my mouth, I'm trying to stay calm, at least on the outside. But this is for real. No amount of training – no matter how professional, no matter how hot it is – nothing can truly prepare you for this moment: the moment when you deploy into the killing zone. Everyone is deafened by the whining 15-ton twin-engine RAF Chinook from 18 Squadron taking us in behind enemy lines. I check my Breitling watch one more time. It is 3.43 a.m. on the dot somewhere over Iraq.

This helo is full to bursting. It is stifling inside and stinks of

8

Marines' sweat. The whole place stinks of sweat. The Chinook has been stripped so it can carry as much weight as possible. All of us are wearing body armour, our helmets on, carrying our weapons, ammunition and water. We are going in low and fast. Our hearts are in our mouths. None of the lads are talking. Every one of us, all warriors trained to kill, is focused on what lies ahead.

I am breathing slowly now, taking deep calming breaths. I keep reminding myself that Royal Marines like me have been kicking arse 'By Sea, By Land' – as our motto says in Latin, *Per Mare Per Terram*, on our crest – for over 340 years. In the Marines you live and breathe past victories of the comrades in the Corps who went before you. Guys out of the same mould as me were at Trafalgar, where we gave the French a good kicking. We recaptured Gibraltar, we stormed the Normandy beaches on D-Day and fought in the Falklands. We kicked the shit out of Napoleon and Adolf Hitler and their armies too. Our history is important, because none of us wants to be the one to tarnish the reputation and memory of the gallant men from the Corps; the heroes who have gone in before us and fallen for Queen and country. Now these Iraqis loyal to Saddam are about to face Royal Marine Commandos vintage 2003, and they are in for a rude awakening. What keeps us sharp is the fear of letting the other lads down. Nobody wants to do that. I know none of us will.

I am sitting on my Bergen, which weighs well over 100 lb toppers with extra ammo, missiles and gear, clinging on to my kit in this white-knuckle ride. I'm in charge of a MILAN (Missile Infantry Light Anti-Tank) weapon, and my SA80-A2 5.56 mm assault rifle is slung over my shoulder. As I look around most of the lads have got their heads bowed, looking at their boots, checking their weapons. They know their equipment is all that stands between them and their Maker. The crew chief is sitting on a box strapped to the floor near the main cabin door. He stares blankly ahead into space. The seat next to him is unmanned: equipment, repair manuals and fluids used to operate, service and maintain the helo are stacked there instead.

It is shaking about inside. But we're used to it. The main cabin – made of extruded aluminium or magnesium panels, riveted together in sections with raised extruded ridges running the entire length of the floor – is eerily silent. There is no buzz. The floor rests on rubber vibration isolators reducing the internal load vibrations. Our kit, ammunition and heavy weapons are just thrown in the back in a heap. I'm completely hyper on the inside now, and I'm sure the rest of the lads are too – but everyone is keeping a lid on it. The last thing anyone wants, especially our OC (Officer Commanding), is a bunch of flapping marines. I consciously hear myself breathing deeply, almost panting like a dog to maintain control over my faculties. We have all been trained to go to the limit; I just hope it's enough.

Our pilot is kicking it now. We are going max speed 170 knots, just 50 feet above the deck; you can tell when you're flat out in a Chinook as the already sweltering heat inside increases massively from the two Lycoming T55-L-7C 2 engines whirring furiously right above our heads. This guy is clearly in the zone. None of us know the pilot from Adam – that's the way it is in the military. Apart from your muckers in your unit, we are a bunch of anonymous cogs with only the top brass knowing how the bits hang together to make it work. All of us on board have to trust this guy; our lives are completely in his hands. We have been training for just over two months now and there has been a dramatic improvement

BULLETPROOF

in the flying ability of the pilots. They were getting more confident and more focused as war approached. This guy is shit hot. We are twisting and rolling so sharply now you literally hang on to your kit as the helo shifts from side to side, then dips. The Chinook lurches from one side to the other. He must know what he's doing. He's trained to fly combat missions and it costs a fortune to put those RAF guys through their paces.

My name is Matt Croucher. I'm a Royal Marine, one of an 800-man assault force equipped to take out three times that number of Iraqi soldiers. We are a deadly cargo. As soon as the pilot touches down we will come out fighting from the word go. Inside nobody is saying anything. But something has focused all our minds. A few minutes before we took off from the deck of *Ark Royal* a US Marine CH53-D Sea Stallion helicopter carrying members of UKLFSG (United Kingdom Landing Forces and Support Group) and BRF (Brigade Reconnaissance Force) went down killing every soul on board. None of us was told the reason, just that it happened. We did not know if this was due to pilot error or an Iraqi SAM (Surface-to-Air Missile) blowing the poor lads out of the sky. But right at the start of the operation eight guys were already dead from HQ 3 Commando Brigade, plus four Americans. Girlfriends or mothers would soon get that dreaded knock on the door and be left to grieve, and the fight had barely started.

I personally knew one of the guys who was killed: Officer Commanding, Major Jason Ward. I met and worked with him during my time serving at Stonehouse Barracks in Plymouth, home to HQ 3 Commando Brigade. He was a likeable man, down to earth and charming. Now he was dead, his life extinguished in a flash along with all his hopes and dreams.

News of the crash of the Stallion is a serious dent to morale right at the start of the op. The only saving grace is that it was probably an instantaneous death. You hope, when your own times comes, it's quick and merciful. We all do.

The pilot puts us into a steep climb. He knows better than anyone that the enemy could engage us with small-arms fire, RPGs or even SAMs. That's one of the reasons why the helo was stripped of all the expensive kit before take-off. The pilot has one job, to get us in and then get the hell out of there. There's no point losing millions of pounds' worth of equipment on a troop drop just for the hell of it. True, it is hard to hit a Chinook moving this fast. But the Iraqi military are no mugs and they fancy their chances. Our pilot knows he has to keep razor-sharp. One minute we are cruising at altitude, the next banking steeply. We continue to hurtle towards our target.

We had all piled in from HMS *Ark Royal* in the dead of night. We weren't issued seat numbers or tickets for this ride. We weren't even issued seats, as they had all been stripped out! I picked a good spot though, right by one of the only windows in the cargo area. I am one of the only guys who can see outside. It's twilight out there, reddish orange sky. It's a great view to go to war on. It's a real ring-side seat to history. I am watching it unfold down below me. I can see blinking shapes as the assault begins. I am part of the same historic moment too, flying in above them. As the Chinook thuds and whirs over the dark black sea I witness 539 Assault Squadron Royal Marines doing their beach landings with their MIBs (Medium Inflatable Boats), hovercrafts and Rigid Raiders. I see the US Navy Seals loading onto their Zodiacs from their stealth boats and inserting onto the beach.

Operation TELIC – the codename for the British ops for the

invasion of Iraq – has begun. I am part of one of the largest deployments of British forces since World War II. Pretty soon I'll be out of the chopper and kicking arse too. I can't wait. The op name means 'purposeful or defined action' and it was picked out of a hat, or actually selected randomly by computer. Unlike the Yanks, who called their equivalent military deployment Operation Iraqi Freedom, ours did not have any political connotations.

Our objectives were clear. Go in fast, minimise civilian casualties and the damage to essential economic infrastructure and get the job done.

Our specific mission as Delta Company 40 Commando is to secure the Manifold Metering Station (MMS) on the far eastern side of the al-Faw peninsula oil fields. Effectively we had to capture the machinery and buildings that allowed Iraq to export its oil from the southern oilfields via the Gulf. We had rehearsed the mission probably a dozen times or more, including all of 40 Commando elements and SEAL Team 3. However, due to bad weather we were unable to participate in the final couple of rehearsals, so in theory had the least practice at the job we were meant to do. We were confident it would be just fine.

Oil flowed from the MMS pipelines out to the Persian Gulf for export. Our key objective was to stop Saddam blowing up and destroying the oil infrastructure. We had been briefed that he had set the Kuwaiti oilfields on fire in Gulf War I, pumping out acrid smoke into the air, causing ecological damage and forcing us to divert our resources. The strategists back at HQ did not want a repeat of that. We had been briefed time and again that if he did this at the MMS it would cause the world's worst ecological disaster. In any war everyone knows that money talks; our top brass knew that the millions from the oil were going to be crucial in rebuilding Iraq after the war. In the tireless briefings we were told the MMS was an area two kilometres square, a collection of several storage tanks, office buildings and big chunks of machinery. But briefings can never paint the full picture. You have to expect the unexpected.

We had been told that the machinery controlled the pressure and split the oil and residual gas. Then it was channelled into massive pipes, which disappeared underground and resurfaced a couple of clicks away at two buildings known as Pipeline K and Pipeline M. It was here that the flow of the oil was controlled before the crude was dispatched out to two giant platforms in the sea, where oil tankers loaded up with the stuff. The plan was that the Navy SEALs and C Company, 40 Commando, would go in first and seize control of key valves and machinery. About half an hour after the initial landings, the SEALs would stand down and the Marines of A, B, C and D Companies would take over, establish a defensive perimeter and get ready for the inevitable counter-attack. Once that was sorted, the guys would move out and capture the nearby town of al-Faw and the surrounding peninsula, which was just wasteland really.

The guys we were up against were Saddam's front-line troops, combat soldiers dug in in the streets and suburbs. We were told they were no pussies either. Our briefing emphasised that we were in for a hard slog. War is a way of life for the Iraqi soldiers. They've had decades of it – against Coalition Forces in the 1990s, and before that for years against the Iranians. We will be the first on the ground. Once we secure the installation, we will have to hold it until relief comes. I've no doubt they will fight to the death to keep it.

I am a Bootneck with 40 Commando and proud of it.

Bootnecks are so called because in the eighteenth century they used to wear boot leather made into collars.

It has been a rollercoaster ride just to get here. I see it like this – you are dealt a hand and whether you win or lose depends on the cards you get. I have been dealt my hand. It is what I wanted and I would not have it any other way.

The pilot is already making a rapid descent now, pulling hard and fast. I am thrust back as we power on. The sea that was once below has been replaced by an arid, featureless desert. I am scanning the landscape like a cat watching a mouse, eyes darting back and forth. I knew the aircrew were on their M60 machine guns doing the same, but another pair of eyes helping to spot the unforeseen is always welcome. Dozens of Chinooks and Sea Kings and Sea Stallions are buzzing backwards and forwards in the air, carrying the 800 of us from 40 Commando and a similar number from 42 Commando.

We are going in.

The loadmaster holds up three fingers: three minutes before we're out of here. We are all busy rechecking our kit, going over in our heads what our first move will be once we debus. He holds up two fingers now, just two minutes away from my first taste of real combat. I'm dead keen to get off this helicopter. I know I will step up to the plate. I'm up for the fight.

I am about to get the ride of my life: real war, real bullets, real blood, real guts and real gore. This is why I had signed on the dotted line. Yes, the training was hard. We had Gucci kit and the banter with the lads. Yes, I had proved to my family I had what it takes to get the coveted Green Beret, but this is the real deal. Just getting here was physically draining, mentally too, but also exhilarating. What I wanted more than anything else was action. Some of the more experienced guys said it should be the last thing we should be wishing. Boy, was I going to find out the hard way.

Before I can say anything it is action I am getting.

I turn to Shorty, whose eyes are out on stalks. I'd known Shorty for about a year. We all knew him as the Little Angry Man as he suffers from outbursts of SMS (Small Man Syndrome). He's a hoofing lad and he is doubly unfortunate . . . his surname is Short! But he's a proper Marine. Bootneck through and through. Hardcore.

'Don't worry, Royal, it'll be a doddle. They'll be fleeing on their camels before the sun's up,' he jokes.

'I'll be fine, mate,' I reply, high on adrenalin. 'I am well up for this.'

'Can you see much out there?' Shorty asks. He was trying to a get a glimpse out too.

'Nah, mate,' I say. 'It looks all right down there to me.'

Shorty nods, but he looks a bit suspicious and can probably tell I'm not telling the truth. I am more focused on making sure my kit is ready to go. I've got the MILAN firing post in one hand and the K115 missile for it in the other. My rifle is slung over my shoulder. The kit feels good. Better to go to war with it than without it.

Then came the signal we'd been waiting for.

'Go, lads! Go! Go! Go!'

Now I am charging down the ramp. This is for real. As the pilot puts the Chinook down the wheels sink into the mud with all the weight of our gear. With our Bergens on our backs carrying in excess of 100 lbs of kit, we jump straight into the soft, damp soil and move as fast as we can to get in position. Vehicles roll out from the back of the other helicopters. Some vehicles were underslung loads on the choppers. Some of the lads are riding quad bikes down the ramps. They will be used for rapid resupply to the rest of us during combat.

The pilot had landed us directly inside the MMS facility. All around us we could see dome-shaped silos silhouetted against the rising sun. There was a tepid breeze in the air, but it was quite balmy. It felt almost surreal. I spotted pipelines running down to my left – a warning of how vulnerable the MMS and we were if Saddam's henchmen decided to blow it. I could make out in the distance the town of al-Faw. Other than that it was soulless, like something out of *Mad Max*.

The enemy were dug in about 300 metres to the south of the MMS facility and were already locked in combat with the Navy SEALs and C Company, who had debussed an hour before us and were getting stuck in.

A few of the vehicles got bogged down. Some of the lads had to put their backs into it to get the Landys (Land Rovers) and WMIKs (Weapons-Mounted Installations Kit combat vehicles) on to firmer ground. The Navy SEALs' DPVs (Desert Patrol Vehicles) were stuck too. They are Gucci-looking vehicles with a mounted .50 cal, but they only have rear-wheel drive and low ground clearance, which wasn't much use on anything other than a half-decent track. We wasted valuable time getting the vehicles out the quagmire.

What was clear within minutes of being on the ground was that the old military rule that no plan, no matter how good, survives real contact was bang on.

I could hear rounds cracking, incoming and outgoing at nine o'clock as we debussed the Chinook. It was high-octane stuff all right, right down to the smell of the chopper fuel. The sound of mortar rounds being fired off with everything else meant that I had to pause for a second or two just to take in what was actually going on. There was no way this was going to be an overnight job. Anybody who thought it would be a pushover was sorely mistaken.

We'd been briefed to expect the conscripts who'd been forced to fight for Saddam to be less trouble. But in Basra the Ba'ath Party were powerful and the Iraqi generals had positioned stronger, well-trained infantry, as well as Special Forces and the Fedayeen. We knew they wouldn't lose much ground in a fight. We had to take them out, break them and then break the spirit of the less committed enemy. We would be outnumbered. But on the plus side we were better equipped, so we knew our intelligence and attack plan was superior.

I'd never really been shot at before, but it didn't take long to break my duck. In fact, coming off the back of the Chinook did that with the odd round whizzing overhead and the occasional nearby mortar landing sometimes only a hundred metres away.

Once outside I quickly assembled my MILAN. After all the training it was like second nature to me. I could do it in my sleep. I put a missile on and then just started observing my arcs. There were reports of two ZSU 23-4s – a nasty Russian four-barrel 23 mm cannon system mounted on a tracked vehicle. This is an anti-aircraft gun which can be fired horizontally. They have a good couple of kilometres range on them too. I was very observant through my arcs to see if I could spot one of them.

Luckily, just before they came within range, a US Spectre C130 gunship took them both out, which was pretty handy as they would have made light work of us on our quad bikes and Pinzgauers (these are high-mobility all-terrain 4x4 vehicles and the lads rate them better than Landys off-road).

I could hear a fierce gun battle in the background as C Company launched an assault on the nearby town of al-Faw. It was apparent that the majority of the Iraqi forces in the area were from the local town and retreated home, only then having the 'courage' to shoot from rooftops and surrounding buildings. We took no crap and it was a task for C Company to go finish them off. The assault incurred the first major casualties for C Company: a couple of the guys got pretty badly injured in the attack.

It was a bit of a cluster-fuck. Inter-regimental and national rivalry aside, even the Navy SEALs would later admit that they had made a hash of the MMS mission right at the start of Op TELIC. Now it was left to our lads to clear up their mess. To be fair they had been caught up in a heavy firefight – shot and killed one Iraqi and snatched half a dozen prisoners – which had caused a bit of a hold-up. To add insult to injury they also cocked up over putting shape charges on the electricity pylons to blow them so they all fell a certain way. This made it difficult to bring in the rest of the Chinooks. It was left to 40 Commando's assault engineers to blow the rest.

After half an hour of being on the ground, the lads to my right spotted a couple of Iraqi soldiers skylighting themselves over a mound just outside the MMS facility. Their heads were clearly silhouetted against the dawn sky. A couple of the lads opened fire before an MFC (Mortar Fire Controller) called in 81 mm mortars onto the target area. This had the desired effect. They were pounded into oblivion.

The battle raged for two hours before we finally secured the MMS. There was no time to waste reflecting on the victory, however. We posted sentries and set up a doss area where we got some scran, and before we knew it, it was getting close to dusk and it was time for some zeds in our doss bags.

Suddenly, it was daylight again and we were back on it. The events of the previous night felt other-worldly. We were then ordered to push on further down the al-Faw peninsula, perilously close to the Iranian border.

Seven miles down the coastline, 539 Assault Squadron and Navy SEALs had landed on the beach. So we pushed down south and got into a small couple of contacts early in the morning. At one location, the enemy had retreated into buildings and with no 'mess tins' we called in a Royal Marines Lynx helicopter, which fired two anti-tank TOW (Tube launched, Optically sighted, Wire guided) missiles directly over our heads and into the front doors. Once we had done that we caught a couple of prisoners and 8 Troop took out a few of the enemy.

During our push there was incoming fire from Iranian gun towers opening up on D Company's advance, down the al-Faw peninsula. They peppered us with rounds – not serious, but it really pissed us off. They were trying to get us to fire back. Sure enough, one of the lads swung a MILAN around and proceeded to lock on to an Iranian watchtower. Other lads took aim with .50 cals and GPMGs. I suppose from where the Iranian border guards were it must have looked like it was all kicking off, so they just joined in.

'Don't open fire!' our boss yelled.

'But they're shooting at us, sir,' the guy on the MILAN said back.

'We've got orders to carry on with our mission and it was made clear not to engage Iranian positions and start World War III.'

We were pissed off but I could see his point. Our boss could see the shit flying if we opened up at the Iranians. His arse and pips would have been on the line. One war front was perhaps enough. But in our defence it didn't stop them firing at us. My view was if they were shooting at us, shoot back. They had declared war on us and fair game. But you can understand the politics.

As they took potshots at us the Iranians even managed to take out some of their supposedly Muslim brothers. They didn't give a damn. As we advanced, everywhere we went, locals told us of innocent people, some of them children, killed by the Iranians shooting over the border. It was always hard to tell when the Arabs were lying. One twat in our group joked that it was whenever their lips moved.

Having secured the immediate area our unit was returned to the MMS facility, now fully under our control. This is how we rolled – push forward, push back, regroup, take stock and push on again. This makes our movement less predictable to the enemy and also means we are never overstretched. We dossed up and resupplied and recharged our batteries for the next onslaught. The second stage of our mission would be to head on towards the outskirts of Basra, securing the route along the way.

As the dawn light rose, we advanced towards Iraq's second city in our Pinzgauers. They're good vehicles but not armoured, so we just had to make do. Unlike the Navy SEALs, who more or less went back to ship, our mission was extended – the push to Basra was an added adventure to our operation. We had Pinzgauers mounted with either .50 cal machine guns or MILAN systems or GPMGs, and quad bikes and trailers attached too. I was on one of the Pinzgauers on top cover and armed with a MILAN. I felt confident with it. I had about 12 missiles, not to mention the other weapon systems. It was a tried-and-trusted weapon used by Marines for the last 15 years. I was ready for any shit they threw at me.

It started quietly for D Company. We kept hearing about other companies – Alpha (A), Bravo (B), Charlie (C) – engaged in heavy contacts quite often and we thought we were missing out. Even after a couple of days pushing towards Basra, we still had not come into any serious exchanges with the enemy. Sure there were mortars and small arms pinging about, but no serious firefights.

If anything, the speed of the coordinated invasion seemed to have caught the Iraqis on the back foot. From the outset their frontline troops were reeling from the ferocity and professionalism of our assault. Our mates in 42 Commando had already won partial control of a strategic Iraqi port called Umm Qasr in the first major battle of the war. Their determined thrust into the town's heart was decisive. The enemy had been no pushover; far from it. In all honesty, despite the bravado we never expected them to be. A diehard battalion of Iraqi soldiers fought back with unexpected ferocity, making their stand at Umm Qasr after we had forced them back from defensive positions. The US Marines had been fighting there for days until Royal rocked up to help them out.

The roar of the guns tore the early-morning stillness of the desert apart as they laid down an arc of lethal fire from east to west. They were firing their howitzers from four battery positions as the Yanks, with some British infantry in support, moved forward. It was both inspiring and terrifying as the road ahead disappeared into thick black smoke. Throughout the night big guns had malleted the Iraqi resistance, and as dawn broke there was a sense that it was their turn now. We'd heard about the resistance at Umm Qasr and we badly wanted 42 Commando to make the breakthrough. All of us were hoping they could do it. 'It is a bit hot over there,' one of the lads said with a grin. Others talked of the huge smoke clouds gushing from the town and constant ripples of artillery fire. It was certainly getting a bit hot.

After a massive aerial bombardment from Tomahawk cruise missiles, naval gunfire and B52 bombers, 42 Commando finally overcame the last resistance at Umm Qasr and established a bridgehead that gave us our second significant foothold on Iraqi territory after the MMS facility.

Marines tended to get int (intelligence) from a digital BFBS (British Forces Broadcast Station) radio we had on the vehicle, and that's how we eventually found out that 42 Commando, backed up by the tankies, had smashed the resistance at the town of Umm Qasr.

We got much more int from the radio than we ever did from our officers, and to be honest I bet they learned a thing or two from it too. The news was more generic as opposed to specific for us, but it was listened to in silence to hear how the bigger picture was developing. The comments from friends and family back home that were broadcast on BFBS kept us amused.

'To my gorgeous hubby who's a chef on *Ark Royal*, keep hanging in there and dodging them bullets.'

Dodging them bullets, my arse – the most he had to watch out for was the complaints about the crap he was serving up. I am the first to admit that it takes all sorts to win a war; everyone is important. But this fella is on the British flagship protected by countless destroyers and frigates over 100 miles away from any front-line action. I doubt he knows what a bullet looks like. It kept the Royals amused anyway, and gave us an endless source of fun, especially when they were serving up the scran.

We were conscious too of possible chemical attacks. At least four Scud missiles were launched against Kuwaiti territory from Iraq, and each time they were detected on early-warning radar the cry 'Gas! Gas! Gas!' went up, ordering everyone to immediately wear their respirators – a pain in the arse at the best of times. One of the lads put his respirator on only for the eyepiece to fall out. We all fell about laughing. It was hilarious seeing his eyes widen with terror as he realised what had happened, then shoving the palm of his hand into the hole to try and create a seal. Lads were on the floor in hysterics, like it's not hard enough to breath in a respirator already, you then have a laughing fit.

Military commanders said the threat was a real one. On the front line we were more relaxed about the menace from Saddam's Weapons of Mass Destruction. The Yanks apparently drafted in some pigeons to provide early warning of gas, like canaries in coal mines, but we just used our noddle or NBC detector equipment, costing upwards of £100,000 a set.

We were now halfway between the MMS facility and Basra and we were closing in on the town fast, about 25 miles away. We were at the limit of exploitation for our Commando helicopter force support, so no more Lynx door-gunners or TOW missiles helping us from this point forward. The landscape started to change. Until then it had all been desert, but now we were seeing the beginning of date palms and slowly the land was becoming more fertile. This was also when we started coming under fire. We returned fire, initiating a contact. It was over in a matter of minutes. We smoked them quickly.

The Challenger tanks raced on ahead and we were tasked with setting up a blocking position to prevent the enemy advancing in the desert behind the tank lines. Because tanks have a fairly narrow optical range, it's possible for infantry to move through the gaps between the advancing tanks, and it was our job to mop them up. The US Marine Corps's ANGLICO (Air Naval Gunfire Liaison Company) team provided vital air support. They were a cracking bunch of lads, even if they did think a little too much of themselves sometimes. Knowing we had that air support was reassuring. We knew they could call up fast air to drop bombs whenever we needed, and if the enemy got close enough we certainly would need them.

Suddenly, intelligence over the radio sent chills down all of our spines. Somehow, several Iraqi tanks, T54/55s, had slipped through the advancing Challenger columns. We were only a light force, no tanks, and only three MILAN systems mounted on the Pinzgauers. This was not good news. And then more int came over the radio: the six, maybe seven tanks charging straight for our position became eight, then nine. We were in for quite a fight. Eventually, the unit commander got the nod that up to 14 had made it through. Now the odds of three missile posts did not seem quite so favourable. We were going to need back-up and fast. I was certain that the Iraqi T54/55s would be able to break for our position, and with 14 of them heading our way I thought my missile-firing skills in this scenario would be the most testing of my life. We were staring down the barrel and it was not a pretty sight. Things were looking pretty grim. I wondered just how I managed to end up in this crap in the first place.

I was 19.

TWO

Lympstone, Devon
Commando Training Centre
Summer 2000

I always knew I had what it takes. From the year dot I would tell everyone who would listen that one day I would be a part of one of the most respected military units in the world: I would become a Royal Marines Commando.

Mum and Dad were convinced I would grow out of it. They thought it was just a boyhood obsession, that I was fixated on war, guns and all the soldiers' kit. They thought one day I'd wake up and want to do something else; it would just fizzle out in time. But it didn't work out like that. I wouldn't let it. The more I read about their exacting standards, the toughest basic-training course in the world, the desire to be the best, the more it inspired me to join the corps. Not once did I waver.

To a young schoolboy from Solihull these men I read about seemed invincible. Like the Spartans of ancient Greek times, they were elite warriors born to fight; their physiques awesome, their unflinching ethos inspiring. Only the most exceptional men, the most dedicated individuals could make it and earn the right to wear the Green Beret. To get there I would have to undergo rigorous training, show initiative, be at the peak of my physical and mental capabilities.

An amphibious force, specialists in Arctic and mountain warfare, the Royal Marines were the core component of the country's Rapid Deployment Force. The Corps was able to operate independently in all terrains, as highly trained as Commando forces. Trained to the highest levels, to make it you have to have a unique mix of capabilities. Those who succeed become part of the best specialist infantry unit in the world. Yes, they are the elite; a breed apart from the regular forces – the Pongos as Marines call them. Where the army goes the pong goes, according to the Marine saying. Booties or Bootnecks are different. Even in the worst environments we try to stay as clean and dry as possible. We scrub our kit, keep ourselves and our uniform spotless. More guys died in World War II due to lack of hygiene than on the battlefield. Trained to be the best, Marines thrive on danger; it comes with the territory. Marines must think on their feet, must react on instinct and take out the enemy without a flicker of thought. I was a 13-year-old West Midlands lad with one passion, one dream – to be a Royal Marine Commando. I never really wanted to do anything else.

As a kid I was always outside. I loved it being in the fresh air. I was the adventurous sort, I suppose. I kept myself physically fit, although I was not a sport obsessive or anything like that, but I loved my footie, boxing, martial arts, running and all that stuff. At secondary school in Solihull I was not a bad cross-country runner. I was good at athletics and rugby too; anything that kept me active. My mum and dad were both teachers, so they pushed me academically too. I did not go to their school, but I didn't do badly either. I notched up eight GCSEs, all with A-Cs, which pleased them. They never once tried to put me off. They just advised, sensibly, that I had to have another option just in case I didn't make it through the tough selection process. There was no point risking everything on one endeavour. I already had, but said nothing. I checked out colleges and went through the motions. I could have gone on to further education and a university degree. I was academic and knew how to handle myself in exam situations. But it did not excite me. I really did not see the point. Nothing anyone said or did would deter me. I was born to be a front-line soldier. I was going to be a Royal Marine, period.

Like most lads I'd read war stories and loved the blood-and-guts war films like *Full Metal Jacket* and *Black Hawk Down*, which were my favourite movies. I was not a violent kid or anything like that. I didn't go around kicking the crap out of other lads; nor did I think it would be good earning a living fighting. In fact, my mum says I was quite a quiet teenager. Of course, I got into my fair share of scraps like most kids of that age, but nothing too bad.

My uncle was a Major in the Army, and my late grandad, Ron Croucher, had served in World War II as Lieutenant Commander and often regaled me with stories of his service. I was fascinated. He may have hammed it up a bit, but it sure as hell sounded exciting to me. Without either of us knowing, he must have instilled something deep inside me, stirring an interest in my young and impressionable mind with his war stories and camaraderie. He had served with distinction with the Royal Navy as a radio operator on the deadly Arctic convoys. He was on board British ships forced to dodge German submarines and battleships, whose crews risked their lives to carry vital war materials to the Russian port of Murmansk. His missions were extremely hazardous, him and his pals facing treacherously icy and gale-force conditions, and the prospect of sinking without trace.

Subconsciously, Grandad Ron had quite an impact on me. I had always been supremely proud of what he did during his war service. My mum reminded me how when I was a six-year-old boy I would wake up my other grandad, her dad, Les, from his slumber early in the morning while we were all on holiday in France, so I could practise marching in front of him. I would insist that he show me exactly what I should do. I would practise and practise until I had got it spot on. It was a taste of things to come. I knew in my heart I would make it as a Marine. I wanted a crack at it as soon as I could, the moment I turned 16.

At 13 I joined 2030 (Elmdon and Yardley) Squadron Air Training Corps, which gave me my first taste of 'military'-style life and the opportunities it gives young people. Apart from playing sports like rugby and footy it gave me a chance to learn military skills such as shooting and fieldcraft. Cadets have the opportunity to fly in light aircraft, gliders, and even front-line RAF aircraft ranging from Sea King helicopters to flights in small aerobatic planes. I had my first go at shooting too, taking weapons-handling tests before firing live on indoor, barrack and gallery ranges. I had a bash at becoming a qualified first-aider as well.

I was hooked. When I wasn't with the Squadron at home I would spend hours trawling through military magazines and books and checking Internet sites about the services. I certainly did not feel I had anything to prove to anyone. I was driven from within. My desire was purely selfish – I wanted to make it for myself. I really do not know why I was drawn, but I was determined to sign on the dotted line for Queen and country as soon as was legally possible. The moment I turned 16 I planned to walk into the recruiting office and apply to be considered for military service. Most of my schoolmates were focused on what A levels to take next term. But for me, school was not only out for summer, but for good. The idea of staying on and picking A Level subjects and then studying for another three or four years after that seriously did not appeal. It was not on my radar. Even though my parents were education professionals I was completely focused on achieving my goal. In hindsight, I was different from my schoolmates in that respect. I fitted in well enough. I was popular with my peers. But all my teachers said I was headstrong. Most of my schoolmates did not have a clue what they wanted to do. They were always trying to cop off with girls, but I was always researching my next career move.

As soon as I read about the elite Royal Marines I knew the Corps was right up my street. They are one of the finest fighting forces in the world, if not the finest at what they do. If I was to join them, I had to be twice as dedicated, twice as fit, twice as sharp-witted. After all, guys from university had flunked at the first hurdle. First I had to be accepted on the training programme, which is far from a shoo-in even for the most dedicated wannabe recruit.

All potential Royal Marine recruits must undergo the rigorous PRMC (Potential Royal Marines Course) if they are to make it to the next stage. This four-day selection process essentially sorts out the wheat from the chaff. They know what they are looking for and the tests are designed to ensure that the pick of the crop make it through to Basic Training.

When the letter inviting me to the Commando Training Centre at Lympstone dropped through our letterbox in June 2000 I was totally ecstatic. I was leaping all over the front room and couldn't wipe the smile off my face for days. To be fair my family were thrilled for me too. I had got to first base at a very young age. Now the real fun was about to begin.

Lympstone itself is a typical English country village with cottages and twee country pubs dotted about the place, joined by winding narrow lanes. You would struggle to find it on a map. To me, however, this place held almost mythical status. Outside the main gate of the camp is a sign that reads *Commando Training Centre*. On one of the gates is a large picture of a commando dagger and on the other one it says *Royal Navy*. We are the elite fighting arm of the senior service, and not part of the British Army as some people still think. An ensign flew over the camp too, and we were coming on board to camp. I underwent a series of testing fitness examinations and exacting interviews. I swotted up on every aspect of the Royal Marines. I wanted to give myself the best chance of making the grade. It was a daunting experience for a teen-ager. I was pitched in with mature blokes in their twenties; some were there for the third and final attempt, trying to convince the selection team they were up to it.

Grim rumours floated around in the dorms on the first night. After listening to the gripes and worries of my fellow wannabe recruits I felt unsettled. It certainly hit my confidence. I truly didn't know what to expect. As the nerves began to take hold I made a conscious decision to keep headstrong and stopped listening to others. What the hell did they really know anyway? They may have been older, they may have been here before, but if they were any good they would not be here, they would already have made the grade and got their green lid. I suppose you could say it is a quality of mine. I can zone out and focus on what I have to do, and cut out all the crap that is blurring my vision. It has come in handy in later life.

It worked. The next day I performed at the top of my ability, excelling in the physical tests, matching the best in the group. But I could see the club swingers (our name for the PTIs) wanted more, they wanted everything I could give. They wanted me to go to the limit and even then push a little bit more. The instructors, with their clipboards in their hands, were checking for mental strength too. They wanted to know we had the psychological strength to face adversity. There is nothing basic about Royal Marine Basic Training. It is 32 weeks of sheer hell. There was no point putting forward lads from the PRMC who would crack up in the first two weeks as a recruit proper.

They gave me the nod, but I did have one setback. I suffered an injury during the PRMC. The selection team picked me up on it, saying that I had gone over on my ankle. They told me to take a couple of months out before starting training to make sure my ankle was all right. As it turned out there was a couple of months between passing my PRMC and starting training anyway, so I was lucky. The next time I walked through the gates at Lympstone I would be a fully fledged recruit.

It doesn't matter when you choose to join the Royal Marines. It lasts for nine intensive months, so you will come across the hardships of both winter and summer. I suppose for training it may be better to start in the winter and do all your drills then. That way when summer comes it is a bit easier and you can concentrate your efforts on other things, as opposed to just surviving out in the open. At the start there are usually 60 recruits in each troop. From that intake, 10 to 20 or at a push 25 recruits will make it past the finishing post.

I had waited for this day for as long as I could remember. Now incredibly it was here. The train journey to the Commando Training Centre in Lympstone, Devon, took most of the day and I had to change trains a few times, which just added to the mixture of anxiety and excitement. I was no fool. I knew the course was going to test me to the limit, but that is precisely what I wanted. This was where I would start living the dream. If I could crack this stage I was on my way to getting the coveted Green Beret; then, and only then, would I be a Royal Marines Commando. I am happy to admit now that inside my stomach was churning, shaken up with first-day nerves. I think it has more to do with the fear of failure, rather than being apprehensive about the conditions or challenges at the camp. I had come so far I seriously didn't want to fail now. I had been told that a lot of recruits drop out in the first two weeks. That is when they 'convert' us to military life and out of our bad civilian habits. Some have left Basic Training in tears. Only the best survive. This was my big chance, and I was desperate to make a good first impression with the instructors. I would do whatever it took to be the best. When everyone got out of the train I could tell who the new recruits were. Their hair was a bit longer, not much, but enough to notice. They were slightly scruffier, and all had a startled rabbit-in-headlights look about them. Every one of us – me included – looked shell-shocked. None of us really knew what was coming next.

A corporal was there to meet us, dressed in Lovats uniform and sporting the Green Beret we were all there to get. The Corporal looked the business, every inch a Bootneck. His boots were so polished you could see your face in them.

He had a clipboard in his hand and a wooden stick under his arm. There had been stories of recruits taking one look at the fella who met them at the station and getting straight back on the train, but I think they were apocryphal. It didn't happen in our case. The Corporal barked out places of interest around the camp as 798 Troop, our troop number for training, was frog-marched to our camp accommodation.

'Medical centre – you'll all end up there at some time. Camp shop – where you can buy extra rations you'll need because you'll be burning off everything you eat!'

Finally we made it to our new home, a stark, scrubbed place with cream walls and highly polished red floors. First up was the two-week Phase One: Foundation. Our first two weeks of training we spent in the induction block, which is a big, impersonal 60-man dorm. We were each allocated a bed, bedding, kit locker and bedside table. The Corporal left us in no doubt that it was our duty to keep it spotless or everyone else would suffer. Next stop was the camp barber, who sheered us into shape with a 'Number One' all over. My hair was short anyway, but I still had to go through the motions. Within an hour we were all in the lecture hall. First we were addressed by a Colour Sergeant. He certainly didn't look like a man to mess with.

'Listen up, lads,' he said in a gruff voice of total authority. In an instant the room went dead silent. This man commanded total respect.

'In the next two weeks we will turn you into military students. You will kiss goodbye to your civvy habits – they will be gone for good. We are going to teach you personal administration. This is vitally important. Some of you will miss your homes, but don't worry, that is perfectly normal. There must be no mobiles, no food and no alcohol brought into the Foundation Block. That is the only time I will say that. We will give you everything you need, loads of kit. Make sure you look after it,' he added. This was an order. It was delivered calmly enough, but every one in the lecture room was clear that they disobeyed it at their peril.

'In a minute the Company Commander will come into this room. When he enters you will *sit* to attention *not stand* to attention. That means you sit bolt upright and look straight ahead. You don't relax until you are told "At ease." Understood?'

'Yes, Colour Sergeant!' we barked in unison. We were already bonding as a troop.

The Company Commander had a much smoother, softer demeanour. He spoke with a clear diction and slightly upper-class, clipped accent. It was not snooty or anything, but decidedly posher than my Brummie drawl. He welcomed us and told us we were now officially the most junior member of the elite Royal Marine Corps and it would be tough, but an exciting and challenging career.

'You have all made an excellent choice. But first you have to pass the most exacting and longest basic training course in the world. It is a prize worth fighting for,' he said with confidence. 'Our aim is for you to pass out as Royal Marines Commandos. If you are good enough we will help you get there, if you're not you will have been long gone by the time of the ceremony.'

The Major was genuine, sympathetic to our plight, even. His words left us in no doubt that fulfilling our goal was down to us. The training team was there to help, but the onus was on us. It would be our fuck-up and nobody else's.

Then it was time to read the oath:

'I swear by Almighty God I will be faithful to bear true

allegiance to Her Majesty Queen Elizabeth II, her heirs and successors and that I will in duty-bound honour faithfully defend Her Majesty, her heirs and successors in person and dignity against all enemies, and will serve and obey all orders of Her Majesty, her heirs and successors and of generals and officers set over to me. So help me God.'

It had begun. I had a restless night's sleep. I kept checking my watch every hour. I wanted to be ready for when the Corporal marched in the room at 5.30 a.m. sharp when our commando training would start for real. For the first couple of weeks the main emphasis is on your personal administration: ironing, keeping your lockers tidy, being able to sew, making your bed to acceptable standards, keeping accommodation spotless. We also had to attend a series of introductory training briefs. It is a fairly fast pace and took its toll on some of the lads. Straight away there was a guy in the bed next to me who quit after the first week claiming he was homesick. If he was to join the Parachute Regiment he would be nearer to home, so everything would be rosier. It sounded a total twat's excuse and I don't know what he did with the rest of his life. There were about two or three in the Foundation phase who dropped out.

First we were taught how to wash, shave, shower and iron like Royal Marines. For a Royal your personal admin is crucial. Time and again we were reminded by our corporal that more people were killed in World War II from shit hygiene than on the battlefield. We were issued shed loads of kit, including the blue beret with red badge with the Globe and Laurel Royal Marine Corps crest. I had read somewhere that once I started commando training, it would feel like I had never trained before. That was spot on. We would hoof down 5,000 calories a day from four large meals, but some lads needed more because the training was just so intensive. We were nicknamed 'nods', because the training and hours were so hard at any opportunity we would nod off. The lecture halls were a dead cert for getting some zeds in. If caught it meant heading down to the assault course called the Bottom Field to dive into a tank full of water, or if you were lucky just a few press-ups. Some of us had arms like Popeye by the end. You would sink into your seat and as the lights dimmed when the slides went on, your eyes would start to flicker and you were gone. I was useless at staying awake!

Physically, the demands of commando training were incredible. Psychologically, it took its toll too. You depended on your mates to big you up when you were down. When a recruit was contemplating throwing in the towel, you depended on the fellas around you for support. You just had to keep going, even when others had given up. You needed every ounce of determination – second best was not an option. We were all pushed to the very limit, but every day I got stronger. With every hurdle I overcame I gained in confidence. Courage, determination, unselfishness and cheerfulness in the face of adversity – yes, I had these Marine qualities.

Every day we had to make our beds in different ways, or bed packs with our bedding, then face daily inspections by our secion corporals. The slightest speck of dust could result in their wrath. They would sift though our lockers looking for inadequacies. If they found one it could lead to all the contents being chucked on the floor. You would get screamed at if you messed up, but it just made you more determined not to mess up the next time. After all, it didn't bother me. It was part of the toughening process. I was now a proper military student. It took its toll though. A few of the lads couldn't take the strict regime.

After three weeks we'd had a few drop-outs, particularly after the First Step – a 24-hour exercise when nods master the basics of living in the field. The men were starting to get separated from the boys. We were also a bit bored with bed-making and cleaning and drill, and ready to get stuck in to the hardcore stuff. The next stage was called Individual Skills Training, which taught us weapon skills, camouflage, map-reading and moving at night. This was followed by Advanced Skills Training, from weeks 10 to 15 and the final module of Phase One. We got to throw our first live grenades, learnt to build survival shelters and rode in helicopters. The exam at the end of this wasn't sitting at a desk writing about Shakespeare. It was a gruelling 32-hour field test called Baptist Run. By the end of it my body was screaming with pain, but I had done enough to progress to Phase Two.

For the first 15 weeks of training we were not allowed washing machines either. Everything had to be cleaned by hand in metal sinks using 'dhobi dust' (our slang for washing powder). You had to earn the right to use the machines. We were now properly bonding as potential Royals and living in smaller six-man rooms. The team with the best room in training was allowed a privilege pass for the evening. We'd get a radio for the evening. A typical morning would start at 5.30 a.m. and sometimes you would be working until 11 p.m. or midnight. Other times you would come out of the field on the Friday evening and you'd got to get your kit ready for the next morning in preparation for drill.

We spent hours down at Bottom Field. The PTIs gave us a good beasting. After every tough session in the gym or in the field we would go to the lecture hall to learn about weapons, like self-loading rifles. You were expected to achieve a speed of six miles an hour carrying your kit and weapons. I got a stress fracture that got worse and worse and broke the fourth metatarsal in my foot. I was unfortunately back-trooped and put into Hunter Company, a remedial facility for injured recruits. A lot of guys get injured – about a third – and have to go through it. It is a bit demoralising, but you just have to get on with it. As a consequence of this I had to put a few weeks aside to rehabilitate myself. I also picked up a strong strain of glandular fever, which set me back a few weeks and put me in hospital for a while.

The second phase of training was more challenging as it involved learning commando skills. The fitness side of things became seriously hard work. We went onto Bottom Field carrying 'fighting order' – everything from pouches with ammo, water, rations which could weigh anything up to 22 lb. We also had to carry our rifle and that weighed in at another 10 lb. It made you feel like you were starting all over again. The extra weight meant we struggled on tasks we thought we had mastered. Climbing the 30-foot ropes was a real effort. It was all in the technique, but it took its toll on many of the lads. The assault course was a new challenge too: a series of walls, nets, climbing frames, rope bridges. We would also firearms carry other recruits, meaning you were carrying his kit too. Again some found this incredibly testing, but I loved it because my fitness level rose significantly even though I felt constantly exhausted. Blisters were common with our webbing constantly rubbing against our skin. Some of the lads were on painkillers throughout the course, but if popping a few pills helped us get our Green Berets we didn't care. By the time we started on the field firing ranges, I felt as fit as Superman. When we started pumping out a few rounds I was at last beginning to feel like a real soldier. We were getting to the business end of becoming a Marine.

And the business end was Operations of War Training. This involved training for all the sharp and nasty stuff we would be required to do in a real world conflict – ambushes, patrol, recceing and marching with 100 lb packs for 12 miles.

Every test we undertook was another step towards passing the legendary Commando Course, which included an endurance course where you had to cross lakes, streams and bogs in less than 70 minutes ending with a shooting test, followed by a 9-mile speed-march to be completed in 90 minutes or less. Then there is a Tarzan and assault course where recruits must perform a 'Death Slide', a rapid descent from a high plateau, complete an elevated ropes course and scale a 30-foot wall. The final exercise is the real killer. It's the 30-mile load carry with full combat gear that has to be completed in under eight hours. We started at dawn and had to endure the harsh conditions of Dartmoor, which is well known for its rugged terrain. We all knew we were on the eve of getting the coveted Green Beret. We scoffed as much as we could at breakfast: it was vital fuel for what lay ahead. This task and terrain has broken many top blokes, but it didn't break me.

Marines are different from the Pongos in the general army. In my room in training there were two crazy South Africans called Dane and Pierre, a Canadian named Jarvis, and Pidge, who can thank me for his nickname on account of him lacking any chest bulk, and whose skinny physique was probably down to the fact that he was a marathon runner. And then there was a giant of a man called Ed, who was 6′ 8″ and weighed about 18 stone. Big Ed was a monster of a man who could carry uber amounts of kit on his back. I have seen him carry three 94 mm LAW (Light Anti-Armour Weapon) on his back at 10 kg a go, in addition to his normal kit. He also had a degree from Loughborough University. We were a well-bonded troop and, in fact, unusually, we all passed out from that room. So we were quite a diverse bunch. And then there was me as the corps-pissed teenager.

Pierre, Jarvis and Pidge went to 42 Commando and Big Ed went to 45 Commando. Subsequently, he went on his Mountain Leaders Twos course, which is probably one of the hardest courses you can take in the British military – those crazy enough to undertake both say it's even tougher than SAS and SBS Selection. Dane was a signaller who now works for the Commando Helicopter Force. Jarvis progressed to a fighting company, and my mucker Pierre later specialised as a Royal Marines LC, operating speedboats.

When I passed out from training and received my green lid it was one of the best days of my young life. My family was there to see me too. It was a long haul, exhausting in the extreme, but I got there. I had been back-trooped through injury, but I had overcome adversity. That is the Marine way. My mum and dad were there waiting in the stands for my troop to be called. The Royal Marines Band played Sir Edward Elgar's 'Nimrod'. It was emotional, stirring stuff. There was a definite lump in my throat. We were no longer a blunt sword, a rag-tag of recruits – but a sharp steel sword ready for combat. Our names were called out one at a time.

'Marine Croucher . . .'

At last it was my turn. My heart was bursting with pride. As the Officer Commanding handed me my Green Beret I could not hide my elation. A handshake, a few words and a salute, and then I marched off to the side. I spotted Mum and Dad in the crowd and flashed a broad grin. Then we headed out of Hunter's Hall and back to the accommodation block to change into our Blues – Royal Marines Number 1 Dress

Uniform, complete with the white-peaked caps – ahead of drill arms parade. We had been rehearsing these sequences for the past nine months. It went well. We were led by the Royal Marines Band and marched onto the drill square. We marched smartly past senior officers inspecting the parade.

'Royal Marines, to your duties, right wheel, quick march!' barked the adjutant.

We had passed out at a time when the world needed men of our calibre and commitment. It would not be long before we would all be asked to put our training to the test.

I had a couple of small drafts. I joined Delta Company 40 Commando. As I was a young lad and fairy fresh out of training too, I got a bit of a hard time at first. It was par for the course. It took a bit of getting used to. I went out on the piss with the lads. They do all sorts to you. You stand in front of a wall in a pair of Y-fronts and they throw eggs at you. I took it as a bit of banter and an initiation to the company. But there was no harm done. Once that's over you're accepted as one of the lads.

This is my story. It's an account of what it's really like on the frontline. It's also a story of comradeship. It is an honest eye-witness account of what really happened. It is not all positive, far from it. Life is a rollercoaster, after all. It would be boring otherwise. It is not about the heroics of battle or crap like that. I just tell it as I saw it. I am not a saint, but I'm not a sinner either. This is just a modern soldier's story. War changes people; sometimes for the better, sometimes for the worse. It can make or break you. Good men on the training ground, men you had thought would be real leaders on the battlefield, crack under fire and never go back. Then there are the guys who you would think would shirk it under enemy fire, who in fact end up performing Herculean feats in combat. War makes men stand up and be counted. It makes you sick with fatigue; it repulses with its intolerable brutality and bloody inhumanity. It pumps you up, giving the greatest adrenalin rush you'll ever experience, and then leaves you on the floor, wiped out, depressed, exhausted and wondering why you are even there as mortar rounds rain down in the desert, not knowing if the next one has got your name on it. What would I be like under fire, behind enemy lines? How would I cope with the prospect of imminent death or watching my best oppos cut down by machine gun fire? It was my turn to find out.

I was 17. Legally I wasn't even allowed onto the battlefield. But I knew my time would come.

THREE

HMS Ark Royal
March 2003

She must have looked quite a sight for those who had gathered on the sea wall as she edged slowly but surely out of Portsmouth Harbour. HMS *Ark Royal*, all 683 feet of her, slipped purposefully out to sea, only those on board and a handful of top brass ashore knew her real task. She would be my home for the next few weeks, along with the rest of Delta Company Royal Marines. We had won the lottery. While the other companies were crammed onto other ships, including HMS *Ocean*, we had more space, better accommodation – and better still, we had women, or Wrens as they're called – dozens of them on-board, so we even had a bit of eye candy.

To the outside world *Ark Royal* was going on exercises. For public consumption the ship – with her 600 crew under the command of Captain Alan Massey – was heading for exercises in the Far East. It was the world's worst-kept secret, however, that she was actually going to get us as close to Iraq as possible, and chopper us into the war zone. We were the British spearhead for Operation TELIC, the invasion of Iraq for Gulf War II.

Every one of us on board knew the seriousness of our task. We all knew we were heading for war. It was only a matter of time before the bullets started flying. Yes, the politicians were still chewing the fat, arguing over the legalities, but every one of us knew eventually we were in for the fight of our lives, and we had better be ready for it. It was only a matter of time.

The sheer weight of our war kit made the ship sink deeper into the water. We had tonnes of stuff loaded on board: weapons, ammunition, vehicles like the WMIK and the Pinzgauer. They looked mean with all their bad-ass kit, plus .50 cal platforms and twin GPMG mounts. God knows who had the task of working out exactly what we did or did not need for battle – rather him than me.

Out at sea something funny started happening. Bits of the ship literally started going missing. No one knew what was up until someone spotted a Royal called Garnet (a bonkers Canadian who had transferred to become a Bootneck) making 'modifications' to his Pinzgauer wagon. He had secretly been hiding out with the ship's metalsmith and they designed and made their own unofficial GPMG mounts. These would prove really effective in the battlefield. Garnet got an official award and £200 from the CO for his ingenuity. It was later adopted by 3 Commando Brigade. We all had a go after that, building bits and pieces, anything to make our vehicles better and more comfortable for combat. Nobody said anything, and I think the boss and Captain Massey fully understood. Garnet did take it a bit far – he ended up looking like the universal soldier! He looked like a cross between a mercenary and a

Navy SEAL. He even looked at proffing and modifying spare aircrew body armour. The standard-issue 6 x 4 ceramic plate didn't really offer much protection in the theatre of war.

Our mess deck was top drawer. The bunks were three high, but we were used to that. The grub was passable too considering the conditions.

The hangar was now stuffed full with vehicles and stores. There was no room to spare.

I joined up with HMS *Ark Royal* in Cyprus. About half of us did, as we had flown over a couple of weeks earlier to undertake various range practices with everything from our rifles to heavy machine guns. This was also a great chance to acclimatise to the harsh desert environment we would be operating in. It was also our first introduction to US Navy SEAL Team 3, the guys we would be going in with in the first wave, and in usual Yank style they came with laptops for their wireless Internet and satellite phones to make calls back home whenever they wanted. We had our 'trusty' Paradigm 20-minutes-a-week phonecard though, so we had nothing to whinge about, gen! I'm not sure living in the comfort zone is the ideal preparation for war. Cyprus was full of its own little adventures, getting pissed and legging it from the ever-vigilant Royal Military Police. Jobsworth arseholes!

We sailed through the Suez Canal heading for the United Arab Emirates (UAE), where we would carry out desert exercises. As soon as we entered the canal, we automatically went operational, with night patrols on deck to ensure detection of possible suicide bombers. This wasn't us being paranoid – it was a genuine threat. Warships had been hit in the past by suicide vessels with devastating effect. The USS *Cole* had an enormous hole blasted in its hull in 2000, killing 17 Yank matelos. A couple of years later the *Limburg* had been hit in the Gulf of Aden. Al-Qaeda would not miss the opportunity to take out the *Ark Royal*, the British flagship. It would be quite a coup on the eve of the war.

GPMGs were mounted down both sides of the ship covering port, starboard, bow and stern. On my sentry I noticed this teenage Wren manning a GPMG. She was a bit of a sance. I was feeling plums and hadn't bagged off for a while and fancied a bit of a chat. There was a serious side to my approach too. I was apprehensive at the best of times whilst watching half a dozen or so small boats a few hundred metres away, and I was specifically trained for this. I wanted to make sure this Wren was OK.

'You all right?' I asked.

She nodded nervously. She didn't look at all confident. I couldn't blame her. She probably joined the Navy to be a meteorologist or something and now she was stuck behind a 7.62 mm machine gun getting ready to blast a boat out of the water should it get too close and be perceived as a threat.

'Well, good evening,' I said as I walked away.

She turned to me and said, 'If anything happens, can I call you to come help me out?'

'Sure,' I said. She looked sheepish, but was a cute blonde and not half bad through my NVGs.

As the *Ark Royal*'s grey hull moved along the canal, the lack of interest from villagers was palpable. Perhaps they knew what was coming too. We went operational. The mood was tense on the ship.

On night patrol, we kept an eye open for smaller vessels. It is well known they use bigger ships like the *Ark Royal* as the bleep on the radar to hide behind and then smuggle drugs or weapons across the Suez. We had to keep our eyes peeled. The Suez Canal was our first choke point, where the water gets very narrow. Next up was the Red Sea and then by Yemen and Djibouti it gets even worse.

Once out of Suez, we arrived at the UAE, disembarked and got stuck in to desert training. Straight away it was obvious that fighting in the desert was not exactly going to be straightforward. One of the guys was stung by a scorpion whilst we were practising section battle drills. He put his hand in one of the ammunition pouches. Inside there was a baby scorpion and it stung him. He was getting a bit worried as he described how his arm was going numb really quickly. It started to paralyse him, so the company medic radioed the team in from one of the neighbouring ships and he was evacuated by a Lynx helicopter. Stings from baby scorpions can be deadly, because they inject more poison into their victims, not assessing the amount the way an adult scorpion would. His war was over before it had even begun and all down to a bug. I think he made a full recovery though.

Meanwhile we were left in the desert with these scorpions, dung beetles and camel spiders, and we were a bit bored so we started racing them against each other. Of course, the officers broke up the fun. They said we had to spend all our time practising on the ranges or doing something constructive. But I never knew how much fun you could have with a dung beetle. It really showed how bored you can get on exercise in the desert.

On the eve of the war we re-embarked and moved north, around 60 miles off the coast of Iraq, and, funnily enough, we had a big piss-up and barbecue on the top deck of *Ark Royal*. The lads were in shorts and T-shirts and a bit of fancy dress. Maybe Delta Company's OC Major Matt Pierson thought it best for us to relax, knowing our destination was the jaws of hell. Letting off steam like this helped boost morale no end, and to have a stand-down day here and there was greatly appreciated by all the lads. Bearing in mind our day would start at 4 a.m. for Phys on the top deck, before the scorching sun rose and turned the metal flight deck into a barbecue grill, any break was welcome. Often we'd be working past 8 p.m. We were limited to two cans of beer a day, and to ensure we played by the rules the fridges were locked by 10 p.m. The Royal Navy was very strict, and to be honest there are good reasons why booze is limited. But that never stops a Royal.

We came up with the ingenious idea of taking off the fridge handle and affixing it to the other side of the door, so when the duty officer came round to give the handle a tug to make sure the fridge was locked, the door firmly stayed shut! You can train a Royal Navy officer for years and give him as many gold rings as you can, but he'll never be able to outwit a Royal Marine. And thus we were able (on occasion) to drink into the early hours. It certainly made for an interesting Phys session the next day, mind.

Captain Alan Massey may have been a bit apprehensive about his cargo, and how his crew and they would get on. He needn't have worried. He had told Major Pierson bluntly, when they shook hands on first meeting on board: 'You're the weapon, we're the delivery system.' He was right.

We were some of the only Marines in 3 Commando Brigade not to muster in Kuwait before the invasion. Rather than go into Iraq by land we were going to be choppered right into the middle of the shitstorm: the front line. Nearing the day of the invasion, Saddam fired a couple of Scud missiles, putting us all on high alert. The ship went into pressurised NBC (Nuclear, Biological and Chemical warfare) mode. All hatches were locked down and the ship ran on filtered air conditioning. This made moving around the ship a nightmare, squeezing through kidney hatches and all. God knows how some of the fat Jacks got through. You'd be locked in one compartment, then your ears would pop moving into another, due to the pressure change. We heard that one of the scuds landed just down the road from where the majority of 40 and 42 Commando groups were located. Things were getting real now! As part of Delta, our job was to make a classic amphibious helicopter assault.

On 20 March we prepared for invasion.

We had gone to action stations. The ship's company's sole purpose now was to get us ashore to begin our mission. My fellow Marines busied themselves, but by now we were mentally in another place. We were in the zone.

Major Matt Pierson, the OC of Delta Company, had got us all together in the hangar for a final briefing. There had been several briefings during our journey towards Iraq, but this was clearly going to be the last. We were in the anteroom and everyone looked dead serious, ready for business. It was quiet too, none of the usual banter. We all knew there was a good chance that some of us might not come back in one piece. We listened to what Major Pierson had to say intently, because it could mean the difference between life and death. Like all Royal Marine officers he was commando-trained. He was fairly laid back, but every one of us respected him.

He went over the plan again. Where we would land, what we could expect when we got there. There was no Churchillian stuff from him. He was not one for big speeches. He was a cool chap and a good officer. This was not the West End stage after all. He told us to believe in each other.

'Believe in yourselves, lads, and the lads next to you as well. You're Royal Marines Commandos and I have every faith in each and every one of you that you will do your duty.'

Our faces were camo'd up ready for action, looking the part at least. The call to mount the Chinooks could come at any moment and we had to be 100 per cent ready for action.

The air conditioning and background noise was loud, but we could still hear the Sea Kings and Chinooks firing up on the flight deck above. Matelots led each group of Marines with illuminated wands along the grey narrow corridors to our assembly point in the hangar, then out onto the flight deck. Our route on the Chinooks would take us right over the sea and along the coast of Iraq. As for the Wrens, the smell of their perfume would soon be a distant memory, more's the pity.

We all checked our kit and checked it again. Marines do that without thinking. Morphine, hand grenades, webbing, all ticked off in your head. We've done this hundreds of times. Water, field dressing, tourniquet, my rifle, of course, an SA80 A2 standard-issue British Assault Rifle; everything was where it should be. We had stripped the kit down to the bare bones for combat. Mobility was key for us, and in a treacherous and stifling environment like the desert the more gear you carry the more vulnerable you are. Still, you had to make sure you had the essentials. I didn't even take a doss bag it was that critical, with the warmers I had and a bivvi bag – a Gore-tex cover – I weighed up the odds and didn't think it'd be too bad. Anyway, it was already warming up in Iraq so I didn't think I needed it.

By now, the sweat was pouring off me under my helmet and body armour. I was drenched. I was ready – more than I had ever been. I went downstairs quickly to the galley to get a last drink of water and mouthful of scran. You didn't know when you'd next get a chance to eat. There were a few matelots sitting around watching the news on telly, along with a couple of the lads. Suddenly, it flashed up on the screen that Charlie Company 40 Commando were coming in to land on the al-Faw peninsula. It was weird, watching war reporters going in and getting live footage of something we were about to be main players in ourselves. We were a bit jealous they were already getting stuck in, but then again they had travelled on the shit ship. You can't have everything.

Shortly after the news item, the signal came to go. I rushed back to the hangar to get kitted up. I didn't care who or what was waiting for us. I was so pent up I just wanted to get off.

'You're up for this, Matt?' Shorty said with a smile. 'This is it, mate, let's kick ass.'

'Bang on, Royal. I'm sweating Royally,' I said.

Shorty nodded. 'This is gonna be hoofing, son.'

We did one final check before we stepped onto the aircraft lift.

There was a mass surge of Bootnecks onto the Chinook. This was what we had waited for. I was half excited and half apprehensive. I was about to get my first taste of war, 21st-century style.

FOUR

Outskirts of Basra, Iraq
Mother's Day, March 2003

In the heat of battle we both knew the rules were simple: kill or be killed. We had had the rules of engagement drummed into us since basic training. In all the briefings subsequently the commanding officers had been clear: 'Only engage if you can identify enemy.' *If only it had been so simple.*

My head was still buzzing from first contact, and it was almost a real-life *Call of Duty*. I had been popping off rifle rounds, and the excitement of it all was coursing through my veins.

And now these tanks were charging straight for our position.

We were staring down the barrel and it was not a pretty sight. We were proper shitting it now.

We were doing our best to remain calm, but clearly the troop boss, a 2nd Lt, knew something had to give. It would have been a tough match for these guys. Fortunately, someone up the food chain with the pips and power to make changes saw it our way too. Our Challenger tanks had managed to turn around just enough to put down some devastating rounds on the Iraqi tanks. Thank God. They fired off round after round, pulverising the smaller, less protected Iraqi T54/55s, smashing into the metal cases and engulfing them in flames. It was a huge relief. We all had mixed emotions: awestruck by the destructive power of the Challengers, and relieved that the enemy were either dead or dying.

The flames engulfed the Iraqi vehicles, lighting up the night sky black and orange. It was cool. We held our blocking position. It was hard to sleep. Mortars were thudding in around us and the howls of dying dogs and screams from wounded men from the Iraqi quarter prevented any chance of proper kip. But we were told we needed to rest. Tomorrow was going to be crucial as we advanced towards our ultimate goal of Basra.

I did not really sleep – not that I remember, anyway. Adrenalin was pumping around my body. I wanted to keep my wits about me at all times. I did not feel tired either. In a war zone this strange buzz washes over you, you keep going until your body cannot go on any more, then it just closes down, as if a switch has flicked.

All night there were mortars and all sorts crashing down, and unbelievably some of the lads slept right through. I guess they were so dog-tired. It was warm, even at first light.

As dawn broke we got our first real look at the place we had travelled all this way to liberate. To be honest it was a right hole, something like a Wild West movie set. White single-height dwellings, date palms and plenty of dust and desert, and that was pretty much your lot. We advanced with caution, aware that the dwellings were perfect ratholes for the enemy, and offered great protection for snipers and machine gunners who would be ready to drop us.

We passed a few tank hulls too. Burnt red-black. Inside were the charred remains of Iraqi soldiers. They looked like charcoal mummies. They were dead still, shrivelled up and suspended in animation behind the wheel. It was weird. No doubt about it, the Challenger boys had done us a favour. If they hadn't done the business it might have been our bodies that would have been burnt to a cinder.

After we passed through the tank carcasses we met up with the Queen's Dragoons Guards. These boys are the armoured reconnaissance, whizzing around the battlefield in eight-ton Scimitars with 30 mm Rarden cannons. They're not really a match for any main battle tank, but they can piss them off, driving up to them and popping off rounds that more or less bounce off. But they make a good dent and they are an excellent nuisance factor and capable with a lucky strike of damaging the enemy tank's optics and armaments.

Orders were radioed through for us to make a slow advance. Along the route we established a blocking position – a defensive position to deny the Iraqis access to a certain area. Nothing was to be left to chance. Back at the command centre, they knew that they did not want to split our forces and give Saddam a chance to reinforce or attack our positions. A day or two later, as we advanced further towards Basra from our blocking position, we met up with these Scimitars that were also pissing off enemy tanks coming through our position.

We were then passed fresh int from the Scimitars that they had spotted the enemy in a large college complex, just on the outskirts of Basra. So we bimbled off to the college to engage.

The college itself was quite odd really. You have a vast

expanse of desert and a college slap bang in the middle of it. It was a series of dirty, whitewashed accommodation blocks with a courtyard in front of it, ringed with a stone wall and fronted by an imposing, rusted iron gate. After the landing on the MMS and the clearing of the al-Faw this was to be our next biggest objective. From the int we had, we knew there were Iraqi forces inside, and in and around the area from the amount of contacts the Dragoons had encountered. The Dragoons didn't fancy getting too close to the buildings at all, so had settled on stand-off contacts with the enemy. Taking the Sabres close to buildings is the last thing the Army lads wanted to do. Couldn't blame them really – all it takes is an Iraqi down a side alley with an RPG and the three-man crew in the Sabre would be toast. This was a job for fast-moving, elite combat troops – guys like us. We would launch our attack in true old-style manpower fashion. To be honest, after a few days of not being in the thick of it the lads were well up for this task. We decided to make a crack of dawn attack on the college, and wipe out the Iraqi forces holed up there.

When H hour came, we knew we would have to go in hard and fast. My vehicle, a 4 x 4 Pinzgauer, was the point vehicle and tasked with leading the dawn assault. I was on top cover, manning the MILAN. I would be scanning all the windows of the college, looking out for snipers and soldiers armed with RPGs, but also eyeballing the general area looking for anything out of the ordinary. My mucker Shorty was in the back with me, and Al and Foxy in the front. Foxy was a Geordie and a great boost for morale with his wicked sense of humour and crazy antics. He had been attached from 45 Commando at the last minute to fill a space on our team, and I was glad he joined us on the gig. We nicknamed him the Combat Gerbil because of his round face and chubby cheeks.

It went down well, all things considered. Foxy floored it and we raced in.

As we approached the college I was frantically scanning the windows and filthy, whitewashed walls and rooftops to spot any enemy combatants who might be ready to pop up and take shots at us. My finger was poised and ready. The MILAN was designed to take on armoured targets, but is also highly effective when fired at fixed positions. It would have made a hell of a mess of the Iraqis hiding inside the school complex. The school janitor would have been cleaning up the mess for days, if he hadn't already pissed off.

The order suddenly came over the radio: 'Go, go, go!'

Foxy was thrashing the Pinz as hard as it would go, moving up through the gears rapidly, second then third then fourth. We came to a roundabout and Foxy took a wrong turn at the island. Rather than turning left he went straight on. I did think that we were approaching the island too fast and at the last minute we all shouted, *'Foxy, left you idiot, left!'*

But instead of him putting the anchors on, he just threw the Pinz at a 90-degree turn at over 40 mph. It was like the wildest rally manoeuvre you'd ever seen. The Pinzgauer was not exactly designed to handle as well as a Ferrari in these situations, especially with all the kit it was carrying with its suspension bottomed out. And Foxy was no Lewis Hamilton. True enough, we under-steered and went straight into the sand and mud. At this point we expected the vehicle to roll and as the man on top cover I was shitting myself – I could have been crushed to death. Me and Shorty had abandoned our weapons and were hanging off the vehicle getting ready to jump, but by some miracle Foxy managed to keep a hold of it, the vehicle levelled out and with its wheels still spinning, we managed to regain our composure and get back en route.

I jumped back onto the MILAN and Shorty took aim again with his rifle. We were racing towards the front gates now, head on. Nothing was going to stop us. Foxy floored it and in true A-Team-style we burst through the gates, taking them off their hinges, and came to a screeching halt in the college courtyard. The vehicles behind us followed us in, coming to a stop to our rear.

The lads on the vehicle all had their weapons drawn and cocked, and I was poised and ready for action on the MILAN. I looked out of the back through the eyesight, keeping my aiming mark on the target. The SACLOS (Semi-Automatic Command to Line Of Sight guidance system) would do the rest. All I had to do was fire. I could see a couple, maybe three, Iraqi soldiers firing off small rounds at us.

We were first out. I quickly recced the lay of the land to the rear of the college, primed to take out any tanks or enemy positions. Our plan was simple. We would bomb-burst off the vehicles. Shorty and me would go left, Foxy and Al to the right. We would clear each accommodation block in turn.

But as we were trying to debus a couple of Iraqis were popping rounds at us, cracking over our heads. I had one guy in my sights, but it was not really worth firing a missile just to hit someone a few hundred metres away. Zigzagging across the courtyard and with Shorty a few metres behind me, I dashed up some concrete stairs inside the nearest college building. My eyes were darting everywhere, clocking every nook and cranny inside the compound. Our footsteps echoed loudly as we ran. Behind each doorway could be the man who dropped me or Shorty. I had to be at my sharpest and I knew it. We both emerged into blinking, blinding daylight. By now the sun was up bright and clear and we found ourselves on a concrete balcony. I did not have to look very far for the enemy.

There before me was the first guy I would ever kill.

He was standing bolt upright in his army rig with a PKM 7.62 mm general-purpose, Soviet-designed machine gun – their equivalent of a GPMG. I thought, *If this guy gets off a few rounds we're both browners.* He was firing from the hip towards us. Instinctively, I popped up and started shooting rounds straight back at him. Instead of diving for cover, he shit himself.

He blinked first.

He knew his luck was up. He must have been looking at the college complex and seeing these shit-hot Marines storming it like Rambo. He knew he was outnumbered and his only option was to get out of there. But before he legged it he prayed and sprayed rounds in our direction. The rounds were bouncing off the college walls and pinging over our heads. The Iraqi, desperate to avoid meeting his Maker, did a runner, zigzagging in the opposite direction. He was still popping rounds off at every given opportunity, looking to slot me and my muckers. Good luck, mate!

This guy wasn't running away. He was clearly up for a fight and just wanted to find cover so he could shoot us up some more. We couldn't take a chance. He could have blown us away at any second.

I looked down my sights at my target. I depressed the trigger and as the first rounds discharged from the chamber I felt the recoil on my right shoulder. I was popping off rounds at the moving target. Lead was flying all over the place and it stank of cordite.

He was in my sights and I was determined to take this guy down before he got me. If he had been a better shot I'd already be a goner. I was not going to give him a second chance.

I was shooting from a standing position, which is the most unstable and challenging firing position, at a moving target between 200 and 300 metres. I pinged 1, 2, 3, 4, 5, 6 rounds off: he had not gone down. Then 7, 8, 9, 10, 11 rounds. By now, thank God, he was stumbling a little, but still making ground away from us.

I had always been a good shot. But that was not in combat, not in a real contact with the enemy firing at you, wanting you dead. This was one-on-one. I unloaded about half a magazine at the target, but he did not drop. I couldn't understand it. I thought, *Jesus Christ, this guy still hasn't dropped!* Either he was on adrenalin or I was a crap shot. It had to be the latter.

I pumped a few more rounds directly into him, but incredibly he still kept going. In war you have to neutralize the target as quickly as possible. You cannot take chances in a combat environment, otherwise the enemy who you thought you had taken down could crawl around the corner and pop one in your or your mate's head. There is no room for error.

This guy eventually went down, dropping slowly before collapsing on the floor. *Got him.* I was sure he was dead, but before I could confirm the kill, me and Shorty had to pull back to safety. There could be any number of enemy ready to drop me. There was no time for sentiment. I had to get out of there and fast. I couldn't believe it took me almost a mag to kill this guy.

That was a good job.

Whilst this was happening, the .50 cals were firing and the other lads were engaged in their own contacts, fighting targets from several different positions. It was deafening, what with all these .50 cals going off inside the buildings and the rifle rounds cracking around us as well.

The lads and I got into a few more contacts; a few more enemy soldiers perished. Then we pushed through to the position where the body of the Iraqi I had dropped was lying, motionless, stone dead, peppered with bullets in a pool of crimson blood. He had 20, maybe more, rounds through him, including four or five through his PKM. A round had struck him in the leg and snapped his leg in two and it lay at a very abnormal 45-degree angle, bending from the centre of his shin. He was a big bloke, probably 6′ 4″ and 16 stone.

He was the first man I had ever killed, lying spread-eagled on the floor. He was a beast of a man, with jet-black hair and a Saddam-style bushy moustache. His eyes starred blankly back at me, dim with death. His mouth was open and bloody. His body was clammy, lifeless. The flies were already buzzing around the body.

I had no emotion really. Remarkably, I had no regret either, none whatsoever. To me this guy got what was coming to him. He was happy to kill me or any of the lads in my unit. To him we were the invaders. In the blink of an eye, it could have been me lying there dead in the dust, not him. That is the grim truth of war.

What amazed me is that he had taken so long to die. He must have been shitting it that much that he was just on adrenalin and legging it as the bullets peppered his body. The rumours of the 5.56 mm rounds not being as powerful as the 7.62 mm rounds may have had something to do with it too. At least he went down and I had stopped him from killing any of the lads. I went back to the lads and I felt fine. I had seen the first bloke I had killed and that was that. They looked at me and asked if I was all right, because I looked as white as a ghost apparently. I felt fine, but perhaps subconsciously it had an effect on me.

There was no downtime. We had to secure the compound, so me and Shorty headed for another one of the accommodation buildings and proceeded up the staircase with our weapons in our shoulders looking over the top of our sights and ready to double-tap any more Iraqi soldiers we came across.

We did not have time to stop and reflect. The dawn assault had been a success, but we could not dwell on it, and we still had a lot of ground to clear to our front. Eight Troop, the light infantry part of Delta Company, was now tasked with another crucial assault through the desert to the rear of the college complex. We needed to take out the positions behind the college and clean up. For this part of the battle Eight Troop went old school, fixing bayonets just like the lads who went over the top in World War I.

As support we manned the .50 cals, and I was scanning for targets through the MILAN. I saw two Iraqi soldiers running towards my two o'clock. They were armed with AK-47s. Now, .50 cal API rounds are designed to pierce APC (Armoured Personnel Carrier) armour so they were going to make pretty light work of a couple of ragheads armed with old Soviet guns.

A three-round burst smashed into the torso of one of the Iraqi soldiers, ripping it apart in front of us. He seemed to explode with blood and body parts splattering everywhere basically disintegrated. I had never seen anything like it. This guy was about 300 metres away, but we could see his arms and legs literally fold in on themselves. It was truly gruesome stuff. All that was left of him was a big pile of bloody body parts, guts and blood on the dusty desert floor. If you hadn't witnessed it you would not have believed what you were seeing. I chanced a glance over at Shorty and his eyes were out on stalks.

'Bloody 'ell! Did you see that, Shorty?' I said, knowing full well he had, as his jaw was on the floor.

'Jesus, it blew the raghead to bits. He's a goner now,' Shorty chipped back.

'Realities of war, mate,' I said.

'Blinding job,' Shorty said.

The .50 cal had an awesome impact. It was a wrath-of-God weapon in infantry terms. The Iraqis who were alongside their mate and had seen him literally ripped to bits in front of them just feet and inches away could not get out of the killing zone fast enough. They were zigzagging all over the place and diving into the nearest irrigation ditch full of human excrement and all sorts. That was the least of their worries. They just didn't want to be the next pile of body parts in the ground.

We moved through the open ground, clearing trenches and buildings towards the rear of the enemy positions. We were now about 600 metres away from the rear of the college when we came across a fairly large building that had been peppered by the .50 cal rounds. The bullets had penetrated through the twelve-inch concrete walls before lodging in the rear wall and to the back of the building. We caught a couple of Iraqi soldiers as prisoners of war. There was a well-rehearsed drill we needed to go through, searching them and tagging them with all the necessary documentation. You could tell they were very worried. One of the prisoners told us through an interpreter that he had several thousand US dollars in cash stashed in the floor of his house, and if we took him home and released him he'd give us the money. Although it was quite tempting, we're professional soldiers with a job to do and we weren't in the business of taking bribes from raghead soldiers. Chances were that he would be released as a prisoner of war at the end of the invasion anyway.

As soldiers this is what it boils down to: blood, bullets and bodies. It's not for us to question the rights or wrongs behind the invasion – that's for the pen-pushers in Whitehall. We're just there to do a job and we like to think that we can make a real difference to the lives of ordinary people. Who knows, the prisoner would probably be thankful that Saddam was no longer his paymaster, and he can get on with leading a life without fear.

FIVE

Fedayeen ambush,
Mother's Day
March 2003
Outside Basra
Op TELIC, Day 10

Saddam's men must have known exactly when we were coming. Either that or it was a bloody good guess.

We had pushed forward several miles up towards the date palms on the road leading to support the Manoeuvre Support Group en route to Basra. I was on top cover of the Pinzgauer, the point vehicle, scanning the horizon looking for signs of trouble. My sixth sense knew the stage was set for an ambush. I did not have to wait long to be proved right. As we progressed through smaller towns surrounded by trees, small tracks and ditches, our patrol was completely exposed and vulnerable to attack in what we call 'close-quarter battle' or CQB. Suddenly, small-arms fire and RPGs ripped in from all directions. AK rounds cracked over my head, snapping in the air. One RPG smashed straight into us, the lead Pinzgauer, thumping into the radiator grille and forcing Foxy, our driver, to slam on the brakes, leaving us right in the middle of the road. We were sitting ducks. All the lads on it should have been browners instantly. Somehow, miraculously, the bloody thing failed to detonate.

Then, just a second or two later, another RPG hit the day sack that was sat on the dashboard, with the comms kit in it. The two RPGs that had been fired against us had impacted before the 20-metre mark, when the RPG fuse is armed. If the RPG hits anything at a distance of shorter than 20 metres, then it usually bounces off because the warhead is not armed. If all the RPGs had actually exploded on impact, the number of lads going home in body bags would have been significantly higher. These guys were lucky sods. Even so, a 2 kg projectile travelling around 75 mph can still make quite a dent in a vehicle or even kill a man stone dead. Instead, this round ricocheted over Foxy's head, missing him by inches and then exploded a few metres away.

We were up against crack troops, extremely mobile and well trained in fast-moving combat situations. This was going to be the fight of our lives. The ambush was ferocious, well planned and brilliantly executed by a group of Fedayeen, Saddam's personal militia under the overall control of his psycho son Uday. They had just finished setting up the ambush, putting the last finishing touches to it, when our convoy came into view, so we were a little bit early for the party.

We were on a road, exposed, being shot at from all sides, as well as ahead of us – the best thing we could do was debus from the vehicle and take cover. All the lads got off and scattered. Some went right, some left, and I stayed on top with my rifle. It was madness, but I was determined to take out some close targets before getting out of there. We were massively on the back foot now in this contact, with three of our vehicles starting to catch fire, peppered with rounds and totally out of action. All we had was rifles and light machine guns on the ground with us. All the heavy weapons systems were on the flaming vehicles, exposed to the enemy. A few of the other lads were on their bellies in shit-filled ditches or folds in the ground, anywhere where they could get out of the line of fire. I remained on my vehicle with only Shorty at my side.

Suddenly, a big white land cruiser with four more Iraqi soldiers came burning around the corner about 30 metres ahead of me. To this day, I do not know why I didn't fire the goddamn MILAN at it, taking out the reinforcements and extra kit in one fell swoop. Instead, I unloaded rounds from my SA80 assault rifle into the bonnet and windscreen. Shorty, who was right next to me, let rip at the vehicle too. By now it was about 20 metres away from us in the middle of the road. The sound was distinctive as I put five, six, maybe seven rounds through the windscreen and aimed at the driver and passenger seats. I peppered the engine bay too in a bid to bring the vehicle to a permanent standstill, right smack in the middle of mine and Shorty's killing zone. That way we could pick them off one by one.

One of the front doors opened and an Iraqi soldier leant out. I did not know what he was up to, I just saw movement. Rounds were going both ways – it was a ferocious firefight. I fired a few rounds into the door. The guys inside stopped moving. Shorty, who was on my left-hand side, knelt down at the side of the Pinzgauer. We peppered the vehicle with bullets making sure all the enemy inside were dead, but as I reloaded my SA80 I spotted that one of the Iraqis had debussed from the vehicle and was limping into a nearby treeline where we knew there were further Iraqi forces. He was clearly injured, but even so he was still able to carry a mortar-base plate. This was serious. If he managed to set this up we were in even more trouble. Every second counted. It was imperative that we took the fight back to them. I raised my rifle and pumped two rounds at him. He was so close I could see the pink mist as the rounds struck him. One smacked into his right shoulder and the second impacted into his torso. Somehow he managed to disappear into the date palms, but I was sure he would die from his injuries. Rounds started coming in now, literally impacting the tarmac next to Shorty, and rounds were pinging off the vehicle I was on, a foot or so away from me.

The Iraqis were specifically targeting me and Shorty, and we had some very near misses. What with us being in the middle of the road using the vehicle as cover, shooting at targets 30 metres away or closer, we were attracting a lot of incoming rounds and RPGs. We couldn't stay on the vehicle any longer without getting smacked, so me and Shorty took the decision to debus, then legged it for cover with the other lads. The mortar guy had disappeared.

We made a dash for a nearby ditch where three or so of the other lads were taking cover. As I ran from behind the Pinzgauer an RPG round spanked into the ground just three metres in front of me. The rocket motor for the fuel at the back was burning ferociously. I ran for my life. The chances are it could have been a delayed fuse. If it was, it would hit the ground and in the next couple of seconds it could explode. Not for the first time, though, Lady Luck smiled on me. She must have fancied me big time. It did not hit the ground hard enough to explode. If it had, without doubt, it would have torn me apart.

We had carried about 14 MILAN missiles along with us and about half a million pounds' worth of equipment. But by now the whole lot – all our vehicles and kit, including a bottle of JD I'd been saving for the ultimate victory – was engulfed in flames. We were on the ground and up above were unmanned aerial drones belonging to the US Navy SEALs. They were filming the contacts we were in for an hour, and they later told us there was an RPG fired every six seconds, 45 minutes since intial contact.

One of them clipped a street lamp and made a big clanging noise as it bounced off it. We all kept our heads down, just lying there and waiting for it to blow. We were still getting rounds off as much as possible. Bullets were raking up the ground just feet away. It was probably one of the hairiest moments of my life.

Commando units as a rule are lightly armed, because they need to move quickly. But we were seriously outgunned, and as we had no heavy weapons it was very hard to compete with the 40 or so Iraqis who were attacking us. There were only 16 of us and our nominated back-up was tied up elsewhere helping with another contact. We were on our own out there. We would have to get out of it ourselves by hook or by crook. It was like the last scene from the film *Butch Cassidy and the Sundance Kid*, when the heroes dash out from their compound into a blaze of bullets.

At the back of my mind all this time was the rogue mortar guy. From his vantage point he would be able to do some serious damage to the guys taking cover. I knew that it was now or never – if I didn't get back-up on the Pinzgauer and whack him with the .50 cal, then it was game over for our team.

We were taking very heavy incoming fire from everything the Iraqis had on them – AK-47s, RPKs, PKMs, RPGs, the lot. It was so frustrating that all of our heavy weapons were mounted on the vehicles that were stranded in the middle of the road. I just wanted to let rip. Something inside me burned with rage. I knew we had to do something or we would all be vittled up.

I said, 'One of us has got to get back on the Pinz.'

One of the lads looked back at me with a big 'Piss off' written all over his face. You could understand it, I suppose. But in a shitstorm like this, someone's got to take the lead.

So, I thought, *it's up to me*. Without thinking about the dangers, I sprinted out from cover to the rear of the Pinzguaer, ducking the rounds that whizzed by me as I climbed onto the back. Bullets were cracking against the vehicle, raking up the floor next to the vehicle. I gave the .50 cal a quick check to make sure it hadn't sustained any significant damage. It looked good to me, and it felt good to hold. Iraqis were getting closer through the date palms at my three o'clock. I cocked the heavy weapon.

The power of a .50 cal M2 heavy machine gun is incredible. It is a truly awesome weapon. Just the sound of the rounds pumping out strikes fear into the enemy. It has a SUSA (Sight Unit Small Arms) sight with a x 4 magnification. It is capable of single-shot as well as rapid automatic fire, with an effective range of over 2,000 metres and can make short work of lightly armoured vehicles and infantry. I knew this was going to seriously mess them up.

As I opened up, the date palms right in front of me about 30 foot away were just falling like matchsticks as the .50 cal incendiary rounds were smashing into them. As soon as I started firing, its distinctive rapid thumping noise had the desired effect. For a split second our aggressors were on the back foot, diving for cover and running for their lives. It struck the fear of God in their hearts and they scattered like ants.

The lads automatically knew they had a great opportunity to fall back or find better cover and they were quick on the uptake. They had already crawled from their position, before zigzagging away from immediate danger. They took up position next to a concrete wall to my three o'clock, and there were guys behind a wall to my seven o'clock, while I provided both groups with valuable cover. Now I was the focus of the enemy's attention. My actions had seriously pissed them off. I had taken out a couple of their guns in the process. They wanted me dead – and fast – before I dropped any more of them.

I had been firing the .50 cal for at least a couple of minutes to devastating affect. I wasn't in the best position – in fact, I was totally exposed. The ammo wasn't quite up to standard, so I had to keep cocking the weapon, which was a bit of a pain and very slow. This meant I was getting plenty of stoppages, which are par for the course, but it was getting hairy as I was so vulnerable to attack. I knew I was a sitting duck.

I could see that the wall to my three o'clock where the guys were in position backed onto the date palms, and there was a high possibility that there were enemy soldiers the other side of it, ready to lob grenades over at the lads.

'Get your heads down!' I shouted.

I put a couple of bursts through the wall. I was firing an unlocked .50 cal literally inches away from my own guys' heads. I doubt there are many people who can trust someone as much as those lads did me in those few seconds. I remember their screwed-up faces looking at me, as rubble and dust fell on them from the fist-sized holes opened up by the API rounds as they crashed through it at over 2,000 mph. Their ears were in bits after that. The stoppages were becoming more frequent now and my wrists and biceps were on fire from trying to control the .50 cal.

'Need some help here lads!' I shouted above the ferocious gunfire.

It was a race against time. Gareth Thomas – Gaz to us in the unit – didn't need asking twice. He was a sprog in combat terms, like me. He was just 18 years old, a dark-haired lad who prided himself on his physical fitness, built a bit smaller than some of the other Royals. But without a care for his personal safety he raced up to join me on the vehicle. He started feeding the ammunition into the .50 cal, enabling me to keep the enemy pinned down. It gave the lads just enough time to complete the pull-back. We both knew it would only be a matter of time before we copped it.

Then rounds started bouncing around and off our vehicle too. We both looked at each other and knew it was time to leg it for good this time, otherwise our number was definitely up. We had clearly outstayed our welcome. The rest of the lads were also screaming at us to get the hell out of there. So we jumped off and dashed towards their shelter, zigzagging all the way. As I leapt off I managed to bust my weapon sling, which was a pain, but luckily it was in my hands and I was spraying off as many shots as I could whilst I ran.

Not for the first time the .50 cal had done the trick. I dived for cover into a honking ditch on the right-hand side. Gaz was not far behind and crashed in a second or two later. As I landed, lead rounds were flying over my head and pinging off the ground to the side of me. It had been a close call.

BULLETPROOF

'Jesus Christ, mate, do you think you could have fired them rounds any closer back there?' one of the lads wisecracked.

That was two of my lives used up – or was it three? I was really pushing my luck, that much was for sure.

But we were not out of the shit yet – not by a long shot.

SIX

Fedayeen ambush
Outside Basra
Under fire

It's hard to describe accurately what it feels like in combat. It is not just the sounds, sights and smells. It is being afraid, sad, angry, upset all at once. You try to make sense of it, while doing your best to stay alive and keep your mates alive too. Then your training kicks in and you just react. There really is little time to think – it's all about action.

We were face down in a ditch full of honking human shit and piss smack in the middle of no-man's-land. AK rounds cracked overhead, sounding like deadly fireworks. We had to keep moving and get out of there as quickly as possible. If we failed, it would only be a matter of time before we were vittled up and overrun. There was only one option: to crawl through the crap on our stomachs, keeping our heads as close to the deck as possible. It was either that or we would be picked off like sitting ducks.

As a last resort, when you are under enemy fire, you send one lad forward to see if he can draw enemy fire. The chosen man pops up as an obvious target. The enemy would immediately start shooting at him and would act as a distraction. Obviously, to be the target man takes real courage and guts, as it is seriously risky. The alternative is to go forward and pinpoint the enemy position.

We now found ourselves in a last-resort situation. We had crawled through the ditch and stank of shit and reached its natural end. Ahead of us was exposed, open ground and no other exit. One of the guys would have to pop up and draw the Iraqi gunfire. I just thought bollocks and decided to go forward to pinpoint the enemy. We were running low on ammo too, making action even more imperative. I crawled forward. I could not really see anything, so I emptied a whole mag in the general direction of the enemy through the date trees. I re-bombed up with ammo and went forward for a second look. This time I pushed forward about 15 metres when I came up to a compound in the trees on the right-hand side.

As I came round the corner, I literally walked straight into the enemy – just 10 metres in front of me. I had no idea the enemy were so close. This guy looked just as shocked as I did. He had an RPG on his shoulder and was flanked by two other Iraqi soldiers brandishing AK-47s. Everything seemed to unfold in slow motion. The Iraqi swung the RPG round in one sweeping movement and looked straight down the sights at me. Simultaneously, I raised my rifle to my shoulder and depressed the trigger. Adrenalin was coursing around my body now. I was proper shitting it. Then, at the critical moment, my rifle jammed.

I was dead meat.

I was in this guy's sights and basically browners.

The Iraqi soldier pulled the trigger, propelling the grenade forward off the launcher at 384 feet per second, the fins along the stabilizing pipe spreading out. The grenade moved like a rugby ball, rotating through the air; the fins stabilising its flight. And then somehow, miraculously, it skimmed off my helmet. It packed a punch though, and while it did not explode on impact, its force sent me flying backwards onto my arse.

Dazed, my ears numb, deafened by the explosion, I was in a total state of shock. Blood was pouring out of my nose. Somehow, more through luck than judgement, I was still alive. I could barely believe it. A guy had fired an RPG straight at me and I was still in the game!

For a second or two I didn't have a clue where I was. Luckily, I could still just about see. I knew instantly if I didn't get my arse in gear and quick I would be a goner. I had landed a few feet away in a crescent scoop on the ground. It was effectively a shell-scrape. As I opened my eyes I could hear very sharp snapping noises, bullets cracking directly over me, and branches and twigs being hit just a couple of feet above.

Bullets were flying, pinging off the mud and trees around me. When I fell back, my weapon was loose, because the sling had bust earlier, and the weapon fell out of my hands. God knows where it landed. I think it flew into the bush at the side, but that was the least of my worries. Somehow, despite all the fire raining down, I managed to scurry back to the lads. My main concern was just getting out of the killing area and back to the safety of the lads and letting them know how close the enemy was. They wouldn't have had a clue otherwise.

They were still back in the ditch, 15 metres away from my

position and utterly oblivious to how close the enemy were. When I got back there was only Gaz and Shorty there waiting for me.

I was out of breath and a bit shook up by my experience.

'What's going on, Matt?' said Gaz

'Where's your rifle, mate?' Shorty quizzed.

My heart was thumping. I somehow spluttered out the words,

'Enemy 10 metres that way . . . Lob grenade NOW!'

They got the message. The lads lobbed four or five grenades into the area I had just come from and we all took cover. A couple of seconds later we heard the bangs as the grenades exploded.

'Where's the other lads?' I asked.

'They found a route out,' Gaz said.

The battle had been raging about an hour now. Our ammunition was running low. Me, Gaz and Shorty had no choice but to lie down for a while. The odd few rounds cracked over our heads. We wanted the enemy to believe we had either already been killed or had scarpered.

After a while of lying low our plan seemed to have worked. The fire from the Iraqi soldiers subsided. At this point Shorty pointed out a barbed-wire fence in the distance. It looked like an alternative way out of there, and although it was on open ground, it couldn't be any worse than the shitstorm up ahead, so we decided to risk it. The only problem was that we didn't have any wire cutters on us. None of us said anything, but we knew we would have to climb the wire fence under fire if we were going to have any chance of making it out alive. All those hours down at Bottom Field at CTC would come in handy now. The plan was that once over the fence we could sprint into the woodline – a date-palm forest, which we believed led towards friendly forces – and find some cover there among the trees and scrub. It was probably going to take us a good five or six seconds each to get over. We stopped returning fire in order to deny the Iraqis knowledge of our exact position. We were still less than 100 metres from the enemy and in clear sight of them.

First up was Shorty. I borrowed Shorty's rifle after Gaz and I covered him. Our rifles were on our shoulders, but we refrained from pinging off rounds, because we didn't want to draw attention to our mucker, as the little fella scaled the 4 ft fence. If they had spotted him, he would have made good shooting practice. As he reached the top of the wire fence an RPG bombed in nearby, exploding, and Shorty jumped off the fence onto the other side. As he did, he ripped the whole front of his combat trousers off, revealing his own Weapon of Mass Destruction. It was hilarious and a bit bonkers considering our treacherous situation. Gaz and I couldn't help pissing ourselves laughing at Shorty.

'You prat!' I said to Shorty.

Once Shorty had cleared the fence, he scampered into the treeline.

I was up next.

The fence was a real bastard to get over. As I scaled it, I caught my trailing left leg and ripped a deep gash about five inches long. Gaz followed at the end and he too made it over and into the trees. We had trouble spotting Shorty at first. I couldn't work out where he'd gone. Gaz located him – he had fallen down a 10 ft embankment. Tit! He eventually managed to drag himself out of it, and we made our way through the forest.

We were all obviously exhausted at this stage, breathing through our arses. We had been in a very heated gun battle for more than two hours. We now found ourselves in front of a waterway next to the Shatt al-Arab river.

As we emerged onto the waterway we were under siege from enemy rounds. I don't know where they were coming from, but they must have spotted us pretty quickly, because the rounds started landing fairly close to us.

If we had any chance of getting out, we had to cross the waterway. It was about 12 ft wide, which was just a bit too much to jump. However, there was a small rowing boat moored just down the bank. If we could just get to that we might be able to make our getaway. Unfortunately, it meant going into open ground where we could draw fire. It was a question of who was up for carrying out this manoeuvre.

We were all in a bad way. I was bleeding and Shorty was breathing out of his arse, so to settle it we played the PO game. This meant that the lad who had been in the Marines the least amount loses out. This isn't Marine protocol, but it's a good way for lads to sort out duties nobody wants to do. Gaz lost, but he's a top bloke and he didn't mind.

'Good luck Gaz, mate,' I said.

Gaz waded in up to his chest and swam demented poodle to the moored rowboat. Sure enough he started attracting rounds. Luckily, they were shit shots and the rounds missed him. Gaz reached the boat in one piece after a good effort and unmoored it, then brought it up back to the bank close to where me and Shorty were sheltering. He then ran up the bank and lobbed a grenade in the direction of the fire. It was a good effort by Gaz.

By the time we got across the waterway the three of us were not exactly looking our Sunday best. I had blood coming out of my nose and ears from that RPG incident and a gashed leg.

I didn't even have a rifle. My combats were ripped, dirty and covered in blood too.

Once across the waterway we made our way back to join the rest of the Company. They were only a few hundred metres away from the other bank. The rest of D Company had just moved into the area. They had seen all our burning vehicles and all the mayhem that was going on and were convinced that there had been quite a few casualties, if not fatalities. They had already linked up with some of the lads, but me, Gaz and Shorty were actually reported MIA (Missing in Action) presumed dead!

No sooner had me, Gaz and Shorty hooked up with the lads and confirmed that we weren't browners, than we were back in action again. D Company was still engaging combatants in the area and I had taken cover in a ditch with an energetic lad called Deano. Rounds were zipping overhead from a lone Iraqi soldier who was making a nuisance of himself. He kept popping up around the Company, on top of buildings or vantage points, laying down rounds. It was only a matter of time before one of them actually hit one of us. I chose to arm myself with a 94 mm LAW. My moment to use it had arrived.

This Iraqi soldier was hiding behind a bunline (a mound of earth) and I decided to use the HEAT (High Explosive Anti-Tank) round and fire it from my LAW. I popped it right over the heads of two disgruntled US Marines and it landed spot on, blowing the bunline apart, along with the soldier too. Bits of him were everywhere.

Minutes later the screeching of tyres was heard and 200 metres away a small white saloon with Iraqi soldiers inside initially tried to pass themselves off as surrendering troops, waving white flags out of the windows. The gig worked until a couple of lads spotted them brandishing AK-47s and putting loads of rounds down on us, it was a cowardly tactic, but one that we were getting increasingly used to. I swung into action. The LAW is only a single-shot weapon, but I found another one just lying about and picked it up. The other lads were training their guns on the car; one lad manning a .50 cal shot one of the Iraqi soldiers, who had adopted a fire position out of one of the doors, and took his leg clean off. I finished the job off with my LAW and the car was blown back about 12 ft by the projectile, blowing the doors and bonnet off.

Once the contact had finished we moved off and set up a nearby patrol harbour. It felt good to be around the lads. We got some hoofing scran down us, then I got my wounds cleared up and was issued with a new SA80 rifle. The QM was going to have an awful lot of paperwork to fill out, what with all the vehicles we'd lost. I got my head down for some vital zeds.

The next day we were assigned to go on a dawn patrol back to the scene of our escape. I have to admit, I was a bit apprehensive about going back into the hornets' nest just 12 hours later. But it was an important patrol. We were Bootnecks after all, and it was vital to get the message out that we could walk back into a hostile area with an arrogant swagger that said, 'Is that the best you got? We're still here and you're not going to stop us from patrolling through.' There were probably 30, maybe 40, Iraqi fatalities. The battle site was cleaned using brushes, but the blood remained, staining the dust. Not a single brass cylinder or any kit was left, though. All the vehicles had been stripped too.

It was soon obvious how lucky we had been – especially me during my run-in with the three Iraqis and the guy with the RPG. Because there had been more than three guys –

almost a dozen of them concealed in a deeper position. If we hadn't lobbed those grenades when we did, we would have all been toast.

I went back to the spot where I dropped my weapon, hoping it would still be there. I couldn't find it though.

Gaz was awarded the Military Cross – granted for acts of exemplary gallantry during active operations – for what he did. The citation focused on the ambush where he had bravely jumped up on the Pinzgauer to feed my ammo on the .50 cal. Another mate of mine called Tommo got an MiD (Mention in Dispatches) for rescuing a full vehicle of kit and equipment from the killing zone. There were rumours that I had been put up for a gong too. I didn't get it, maybe for reasons I will explain later in the book. I would never drip about it. The lads who were there knew what I did and to a man recognised what happened for them. That's all that matters. As for Gaz, I was thrilled for him. He is a brave Marine and deserved it.

SEVEN

Operation Pussy Galore
Abu al-Khasib, south of Basra
April 2003

Hanging out, we had been on our feet for 15 hours.
I had lost all track of time. None of us had slept
properly for 24 hours, maybe even more. Our unit was
advancing towards Abu al-Khasib running parallel to
the Shatt al-Arab waterway, which literally means 'Beach of
the Arabs'. At night, the temperature would drop dramatically, but during the day it was red pigs, especially when
weighed down by combat kit.

The MSG (Manoeuvre Support Group) advanced to the
western outskirts of Basra. The city, our mission objective,
was now in our sights. Delta Company was in support. Our
op codenames followed James Bond themes. There was Op
Blofeld, Op Goldfinger. Ours – Op Pussy Galore – was clearly
one of the most important and demanding.

Delta was tasked with securing a crossroads that linked

Abu al-Khasib to Basra. HQ believed that this was clearly the route that Iraqi reinforcements would pass on the way to Basra. We were tasked with taking it and holding it – a double whammy in theory, but not so easy to execute in practice. It would stop the Iraqis reinforcing Basra and give us a chance to take out troops retreating from the city too. Of course, if they came out in nothing but their pants with their hands up we would take them prisoner, but we were dealing with the hard core now, and the chances were that they would come out fighting, and fighting to the death.

We all knew the chances of serious casualties were high in any war zone, let alone going into a probable deliberate attack. By nightfall, we had taken our 'consolidation position' in the suburb of Abu al-Khasib, which was primarily Sunni and full of palm farms. We would press on in the morning further along the Shatt al-Arab river.

Pussy was a key objective. If we were to take Basra, Iraq's besieged second city, we had to tick this off first. If we got it right it meant that Op James – a mission involving hundreds of commandos – would have been a success. The idea was that if we could demonstrate that Saddam's forces were vulnerable, that would ignite an uprising by Basra's large anti-Saddam majority. We had taken out around 22 Iraqi tanks and dozens of prisoners, but there was still a lot of fighting ahead. Under cover from smoke shells fired by British gunners, we resumed the assault. As we pushed forward over the Shatt al-Arab waterway we heard reports that two boats crammed with soldiers had come under heavy mortar fire and helicopter-borne missiles. This fight was far from over.

While there were some Marine casualties from the battle for Abu al-Khasib, only a select few were caused by direct enemy fire. Looking at the devastation around the town, that seemed astonishing. Under plumes of black smoke from two burning oil tankers, more than ten destroyed Iraqi tanks could be seen in one stretch of road alone as we advanced. Each had been stopped in its tracks, its thick steel armour peeled open. There did not appear to be any Iraqi dead inside, but all of the tanks had gone up in a blaze of flames once a HEAT warhead had hit them.

Reinforced trenches and earthworks were built to the south of the town, where it faces the salty marsh flats of the al-Faw peninsula. No matter how elaborate the Iraqi tank positions, nothing could stop 600 Royal Marines commandos facing them down on foot, backed up admirably by tanks, artillery and air power. The 105 mm light guns of 29 Commando Regiment, Royal Artillery, had fired an unprecedented barrage ahead of our advance. Each of the eight guns from 8 Commando Battery fired more than 100 rounds, and their gun pits out on the flats were each surrounded by a small mountain of burnt brass shell cases. In one night alone, 40 Commando Mortars fired a cocktail of more than 5,000 rounds in support of one of Delta Company's battles. On the roads within the town there were heaps of spent British ammunition cases, each one telling part of the story of the 15-hour battle for Abu al-Khasib. An Iraqi anti-aircraft gun lay destroyed next to a bridge, and mortar impact splashes pockmarked the roads. We were winning this war and nothing was going to stop us now.

The Challenger 2 tanks from C Squadron the Royal Scots Dragoon Guards were crucial to the battle. Plenty of rocket-propelled grenades were fired at our call signs, but they simply had little effect against the Chobam armour. Chobam armour is the most advanced heavy armour composite on the market, even better than US, French or German counterparts.

A British armoured vehicle was attacked by 70 RPGs, but it was not destroyed and its occupants were unhurt. On the other hand, we had hit them where it really hurt, devastating the local forces and leaving them totally exposed and making a siege of the city impossible.

This way Saddam's top thugs would get a thumping great signal of our intent. By now we were flying. The ambush – and the fact that we had got out of it alive – had given us all a big adrenalin rush. We were right in the thick of the action and loving it. The area was previously used by locals, and a couple of wealthy Iraqi generals' houses made for a very good HQ for Delta. We had pushed approximately two miles further ahead of the main advance of British Forces, we knew it would be risky and wanted to fortify the area of houses and compounds we occupied as best we could. We mounted .50 cal machine guns at each corner of our patrol harbour in this built-up area at Op Pussy.

We had three .50 cals pointing down each of the roads to give us maximum firepower if an Iraqi advance came from those directions. We deployed Claymores in blind spots and crucial areas, and snipers on the roofs on 24/7 sentry. Co-located with them would be the MFC and TACP to bring in instant mortar, artillery and airstrike support. Also located on the roof would be the 51 mm mortar man, for the 'token' effort if it all kicked off! The sentry posts were backed up with MILAN teams, 94 mm LAWs, and GPMGs. We had this place screwed down and it was a fort, waiting for the inevitable Iraqi counter-strike.

We went out pilfering food from the local deserted houses – like chickens, rice, potatoes, tomatoes, flour and cooking oil. It was enough to keep the hunger pangs at bay. A lot of our supplies had been blown up along with our three vehicles in the previous contact, so needs must. You can't beat fresh food and although a lot of people have the perception of Iraq being like a Third World country, so the food must be dodgy, I can tell you from experience it's far from the truth. We were running low on rations and it was too dangerous to get a resupply as far forward as we were. Shorty and me managed to get some kit off the Yanks, including a new set of combat pants. From then on we looked half Yank, half British.

The US Marines couldn't believe what we were doing, but after a day they were saying, 'We'll just go hungry.' More fool them. We were living the life of Riley, cooking these great big chapatti things, plus banjos (our slang for eggs) on bread in the morning – it was better than living on rations really, and it beat Marine scran hands down.

'Are you really gonna eat that Iraqi crap?' one of the Yanks asked.

'Well, mate, what have you got as scran then?' I said, before answering for him. 'Sod all!'

A couple of days later the same Yank came up to me. He looked really hungry and sorry for himself.

'Sorry for taking the piss, man, but can we have some of your food?'

'Sure, fella, tuck in.'

He took one bite of my makeshift scran and his face lit up.

'Jesus, this food is good!'

The Yanks couldn't believe how proactive we were. We didn't mind, cracked a few jokes, took the piss out of them for a bit, before cooking them some eggs with garlic bread. Not the most famous of dishes, but Gordon Ramsey would have been proud considering the circumstances. The only thing that we did mess up was the three small chicks. We were going to feed them and fatten them up for a nice roast. Unfortunately, they died after the first night. It was a freezing night and we left them outside. It must have been too cold for them, because they were dead the next day.

Royal Marines are thinking soldiers and pretty self-sufficient. We just got off our arses and did our own things. As night fell the sky was lit orange with a burning building. That was the handiwork of the lads on Op Oddjob, who were tasked with blocking our exit line. There was a stink of burning rubber too, and wafts of black smoke.

We experienced contacts during our stay at Objective Pussy. There would be some almighty contact kicking off, and then suddenly some bloke with a donkey and a load of fruit or something would appear in the line of fire. It was like something out of a Monty Python skit. They didn't seem to give a shit if they were hit or not, just going about their daily business of making a few quid, as if everything was normal.

We were well forward of the main front-line advance, maybe as much as two or three miles. We were now within spitting distance of Basra itself. The presidential palace on the banks of the Shatt al-Arab river was now within our sights. It looked like something out of *The Thousand and One Nights.* Gaudy and totally over the top. We held our position, despite coming under constant attack from enemy fire. Then we got intelligence that we were seriously under threat.

Two thousand Iraqis were just down the road, maybe a mile or two. The officers and lads tried to play it down.

'Can't be that many lads, maybe 200,' one of them said.

'You sure about that, Boss?' one of the guys quipped.

'You heard about all them Iraqis up the road?' Shorty asked me. 'Sounds like it's all really going to kick off.'

'Looks like it, don't it? Might not be a bad idea to start double-manning on the sentry positions, mate. We want to be ready.'

Whatever the true numbers we knew we were in for a fight. All we seemed to be doing was pushing the Iraqi forces back, further and further. Our call sign had already discussed this, making a presumption that eventually they were going to realise, *Hang on, there is a few hundred of us now – we have enough to fight back.*

This was pretty nerve-racking. At the fort we had more time to reflect and dwell on the possible contacts, and that played on your mind a little bit, considering we had experienced such a close escape only a few days before against a far smaller enemy force. I had just turned 19 a couple of months earlier, and I was experiencing the most terrifying, dangerous, mind-blowing experience of my life. Now we had been told that 2,000 heavily armed Iraqi soldiers were right on our doorstep. We were a couple of miles away from any other coalition forces and support. All we kept thinking was: *It was hard enough with 16 of us against 50 of them, so 60 against 2,000 doesn't sound so hot.*

We were heavily outnumbered. This was in danger of turning into a modern-day *300*. I wasn't flapping. I have always been a realist. I took a moment to think before being proactive and deciding what to do. I went around the sentry positions, realising they could be improved. So me and the lads bolstered up the defensive positions with extra sandbags and more ammo. There was no way we were going to extract. Vehicles were tight at full strength, and we already had three down. As a manoeuvre support company, we were armed with the big guns. This meant we needed vehicles to operate as efficiently as possible. If we allowed our position to be overrun, we would be unable to do our jobs properly.

The first wave of Iraqi soldiers formed up behind a sprawling school complex, waiting and ready to attack in their dozens. The final protective fire position was established. It was shit or bust. The 81 mm mortars flew in, striking right behind the school where the enemy lay in wait. It was carnage, just 100–150 metres or so away. The noise of the assault was deafening. So were the screams from the injured and dying. Flashes of yellow and white lit the sky, and we all dived for cover to avoid being peppered by bits of shrapnel from mortars and RPGs.

The .50 cals were singing. So were the GPMGs. Lads took up post on the MILAN, looking for any vehicles or machine-gun positions to take out. Snipers were sniping and the MFC was hard at work calling in fire missions on multiple targets. It was a different call sign taking the lead on this contact. Our sentry post was quiet, facing towards the south-east, but we still needed to be vigilant. There were 2,000 of these Iraqis apparently out there, and they had more than enough numbers to surround us. I was running back and forth ferrying ammo to the .50 cals and GPMGs.

We weren't in a position to assault the Iraqis. We had no reserve, and hadn't done any in-depth previous recces of the ground in front. We had no idea of enemy numbers, and to be honest we were receiving so much incoming fire, we needed to keep our baseline and win the initial firefight. We were taking as much incoming fire as we were dishing back out. Sandbags were taking rounds and walls were crumbling or collapsing from RPG hits. We relied heavily on the indirect fire taking out the majority of Iraqi forces. The Mortar Troop of 40 Commando were awesome, and had assisted 40 Commando battle group over the previous days in all of our many contacts.

Mortars were raining in now, some impacting just 100 metres away, which is very close considering the damage they can inflict. But that was where the enemy were and that's where we needed them. The majority of Delta Company had to get out of direct line of sight from the impacting rounds to avoid shrapnel from friendly mortars. Mortars did the job, and the remaining Iraqis chose to count their chickens and retreat.

There were a few injured survivors, along with the many dead: charred black with smoke, their faces dazed and destroyed. It had been the most horrific lesson, and they had learnt it the hard way. It was an important battle for us. They probably thought of us as a soft target. Perhaps they even had intel that we were the only invading troops in the area – out on a limb and vulnerable. We had to stand and fight. We had to show them who was boss and that we could pack a much larger punch with a lot fewer guys than they could. I think we were fortunate, though. It was feared that this could have been a probing attack with no more than possibly 20 or 30 Iraqis, just testing to see what punch we packed, in order for their commanders in Basra to assess and overrun our position in a well-planned and well-executed attack.

For a while we stayed alert, just in case there was going to be a second wave of attacks. After a while we were stood down, all tired, splattered with weapon oil and smelling of cordite. We still had to admin the sentry positions, though, one covering the other. We also had to give the weapons that were heavily used a quick boogey, replenishing the spent ammo with new boxes and also tidying the areas of used ammo tins and brass. If we didn't, before we knew it we would end up in a similar state to Charlie Sheen in the film *Hot Shots!* when he was stood on a mountain of brass, still firing. All was done and we could settle back into our routine, which was of course scran then sleep – until you are rudely interrupted by the 'duty' shake at 2 a.m. to do your stint on sentry for two hours.

It wasn't all bad though; we were all doubled up because of

the threat, and you could have a bit of a chinwag so long as you weren't too noisy. But then we were woken up just before dusk to all stand to. So actually I got no sleep, and I couldn't sleep in the day as it was too hot and there was stuff to do, such as clearance patrols. I was beginning to experience the 'not so' fun side of being a Marine. I just remembered to take the good with the bad.

The next day we got into a routine. We knew we'd be there for a couple of days, so all we could do was prepare the area better for the inevitable future attacks on our position. All neighbouring areas were derelict. On the deserted road that went through our position lay two large craters caused by a coalition airstrike, most probably aimed at the nearby generals' houses, but missing the target by a couple of dozen metres. Later that day a wounded cow walked into our position, suffering a nasty head injury, either from last night's contact or possibly some shrapnel off the previous airstrike. The cow wasn't best happy and decided to locate herself in the middle of our harbour, refusing to move. I think in the end it took seven or eight of the lads to push that stubborn cow out of the area. I can't remember off-hand if the lads put a round in her head to put her out her misery. A couple of hours passed with not much happening, the sentries going through their rotation; some cooking, food-hunting, the odd clearance patrol. I decided to take a wander onto the flat roof of one of the generals' houses; there were a few other lads up there too, carrying out whatever job they had or just to relax.

All of a sudden, several rounds were fired; they must have been about 30 metres away from us. With the trees and walls in the way we couldn't see what was going on from the roof. There was a bit of shouting, the lads standing to, and a little uncertainty as to what was going on.

An hour of daylight was left. The anticipation was written on everyone's faces, wondering what the Iraqis had in store for us. But dusk came and went and the lads settled into their night routine of manning defensive positions and getting their heads down. It was expected that the Iraqis would attack us, but not a total surprise that they had decided against it. We had given them a kicking the previous night and perhaps they were just not up for it again. I managed to get my head down for the first time in a few days. I used to go most of the night without any sleep. I physically couldn't sleep with the noise of gunfire, mortars, artillery and jet fighters constantly around us. In the end I think I was so tired I just fell asleep from exhaustion, and, to be honest, I think most of the lads were the same.

I was woken up at around ten o'clock to carry out my duty on sentry. I was sat behind one of the .50 cals with Foxy for the duration.

He kept banging on about Newcastle United all the time.

'I've got a good feeling about next year with Sir Bobby [Robson] there, man.'

'Bollocks, Foxy, you've got no hope . . . you haven't won anything in years.'

'I suppose Birmingham have then, mate?'

We'd spotted heat sources in our arcs with the SOPHIE thermal-imaging device, about 300 metres away.

They confirmed there were no friendlies in that area. We looked through the Maxi-Kite night-vision sight, which was attached to the soft mount of the .50 cal to give a different perspective of the target. It was hard to see, as these shapes and heat sources seemed to come from a treeline, so it was very hard to identify what they were. After about 20 minutes or so the heat sources moved into more open ground, and we clearly identified them as cattle – and very lucky cattle at that. I was close to sending .50 cal slugs their way.

Another hour passed and I was soon off sentry, when all of a sudden: WOOOOSH . . . BANG! An RPG had impacted directly above me and Foxy into the wall of the HQ building. Our ears were ringing, but fortunately we took no shrapnel. Looking up at the wall, the RPG had taken out a big chunk of concrete, which potentially could have landed and hit the lads below. They would be awake now and sorting them-selves out anyway. A few cracks went overhead as incoming fire rained in for a second night in succession. I was desperately viewing my arcs with the Maxi-Kite and SOPHIE, as was Foxy. The rounds weren't coming from our position. Then we heard the .50 cal and GPMGs from around the corner opening up. We'd been hit from the same direction as the previous night.

I asked Foxy to man the .50 cal, while I went to check on the lads and give them a set of QBOs (Quick Battle Orders), so they knew what was going on, where to go and what to do when they were up. I looked over and saw no movement. I went and shook a couple of the lads and realised they were all fast asleep. I was baffled that they had managed to sleep through the RPG exploding 10 or 20 metres away, and all of the gunfire that had now erupted. It just shows that when you're that tired, there's really nothing that's going to wake you! It made me wonder what potential situations I might have slept through.

The lads were up by now, still a bit dazed, but doing their admin as quickly as they could to get out to the battle or wait in reserve for another tasking. Gunfire subsided for a time. The lads still all stood to, waiting for the Iraqis' next move. All of a sudden there were two almighty bangs that came from a nearby treeline. It turns out that the lads had heard rustling and movement from that direction, so decided to detonate the claymores. These are mines that have 700 ball bearings in each, packed into 1.25 kg of RDX TNT. It makes for a formidable defensive weapon. Any troops that would have been in the vicinity would have serious injuries, if they weren't already dead! A couple of minutes later two whimpering, injured dogs came out of the treeline. Looks like they were trying to escape the battle and took the wrong route. The lads had thought the Iraqis were pulling a right-flanking manoeuvre. There were no more Iraqi attacks on Pussy.

The next day we were relieved by Bravo company and a Chinook flew in and extracted us a few miles to the rear of Objective Pussy to Umm Qasr port, where we were meant to get 24 hours of 'forced rest' – decent scran, a hot shower, soft arse paper and a general replen. It was a welcome relief from the non-stop intensity of the front line. However, after sorting out all our kit, post and admin, we had very little time to ourselves, although a warm shower was welcome before heading back out.

Next stop: Basra.

After the battle for the Abu al-Khasib suburb, there was a real buzz of excitement and anticipation among the Royal Marines. Many were busy exchanging stories about the contacts they had been in. One of the stripeys was getting patted on the back after he told how he was hit in his ceramic plate by a 7.62 round fired by the enemy just 50 metres away. Another Marine told of a grenade glancing off his helmet, and another told of how an Iraqi colonel driving a car with a briefcase full of cash refused to stop and was shot dead. 'I didn't know what to do with the money,' he said, 'so

I gave it to the kids, bundles of the stuff, it was worthless anyway.'

We all knew we had been lucky to get out with our arses intact. The locals appeared happy to see us. Everywhere we went we discovered evidence of the brutality of the regime. In a police station in the suburb the lads found what appeared to be a torture chamber. If any proof was needed of the nature of Saddam Hussein's reign of terror we didn't have to look any further. Local people openly discussed the past, but life appeared to be returning to some sort of normality in the suburbs and the majority seemed pleased to see us. Certain villages we passed through had been banned from having electricity for the last couple of years under Saddam's regime. They were overjoyed they could turn on their generators once again.

Shops opened, selling bags of flower and rice, and bakeries were producing fresh, unleavened bread in clay-fired ovens. Our boys patrolled the streets of the town and reported good relations with the local population. Our intelligence got a boost too. We started getting accurate tip-offs about an ambush being prepared by Saddam loyalists. We received a message from our OC, Lt Col. G. K. Messenger OBE.

The message read: 'Quite simply, you were magnificent.'

We were hard as nails and up for the next fight.

I'm not bigging up any one of the lads – all of them rose to the occasion. It may sound bonkers now, but I remember we were actually laughing and joking half the time in the heat of battle. It may have been bravado, covering up for the fear we felt inside, but actually, as the fight went on it was as if we had our second wind. And to be honest, it's all good fun, until someone gets hurt.

EIGHT

Outskirts of Basra
Week 3
Operation TELIC

The message came down that Major General Robin Brims at Brigade Headquarters wanted one final push for Basra. But only when he thought the time was right. So far our forces had refused to be drawn into fighting in the centre of Basra until it was the right time. We had kept a loose cordon around the city, which allowed controlled movement in and out. This was a chance to spread our propaganda.

We were getting the reports that the Ba'ath militia and Fedayeen were capitalising on this by using the fleeing civilians as human shields. They also mortared these civilians as a brutal and bloody warning to those left behind that they still had control. It was all part of Chemical Ali's strategy to try and draw the British into a firefight on the streets of Basra. But that was not the way our commanders wanted to win this battle. Some locals were being force to fight, because

Saddam's henchmen were threatening to kill or harm their families. Yet the locals still weren't committed to over-throwing their Ba'ath Party oppressors and still had not come off the fence.

Delta Company was under strict orders to hold our position and keep the suburb of Abu al-Khasib with its 30,000-strong population. The strategists were convinced that as soon as word spread that Saddam's troops had suffered a serious bloody nose in the suburbs they would rapidly lose their hold on power. After three days of fighting news had reached the Shiite Muslims that Saddam was losing his grip. We were left to fight around 1,000 or so die-hard Iraqi loyalists, but we knew it was only a matter of time before the Shiites rose up and attacked members of Saddam's Sunni Ba'ath Party and their loyal band of fighters. The enemy's morale had been sapped. All of their plans were more or less out the window, and I think the majority of the 1,000 thinned out and went home.

While Prime Minister Tony Blair was on his feet telling the House of Commons that he would offer support to the insurgents, we were dead on ours, relying on adrenalin to take us over the final hurdle and into Basra with its 1.3 million inhabitants, a tinder box of terror. After years of suppression and religious persecution, the Shiites were ready for a fight too. Running low on food and water, and sick to the back teeth of the tyranny of Saddam, it was their moment and their revolution would get us over the finish line.

As the commando force pushed forward, Saddam's loyalists were firing artillery from the heart of the ancient city. We had been instructed to do our utmost to avoid civilian casualties, but there will always be innocent victims of war, no matter how diligent we are. The desperados who had been running the city with an iron fist had made their last throw of the dice. Desperate measures for desperate times. We had to neutralise them as soon as physically possible without putting our own men in unreasonable danger.

US war planes threw their considerable weight behind us too. Satellite-guided bombs smacked into the heart of Basra. Intelligence had singled out specific military targets, sites that were hidden in civilian buildings. Saddam was using human shields right up to the end.

Some targets we simply couldn't engage. For example, our intelligence showed Saddam's army were using hospitals and built-up areas to refuel their tanks. It was a dirty trick. The risk to civilian life was just too great. As we pushed forward the 7th Armoured Brigade – the famed Desert Rats – were poised to enter the heart of the city and write a new chapter in their illustrious history. The commanders knew it was a risk to go in so quickly, but it was a calculated risk that they thought was worth taking.

We could have pressed on more quickly, but the strategists at HQ were determined to avoid getting us caught up in urban warfare, and they were waiting for Basra to implode. There were an estimated 1,000 militia men still active and ready to fight to the death from street to street and house to house. You have to expect a 60 per cent casualty rate in these fighting environments, and whereas on your XBox it can be the most exciting environment to fight in, in reality it is one of the most dangerous. The enemy can come from above and below you, as well as from 360 degrees around.

By early April the exiled Iraqi National Congress opposition party had got word of mouth out too. They were urging the locals onto the streets, leading to bloody hand-to-hand fighting and bayoneting. Saddam's men were so alarmed that they started mortaring them. From our position, intelligence was seeping back that the inward collapse of Basra was starting. Basra was on the brink.

Raids were carried out by Warrior armoured vehicles, targeting specific sites singled out by British intelligence as Ba'ath hideouts. Taking out these targets would have a dual impact: not only weakening the resolve of the Ba'ath militia, but also encouraging the Shia to rise up. Propaganda leaflets were scattered around the city, urging the Iraqi people to be patient and trust us. 'We will not desert you this time,' they read in Arabic.

The city's electricity supply had been taken out during US and British bombing raids. That, in turn, shut down Basra's water-pumping and treatment plants. We were itching to finish off the enemy, but, wisely, the commanders told us to hold our position. If Saddam and his generals wanted to reinforce the city, they would have to come through us. Equally, if his battle-hardened troops decided to escape, they would walk straight into us.

If we were going to have any chance of rebuilding this devastated country, first we had to win the war decisively, without too much damage being inflicted on the innocent population by Saddam's bitter retreating army and his political cronies who had enjoyed savage power. Thousands of innocent children were now at serious risk due to poor sanitation and unsafe water. We knew a swift victory was imperative if a new Iraq was to emerge from the blood and flames.

It was not all plain sailing – it was never going to be. In a ferocious counter-attack, three Iraqi patrol vessels launched an intensive RPG assault on one of the marine landing craft on the Basra canal, 30 kilometres to the south, setting it ablaze with a direct hit. One by one they managed to take out each of the Iraqi vessels with anti-tank missiles. But the Marines under fire had a close call.

On 6 April the British launched a decisive, three-pronged attack on the city with battle groups of the 7th Armoured Brigade, consisting of Warriors and Challenger IIs and 42 Commando. 40 Commando were a 'cut-off and blocking force' to the south of the city, overlooking it. Delta had a good view towards Basra Palace. The objective was to penetrate deep into the city during the day, then retreat at night, again exposing the enemy's vulnerability.

It was now only a matter of time.

When word reached our lines that victory was ours – only a few hours after the assault began – it was a bittersweet moment. I cannot deny that I had enjoyed the thrill of the fight. Maybe that was wrong, but I was charged up when combat operations ended.

We would not be able to stay long before being relieved. The Geneva Convention says something about not having fighting troops conducting peacekeeping operations straight after taking control of a region. It made sense. Action is like a drug, and I was as high as a kite after being in the thick of it, although I was thoroughly exhausted. Every one of us was still in fighting mode. Not trigger-happy – we are too professional for that. But the rules are written for a reason, and with hindsight I can see why. We were all so charged up.

It was only a matter of time before we were shipped out and replaced by a fresh unit as quickly as possible. A Spanish Armoured Cavalry regiment moved into the area after us. It was weird. The place took on a whole new ambience. There was the occasional explosion from mortar fire, but the screams of dying dogs and humans had subsided. It is amazing how quickly you can adapt to situations. The lads were almost in holiday mood now. At a new complex located further south in the country, the position we had been ordered to hold, we caught up on a few rays. The lads stripped off and were sun-bathing to top up on the power tan before going home. One of them, Ben, managed to turn his arse red-raw through 'naked' sunbathing.

The officers were all for us having a bit of downtime after so much stress in combat. They were proud of our performance and realised that after all we had been through it was important to unwind. We did a few workouts. I got my max rep up on bench presses, played a bit of chess or cards and had time to write letters back home. I wrote to my mum to reassure her I was OK. I told her it had been a walk in the park and there was nothing for her to worry about. There's no point worrying your loved ones unnecessarily. She also informed me my Grandpa Croucher had died whilst I was in Iraq. I remembered him telling me all those stories about his time in the Navy. I was sad.

We were also inundated with post from well-wishers from the UK; it was really good to feel appreciated. There were sacks of letters from women back home, which didn't go amiss with the lads. They were delighted with the potential trapping power the war had given them. Some of the lads wrote back too, and got the pen pals thing going. Some of them even scored – or so they said!

Days blurred into each other. It was a big difference from the intensity of the previous weeks when time passed so quickly. We could get some real zeds in now for the first time since we were choppered in.

As soon as the order for extraction came through, half the company were pulled out by helicopter straight into neighbouring Kuwait. I volunteered to go on one of the road-and-vehicle convoy moves back into Kuwait, which in some ways was probably a better option.

I saw a bit more of the Iraqi countryside. When it's your combat zone you tend to see it in pure battle terms – cover, lie of the land, defensive positions, exit routes – and you just want to get out of there alive. Now, without the direct threat, I got to see it through different eyes. For a West Midlands lad from Solihull it was like being on Mars. I'd never seen anything like it. But I started to think this place could grow on me, and I hoped my part in the liberation would give these people another chance. I wasn't holding my breath though.

We crossed over the Kuwaiti border and into Kuwait City, where we managed to go and have a drive-through at Kentucky Fried Chicken. We had to drop off all the vehicles at the port where the Royal Fleet Auxiliary ships would pick up all the equipment. We boarded the *Sir Bedevere*, and sailed down to the UAE towards Dubai for two or three days' chill-out away from the war zone. We would have to come back to Kuwait afterwards, so it wasn't quite goodbye, but it was good to let our hair down.

We had a bit of a piss-up and relaxed. It was long overdue. There was a sense of euphoria and real pride in what we had achieved. Now it was time to celebrate. We got back to Kuwait and were held for just a few more days. Most of the lads stationed there were US Marines and most of them, through no fault of their own, had not been engaged in any contacts in Iraq itself. They couldn't get enough of our war stories and we soon made a few friends while we were there. We spent hours just chewing the fat and swapping kit.

The Yanks found it difficult to get hold of alcohol, but we helped by getting it posted out to us. We could do them a favour by getting them a bottle of Jack Daniels, which was worth up to $300 a pop. This was a nice little earner, especially as we were about to pull out of the country and they would probably be there for a few more months.

That camp came under attack from a Scud missile. It landed about a kilometre away, but it got them all excited. Astonishingly, the Yanks that hadn't seen any contact on the front line were put up for a medal just for being under enemy fire. To be honest, I thought they were having a laugh given what the Marines had been through, but it was for real.

After all the excitement of fighting the enemy, the boredom was excruciating. We were hanging around kicking our heels just waiting for the order that we were being flown out. I got bored. I ended up going to a US military barber without giving it too much thought really. The lads pissed themselves when I emerged complete with a jam jar high and tight. I looked like something out of the film *Jarhead*. I looked a total prat, so went back the next day and told him to shave the whole lot off. I couldn't cope with all the jibes about looking like a Yank.

The RAF were flying troop planes into Kuwait to take us home. It was a toss between 40 Commando and 42 Commando over who would be flown out first. To be honest, that was the only tension around the place. There were a lot of lads who were praying that 40 Commando would get the nod. The prospect of another two or maybe three weeks in theatre was not appealing. As far as the lads were concerned we had done our job and sitting around chewing the fat with the Yanks for weeks was not our idea of having a good time. It was up to the Pongos now to do the mop-up job. Commandos are combat troops, not policemen.

A cheer went up when we heard we had got the nod. I felt

for the lads from 42 Commando, but there was no time for niceties. I was going home. We scrambled our kit together and before we knew it we were on the tarmac loading up. As we boarded the aircraft I felt a bit weird. I had been waiting for weeks to get that plane home, as I was so bored out of my skull. I was glad to leave, no doubt about it, but I fully expected to be back here again soon. It was clear this would take a long while to clear up. And I was leaving with a feeling of satisfaction at a job well done. Some of the lads back home, experienced stripeys, had not seen what I had seen or done. It felt good to have achieved my life ambition, to be a Royal Marine in war. That's what I had joined up for in the first place.

We flew back into Exeter Airport, which was right next to our base in Taunton. There was a lot of press, a lot of phots, and some of the lads' families too. The majority of the families were waiting back at 40 Commando at Norton Manor camp. It was a surreal experience. We were still in desert rig, but for us dusty warriors the war, for now, was over. Blinking in the sunlight, as I descended the steps I knew life after Iraq was never going to be the same. How could it? We were blooded soldiers who had stared death in the face.

NINE

Exeter, UK
May 2003
Back home

As we peered out of the windows of the Tristar, we saw the old familiar green fields and thick forests of England. It looked a lot better than Iraq.

We disembarked at Exeter Airport and it was time to head back to our homes. Shorty lived down in Bournemouth, and Foxy up in Newcastle. I had to get back to Birmingham. Shorty had a bird to go back to, but as Foxy was heading in the same direction as me we decided it was a great idea to get on it Sandy Bottoms-style and have a proper hardcore session. Me and Foxy went up to the Company Sgt Major and asked him if we could skip going back to camp. He knew us well and must have thought we deserved to get shiters.

'If you get someone to get your Bergen and baggage off the other end I can't see why not lads,' he said.

What a top man, we thought.

Foxy called a taxi straight away. We were buzzing. We just wanted to get bang on it. Foxy's missus and little brother had come to meet him, and we didn't see the point in hanging around. We were still in our desert rig and at the time there were rules about wearing it in public. We didn't even go out in uniform, apart from exceptional services like Remembrance Sunday, although the rules have since been more relaxed.

We thought bollocks to it and went to Exeter train station in a taxi to get the train north to go home. There was another Royal Marine at the station. I recognised him from Lympstone. I knew he had not been out in Iraq. He must have been kicking himself that he had missed the deployment. Some people who had been in for 15 years as corporals or stripeys hadn't had the chance to go to Iraq. This guy gave me a funny look.

'Bloody hell, guys, you're in rig at the station. What's the dit?' he said as I passed him.

'I just don't give a fuck, mate,' I said, turning around. 'I just want to get home.'

He didn't say a word after that.

Me, Foxy and his family jumped on the train and straight away got tucked into shedloads of Stella. We were necking them like apple juice and it tasted great. As soon as it hit the back of my throat my head was buzzing even more. Me and Foxy tore into the lager just like we tore into those soldiers back in Iraq. We got some funny looks on the train as we were still in our desert rig, but by this time we were flying.

A couple of guys were sat opposite us with their birds.

'You guys just got back from Iraq?' one of them asked.

'Yes, mate,' I said.

We struck up a conversation. They were OK so we all got pissed-up on the train. They thanked us for what we had done out there. It was good to know we were appreciated.

I jumped off at Birmingham New Street and climbed into a taxi and headed home to Mum and Dad. At this time I used to spend my leave at home or at a mate's house. There didn't seem any need at the time to buy a flat or rent anywhere, as the rest of the time I lived on camp.

My mum, Margaret, opened the front door. She had a beaming smile on her face and was really happy to see me. I gave her a great big hug.

I think she and my dad, Richard, could tell I'd been on the sauce a bit. But they didn't care at that point. I was the returning hero.

'How was it, Matt?' Mum asked me.

I told her about the missions and the country and the heat. I didn't tell her about the guy I slotted with the .50 cal or the car I'd blown to shit with my LAW.

I didn't know it at the time, but this was the start of almost three months' worth of leave, which was a great surprise to all the lads. We certainly did not expect to get that much, but it was well appreciated.

It was very odd being back, especially in the first few hours. A few days before we had been killing enemy soldiers. I was in the thick of it with a real chance of dying at the age of 19. It was bizarre coming back to what some call normal life. But what was soon clear to me was the general apathy about what was happening in Iraq. Maybe I was supersensitive, but it seemed to me that nobody gave two hoots back here. I could have been killed at any time – and for what?

Perhaps the experience had taken a greater toll on me than I knew. There was a sense that people back in the UK kind of owed us a favour or something. We had been over there fighting for the country, for democracy and freedom, and they were more concerned about the price of their new car or

With the lads from 2030SQN Air Training Corps, Remembrance Sunday 1999.
Left to right: Mark Kenny, me, Grant Sirret, Dan Castro and Matt Cox.

At the Commando Training Centre the day after our 30 miler and still four weeks left of training to go!

The infamous Bottom Field at CTCRM, Lympstone.

Me and a lad we knew as Cyclops putting some rounds down on the ranges with the .50 cal.

The .50 cal is an awesome weapon. You can see there's a 2ft channel dug underneath to catch brass and it's overflowing with spent rounds.

(*Left and below*) Practising my helicopter abseiling skills. We trained in this technique for situations inserting through tree canopies and onto waterborne ships as a boarding force.

Royal Navy door gunner letting loose with a GPMG (General Purpose Machine Gun) on the insertion into Iraq from a Sea King helicopter.

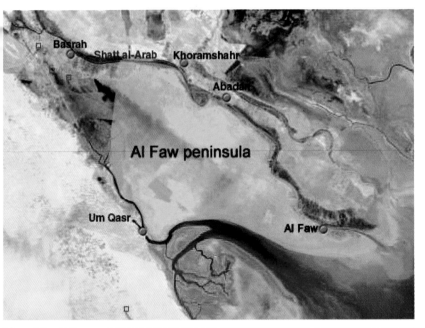

Map of the Al Faw peninsula area that 40 Commando were tasked with securing.

Me with the other 'Matt Croucher', a guy from US Special Forces' Force Recon, May 2003.

Final preparations from HMS Ocean before going into Iraq. The lads are zeroing Barrat .50 cals and .50 cal Browning HMGs to make sure they're accurate.

The lads in B Company fire off a K115 HEAT missile from a MILAN firing post during ops in Iraq.

The 94mm LAW is a mean bit of kit. I did some serious damage with this on tour.

Launching a final assault on an Iraqi Armoured Personnel Carrier. A grenade being thrown in for good measure to take out any remaining enemy.

Me, Bungey, Shorty and Foxy on the back of our MILAN-armed Pinzgauer, toppers with about a million quids' worth of equipment.

Our blown up Pinzgauer surrounded by locals the day after the ambush, as you can see there's nothing left of them! A close shave.

shopping bills. I felt that we were worth a lot more, certainly worthy of more recognition.

All I wanted to do was let my hair down when I got back. I started going on the piss regularly, perhaps a bit too much. I wouldn't say I'd turned into an alcoholic, but the war had obviously had quite an impact on me. Was I drinking to forget? No, not really, but it was a way of dealing with what I had been through – the killing, the blood and gore, and facing the stark truth that at any moment my life could have been ended as bluntly as I had ended the lives of others. There was a sense of boredom when I got back. All my civvy friends were either at college or university or had jobs, so I think going out on the piss or to the gym, for me, just passed the time.

Yes, I had done it without thinking. I had done it for Queen and country – yet at the time it did not sink in. But back home with all the mundane normality around me what had happened in Iraq seemed surreal. I thought the best way of dealing with it was to go out on the piss with my mates. They loved hearing the stories. It was unheard of in our adult lifetime. Campaigns like the Falklands or even the Gulf War were in our chilhood. My old mates from school – some of them now at uni – were just relieved that I had made it back in one piece, and they wanted to go out on the piss with me to celebrate. It was nice to have a good few jars every now and then.

But 'every now and then' started to turn into every night for the first two weeks of leave.

My mucker, Pierre, from 42 Commando, who was in my troop in commando training, was more like a brother than a mate. We were very close. I could pretty much tell him anything. We just kept going out on the piss. Nothing could stop us. Neither of us reacted too well to people back home.

We were proud of what we had been doing for the country and despised their apathy about what was going on in Iraq. With hindsight, perhaps we shouldn't have been so hard on them. At that time the media weren't giving us their full support. It wasn't a sexy story – they seemed to think Jordan's tits were more important than lads dying for their country thousands of miles away. Still, we were not shy to let people know what we had been doing out there. We would chat to bouncers at nightclubs and say we have just come back from Iraq, and ask if they would let us in free and stump up a few beers. Nine out of ten would be happy to oblige, and we had some cracking nights out on the back of our front-line service.

But it was only nine out of ten, and the tenth could be trouble. There was always the one and that is when it could kick off. We must have had quite an attitude post-Iraq. We would look at the people in the club and be dismayed that they were the ones for whom we had put our lives on the line. Frankly, some of them didn't seem worth it. I became disillusioned. They were behaving like arseholes.

'Look at that wanker,' we'd say to each other, nodding towards some guy totally smashed off his face.

'Can you believe we went to war for that?'

I shook my head. I couldn't.

Perhaps our reaction was normal. Perhaps returning soldiers throughout history have felt the same sense of abandonment. We had not been prepared for it. During some of those nights out, we would end up getting in scraps. We were minging, off our heads half the time. The fights were pointless, really. Half the time we didn't know what it was all about. It just kicked off for no reason.

I suppose I had the mentality that I had survived Iraq, I had made it through that war alive, so what was the worst thing that could happen in a fight? I could handle myself pretty well. The worst thing that could happen was getting hurt pretty badly. That didn't bother me. Perhaps I was losing perspective, but I'm sure I wasn't the first battle-hardened soldier to bring the violence back home from the war zone. Most I won, a couple I lost.

That summer me and Pierre hit it off with two gorgeous girls. We kept it simple at first, but actually got to know each other and we had a real *craic*. We spent most of our leave with them just chilling. We would go out, the four of us, to the movies or clubbing or having a barbecue. It was great being normal again. The girls were able to take the edge off our aggressive temperaments. But sometimes this girl complained that I could be distant. The war was never far from my mind. Clearly it had had a bigger impact on me than I thought. She was a great girl, though, but it was never going to be anything serious.

I hadn't had any serious or long-term relationships at that point. As a Royal Marine I didn't see the point, what with me being away all the time and totally committed to my job. So what with Iraq on my mind, coming back to three months of downtime, and having a girlfriend, it was a lot to take in.

With the money I had saved up from serving I bought myself a Subaru Impreza Turbo STI. I felt fantastic at the age of 19 that I had earned enough to splash out on this cult car. I was delighted that what I had done in Iraq had earned me this money to buy it outright. I was made-up.

Generally, life was good. I had the wheels, I had the bird, and my oppo Pierre to go drinking with. But something didn't feel quite right. There was a dark side to a lot of the nights out with me and Pierre. The girls said we would snap too easily, at the slightest provocation. It was only a matter of time before things really kicked off.

The final straw was a couple of weeks back at camp. Pierre got into serious trouble for fighting down in Plymouth. Some nonce drove past and shouted some abuse at him out of a taxi. He should have just let it go, but it really pissed him off and so he chased this taxi through Plymouth for a couple of miles until he eventually caught it up at some traffic lights.

He was in a rage by now. Nothing could stop him. He punched the rear window of the taxi and dragged out the bloke who had stuck his fingers up at him. Pierre gave him a right hiding, and all his mates were begging him to stop. He did eventually and just walked off back to camp. The police caught up with him, but in the end, the fella he whacked refused to press charges. Again, the incident was booze-fuelled. In reality, we should have just let the insult go. After Iraq, maybe Pierre was hypersensitive to these wasters. It was costly though. The taxi driver needed £600 to fix his taxi.

Pierre did not help himself, really. When they loaded him into the police car he was pissed off and gave the handbrake an almighty boot, so the police car rolled down the hill. The two coppers had to leg it after the car. He did himself no favours, and was given a police caution. It should have been enough, but worse was to come.

A couple of days later we came out of a club and saw a bunch of teenagers kicking the crap out of a bus shelter, and it really pissed us off. There were a couple of other lads picking rubbish bags out of the bin and chucking them all over the road. With hindsight, we should have just walked away. It was nothing to do with us. Pierre and I had exactly the same mentality: we thought those kids were bang out of order.

We stepped back and thought, *Are these the arseholes we've been fighting for in Iraq?* They had no respect, so why should our lads put their lives at risk for people like these wasters? We walked over to them, and Pierre asked, 'What the fuck do you think you're doing?'

They were full of it. They started gobbing off back at us. That really got our backs up, and we lost it with them.

'I wouldn't push it, mate, if I were you,' I said, but they didn't give a damn. They were determined not to back down. Pierre, whose size can be quite intimidating, forced two of the other lads to go back into the road with the bin bags they had emptied and pick up the rubbish strewn all over the place. Just then, a police patrol car rolled up at a nearby junction. The two coppers inside had obviously looked over, saw these lads collecting the rubbish and deduced something was up. They pulled up and got out.

'What's going on here then, lads?' one of the coppers said. He gave Pierre and me the once over and didn't seem to like what he saw. Before we could explain, these four or five lads chipped in and said, 'These two big lads said if we don't start collecting all this rubbish they were going to kick our heads in. Honestly, sir, we've done nothing wrong.'

It was bollocks, of course. We were just putting right what they did wrong. The police told us both to move on.

One of the worst things you can say to a copper or anyone in a professional position is that they are not doing their job properly. It didn't stop me. Perhaps it would have been better to just sod off and go our separate ways, but I couldn't leave it. Neither could Pierre. It was like a red rag to a bull.

'You're not doing your job properly, mate,' I said. 'These lads have trashed this bus shelter and emptied the rubbish out the bins, it's a disgrace.'

I could see immediately that it was unwise. One of the coppers took offence. He was clearly in no mood to be lectured by me.

He looked me squarely in the eyes, and said, 'Listen, mate, don't tell me how to do my job. Do not start pushing it. Do yourself a favour and go on your way.'

Maybe it was the booze talking. Maybe, post-Iraq, I somehow felt indestructible, above the law. But I was not having it. His attitude got right up my nose. As far as I was concerned, he was letting these hooligans get away with it. It was just plain wrong.

'If you look at that CCTV footage you'll see what they were up to. You're obviously not doing you're job properly if you're not going to arrest these guys and prosecute them. What is the point of you?'

It was a step to far. He got all arsey about it. Eventually, the lads who had been the catalyst of the situation just pissed off and left Pierre, the two officers, and me in a stand-off. Pierre's fuse, which was short at the best of times, just snapped. The copper did not like his attitude, the anger in his eyes, and grabbed hold of him to arrest him.

Pierre, with real force, pushed the copper away and shrugged him off. He ripped his shirt off his body and took off. This copper gave chase after him. Then the one that was chatting to me ran after him too. I knew Pierre was in trouble, and I suppose instinct kicked in and just like back in Iraq I felt compelled to protect my oppo.

Foolishly, I just grabbed the copper and got him in a headlock. I did not intend to harm him. I was trying to defuse the situation. I said, 'Listen, mate, look, leave him alone. I'm not going to hurt you, just leave him be. We'll call it quits and we'll go on our way.'

It was a big mistake. As soon as I loosened my grip on him,

the copper turned round and pepper-sprayed me in the face. It hit me right between the eyes. As the spray hit me, my eyes closed and started to swell up, and it was a while before I could open them properly again. My nose was running continuously and the spray went into my mouth. It was burning and I was coughing a lot.

Simultaneously, he tried to arrest me, which really pissed me off. Despite being disorientated and in pain I managed to grab him. I could not see, but I could hear him calling for back-up assistance on his radio.

I admit this was not my finest hour.

He was grappling with me to try to arrest me, so, despite the pain, I managed to twist him up and drop him face down on the deck. In Royal Marine basic training I became proficient in hand-to-hand combat. My reaction was instinctive and for a second or two I thought I was back in the war zone. Without doubt, I had lost all sense of propriety. At that moment, I was a mess. Everything that had been going through my mind since we got back from Iraq, the alcohol and the late nights, it all exploded. In the course of the scuffle, the copper dislocated his knee and ankle.

Meanwhile, Pierre and the other copper had squared off at each other. He just turned and thought, *Why am I running away from this prick?* He stopped and told the copper, 'Let's have it then, mate!' The copper was obviously more clued-up than his mate was. He did not fancy a ruck with Pierre, in case he came off worse.

'Oh OK, mate, just carry on,' he said. Pierre had got away with it, and just legged it.

Apparently, Pierre hid in a bush all night as the other police patrols were out looking for him. I kept schtum. I was not going to grass him up. But he came forward later that week when there was a warrant for his arrest. Meanwhile, the situation was getting worse for me. I had this copper pinned on the deck and my face was in bits from the pepper spray. By now, my vision was blurred and tears were streaming down my face. The pain was excruciating.

Through the blur, I clocked four or five police cars – the blue lights – and a load of people running towards me with their extending batons out ready to give me a solid whack. I thought, *Bollocks to getting beaten up*, so I lay flat on my face with my hands behind my back. It worked. The officers could see I was in a passive position. I was cuffed and unceremoniously carted off to the police station, then charged for assaulting and injuring an officer in the line of his duty. It was bound to get messy, and I knew no matter what action the police took, the Corps was going to throw the book at me.

One of the policemen who questioned me was ex-military police, who knew where I was coming from and was a top bloke. He was very understanding and, although he could not condone what I had done – no one could – he could not thank me enough for what I had done in Iraq. Even though they were the prosecuting coppers, they were still quite chatty and friendly to me. There was no question that I had been very wrong to react the way I did, but they didn't treat me like an animal, which I appreciated.

Looking back now, I think this moment in my life had more to do with the way I was feeling after returning from the Iraq war zone. Maybe it was psychological. Who knows? Shrinks in the United States have claimed that thousands of returning service personnel suffered terribly from flashbacks, inability to relax or relate, restless nights and more. The symptoms of combat stress are more commonly recognised now than they used to be. This is not an excuse, but a fact, and possibly the reason why I ended up hurting that policeman. I don't usually go around bashing coppers. I hadn't before and I haven't since. The one time it did happen, I was 19 years old and just back from my first taste of real war. It's not difficult to work out what was going on in my head. Nonetheless, setting all that aside, I am responsible for my actions and I am truly ashamed of what happened that night.

Nothing could excuse my behaviour, and I fully deserved the sentence I was given. Luckily, it was not custodial, but it so easily could have been, which would have ended my career in the Royal Marines. The judge handed me a sentence of 200 hours' community service and £1,000 compensation fine. In addition, I had to attend alcoholic awareness and anger-management classes.

My troop boss, who was about two days out of Royal Marine training, was sent to represent me in court, and frankly did not know me from Adam. He had to come up with a character witness statement sharp. After the court hearing, I got a severe dressing down from my CO, but my record in the Corps and in combat must have counted for something. Rightly, he left me in no doubt that it was not acceptable to bring the Corps into disrepute. I could hardly argue. My career was on a knife edge. Future slip-ups simply would not be tolerated. I would be out on my ear and I knew it. I was put on a career check for the time I was carrying out community service.

It was soon apparent that I would pay for my crime in another way. Before the incident, there was a strong rumour circulating around Delta Company that I had been written up for a citation by my OC regarding my actions during the ambush in Iraq. Apparently, the citation was in the process of being considered further along the military chain of command for consideration.

My arrest and conviction put paid to that. I will never know if I was in line for an award. If I had received it, I would of course have been honoured, not only for me but also for the lads I had served alongside. I was never told if it was true or not, but when Gaz Thomas did receive an MC for bravely jumping on the vehicle with me and feeding the ammo as I pumped out rounds to allow the lads to retreat, most of the lads were very surprised that I hadn't been awarded anything.

He had also got the boat for us to cross the Shatt al-Arab waterway too. I do not in any way resent what happened. However, most of the lads were pissed off about it. Gaz included. I think he felt a bit guilty, but I told him not to worry and that he deserved it, and shouldn't think otherwise. Frankly, the lads that were there knew what happened, and in my book that is all that matters, really.

My parents were equally unimpressed with my conduct. They were both convinced that if I didn't tone down my drinking and fighting I would end up getting into prison and going completely off the rails. They were right. I knew I had to calm down and fast. I needed to focus, to get back on track.

I knew I had to shape up and I hit the gym harder, started boxing again, up to four or five times a week, and managed to tone up. I needed to. Five months after Iraq I knew I needed to focus again. I certainly calmed down after doing that to the copper. I had to really screw the nut and avoid any more trouble, but that is easier said than done. You cannot change your character overnight. All that I had achieved serving in the Marines was in danger of being destroyed, and for what?

I returned to Norton Manor Camp (NMC) late August. It felt great to be back with the lads. We were kicking our heels for a bit, just trying to get used to military life again. The one big drama we had when we got back was bringing all the ragged vehicles that had been in theatre back up to scratch. All the kit and equipment came back to camp too and had to be de-serviced and cleaned. Many bits of kit were broken or in need of service and it took a good few weeks to sort them.

The Sgt Major and officers were constantly reminding the Company that we had to be ready for the unit's next role. We were to be lead commando unit in the next few weeks, meaning we'd be on a heightened state of readiness to deploy across the globe at a moment's notice. As soon as you are back from leave, you have to take the responsibility and be back up to R1, the codename for Readiness 1. It means you have to be fit to be the lead commando unit, so that if anything happened anywhere in the world we would be the first guys to be deployed.

That role is usually swapped between us and the Paras (1, 2 and 3 Parachute Regiment), or the Army guys in 16 Air Assault Brigade. There is therefore always a commando unit or parachute regiment on various levels of readiness, which means anything down to four hours' notice to move.

Even on your weekends, you cannot go anywhere further than four hours' drive away from your camp, so you can get back in time. Sometimes, on leave, you are called back in a practice to ensure everyone can make it in time. It may piss the lads off, but it is essential from a strategic point of view for the higher ranks. Anyone who turns up late gets a severe dressing-down and it is drummed into them how serious this can be.

Then news came through we had a posting. However, it was not another operation as we had hoped. We were off to Norway. It was going to be icers.

Ten

Narvik, Norway
Artic training
January–April 2004

We were ready to let off steam after several weeks of Arctic training, freezing our cods off up some godforsaken mountain. The thrill of 20 mile-long ski yomps had worn a little thin by now. Some of the lads were also desperate to try and get fixed up with some Norwegian women, too, even though it's well known amongst the lads that it's ninja to pull in Norway. I don't know why, but for some reason they're not really up for it.

The Bier Keller was pretty busy, so it got the thumbs-up. Each of us nursed a beer. It was too costly to buy rounds so we bought our own. We had had a decent skinful of duty-free booze back at camp, too. Inside, we bought orange juices and tipped in vodka from the hip flasks we had smuggled in.

Straight away a group of Viking-like blokes kept eyeballing

us. They didn't seem very impressed by our behaviour. We were a bit rowdy, but we were just having a laugh. We were chatting away to birds, but not really getting anywhere. Yet these blokes seemed pissed off about something. We didn't care. If they wanted to have a ruck, we were pretty sure we'd take them if we needed to. None of us really gave a toss about anything much that night. It was time to let our hair down and have a *craic*.

One of the lads – Ben – thought he had got lucky with some sance, apparently called Aasta or something else I couldn't pronounce. He was clearly hoping to bag off with her. Normally, I wouldn't touch any of Ben's with a bargepole. But she was different. Blonde and blue-eyed, I have to admit she was pretty fit. She must have been in her mid-thirties, but well trim. None of us would have kicked her out of bed. Obviously, Ben thought he was in there and had targeted some kind of Norwegian spunk bowser, but he was about to find out that talking to these birds got you nowhere. I would call them cock teasers, but they never even seemed to get round to teasing. Needless to say, Ben came home with us in the end, wearing the look of a stray dog.

As for the rest of us, we were too shiters to get anywhere with the girls at the Bier Keller. In Norway my normal trapping powers deserted me. By the end of the evening the situation was in danger of getting out of hand. One of the locals, from the group of Norwegians who had been staring at us, must have called the Royal Marines Military police, our wing of the MPs, because when we emerged from the bar they were waiting for us.

We were all pretty minging by then. Bimbling along, heads down as we left the Bier Keller. One of the lads clocked the two RMPs in their wagon. They looked like they meant business. Another one of the lads shouted for us to thin out, but by now it was already too late.

The RMPs jumped out of their Landy and started walking meaningfully in our direction. In the Corps the lads, perhaps unfairly, saw these guys as traitors for taking a police job when they are fully trained commandos. Many of us thought becoming MPs was a cop-out, and they often got abuse for it. That night they got it both barrels from us.

'You're supposed to be Marines, you wankers!' one of the lads shouted at the RMPs. They didn't take the abuse very well.

But the closer they came the more abuse they got. Perhaps we were just spoiling for a fight that night and it was just their turn. By now we had all started gobbing off at them. This could only end in tears.

'Shut it, you gobshite!' one of them said. 'If you carry on you'll all be nicked.'

By now the alcohol must have kicked in, and it was about to seriously kick off. The RMPs suddenly developed a sense-of-humour failure. When one of them threatened to arrest us it was like a red rag to a bunch of raging bulls. In unison we told him to piss off. It clearly wasn't the wisest crack.

They came straight for us. The best thing to do was make a run for it. We jumped into a taxi we had luckily pre-booked, a converted big Sprinter minibus, complete with local driver. That was our saving grace. As it turned out, it proved a touch of genius. Without him we would have been nicked for sure.

The RMPs were now seriously pissed off. They could see us making a getaway and were determined to cut us off. They jumped in their Landy and the race was on. They wanted to beat us back to camp, summon the duty stripey and then throw the book at us. At best we would have been given a serious bollocking the next day, maybe even put on a charge. None of us could be bothered with that.

As true Marines we were determined to go down fighting. If we could kick Saddam's backside in Iraq we were confident we could give these two pricks a run for their money. We were going to have a damn good go anyway.

As we sped off the lads and me were pissing ourselves in the back, just laughing our heads off uncontrollably. We told the driver to go hell for leather to lose the military police car giving chase. We needn't have worried. This guy could have given Lewis Hamilton a run for his money.

'You do know what you're doing,' I said to the driver. 'You're running from the police.'

The driver was ice-man. He didn't seem the slightest bit bothered; if anything he was up for the *craic*.

'I know how I drive these roads, gentlemen. Stay cool, hold on tight,' he chipped back in broken English.

He was clearly well up for the challenge. If he couldn't give them the slip, no one could. The driver was as good as his word, drifting around the bends as if he were a top-class rally driver, even with his studded tyres on. He was awesome. All the boys were well impressed.

At one point, the RMPs' Landy raced passed us, but just when it looked like we would have to wrap, they spun out into a snowdrift and were left stranded. They were furious, arms up, gesticulating, each blaming the other for the cluster-fuck. Pissing ourselves, we all gave them the finger in unison as we whizzed by.

When we pulled up at camp we happily handed over our cash to the driver. He had played a blinder. He got a big pat on the back from the lads, but victory was not ours yet. There was still time for the RMPs to catch us out and pull us in. We all legged into our dorms and had just enough time to get in and get our heads down before the MPs stormed in. They scanned the place, seeing if they could recognise any of us. Of course they couldn't. One Bootneck looks just like another from a distance at night.

We stiffed them, because, being tactically aware, we shoved our boots in the drying room with all the others. If we had left them by our doss bags with fresh snow on they would have rumbled us. Luckily, that night we came out on top and got away with it.

It was typical of the scrapes we got into during our three-month deployment to Narvik, in the north of Norway, about 140 miles outside the Arctic Circle, where we were specialising in Arctic and mountain warfare.

Although there was time for drinking and trapping it was serious stuff. It was icers. Just getting used to the freezing conditions was tough enough. You have to take in twice as many calories – up to 5,000 a day – and carry loads of kit. You have to learn how to ski with all the kit, too, going out each day for nine hours, from first light till last light, with some night-time skiing thrown in for good measure. You would come back with an aching back and legs, and just desperate for some zeds.

It was a very different level of war-fighting training to Iraq. There was a new set of challenges, not least coping with the extreme temperatures, which regularly dropped below minus 25 degrees Celsius in January. At this point we were living in 12-man tents. We needed to listen and learn quickly. The CWSC (Cold Weather Survival Course) was the minimum requirement for all ranks deployed.

It entailed days of learning how to build various types of shelters, how to survive in extreme conditions, and how to prepare the various food types available in the local area. For me, this was my first experience of living 'in the field' in such extreme conditions, and it proved an 'eye opener' as to what is expected of a Marine. You really cut your teeth as a young Marine. It is fair to say that if you can survive and fight in these conditions, then you can do it anywhere.

I personally loved it. It was a new challenge, a chance to pit my skills against the elements, to test myself to the limit. It is easy to underestimate how much knowledge you need to live in such harsh conditions. The instructors gave us the pointers and taught us the basics we needed to survive in that extreme cold weather environment, but it was really down to you and how you coped. Above all, supreme fitness was critical to your survival. Without that you were screwed.

Within a day or two of our arrival we were out on our pusser's planks (service-issue skis), as it was imperative that we made it through our novice course as quickly as possible. If you are out skiing from morning until night – nine hours a day, six days a week – it takes about two weeks before you are skiing up to speed.

It is hard to ski on the military skis, as they are cross-country skis rather than downhill skis. Your feet are not locked in as they are on the downhill ones, which makes for easier cross-country skiing, but going downhill on them is a nightmare. The lads were quite good, but there were a few Bambi Marines who could not ski to save their lives. But eventually we all cracked it – there is no room for failure. Even Big Ed managed to pass, and he was one of the worst skiers out there. Bizarrely, he went on to take the Mountain Leaders Course, becoming a specialist in mountain and Artic warfare techniques.

We were in log cabins, not on bases. You would get pissed

up on cheap booze, because alcohol in Norway is hugely expensive, about £5 a drink, which is a bit of nightmare. Plus, when you're pissed walking on the icy roads you always fall over. There have been cases where lads have been drunk and paralysed themselves from just slipping. Alcohol and ice never seem to be a good combination.

The thing that pissed the lads off most of all on a Friday – because we had put so much effort in during the week – was when we had de-kitted and were chilling, some bright spark would volunteer us into all these stupid ski races or biathlons. There was one ski race that was about 20 miles, which left all the lads with a bit of a sense-of-humour failure. I suppose it comes with the territory.

On one Saturday morning before one of these ski races, we decided to have a laugh with Cyclops, a Shrewsbury lad who we always used to see off whenever we got the opportunity. He was always game for it too. Before each race you have to scrape the old wax off your skis and apply the new wax appropriate to the temperature and snow state. This one Saturday we saw Cyclops's skis propped up in the snow. We seized our chance. Grabbing his skis, with one lad keeping watch, we coated them from tip to tail in a soft wax, so that the skis wouldn't glide on the snow.

We were set off in time intervals. Broosky went before us, totally baffled as to why he couldn't get into a kick-and-glide rhythm across the frozen lake. We were pissing ourselves watching him struggle, and I think he might have realised what had happened. Eventually I caught up with him at the five-mile stage. He was hanging out of his hoop, sweating his tits off, totally knackered.

'What have you bastards done?' he shouted.

I only just stayed on my skis. It was all I could do to stop myself from falling over and laughing. I skied on and left Cyclops behind.

'Bastard! Come back here, Croucher, you nob!' he yelled.

We had all long finished by the time Cyclops finally shuffled over the finish line. He didn't look too happy, but he was too shattered to do anything except collapse in a heap on the floor. This brought a much-needed morale boost to our ski races and everyone made sure to check their skis before the next race!

It was a relief when it was over. Already there was an undercurrent of excitement. The buzz was we were going back to Iraq for a second tour.

I for one couldn't wait.

ELEVEN

was back on the front line. It felt like revisiting an old friend. Ever since I'd returned from the original Op TELIC tour I had been trying to chase the same adrenalin buzz. So when the news came in that we were heading back to Iraq for a second tour of duty I was elated. I couldn't wait to get stuck in again. But I was not to realise that things had changed so dramatically since the invasion. This would be a very different type of war.

40 Commando's mission had several objectives in Iraq. The unit mostly operated in the south of the country, where we helped protect oil pipelines and other infrastructure. In late October 2004 a section of 40 Commando was deployed north to Baghdad. We were also tasked with carrying out peace-support ops. Our commanders were Lt Col. Watts OBE and KSM King.

Me, I was stationed in Baghdad for the British Support Unit as part of the close-protection team for visiting generals and diplomats. We would regularly travel down 'Route Irish' – probably the most dangerous road in the world – in convoy. Everyone would always have to be on high alert.

Mum wasn't too keen on me going back. But she knew it was what I wanted to do. Being a Marine was in my blood.

And suddenly here I was again, caught up in a shitstorm and putting my neck on the line for Queen and country. But this time there was no charging off the back of a Chinook behind enemy lines. That didn't mean Iraq was any safer. In fact, quite the opposite.

I spotted them out of the corner of my eye. Cool as you like, two ragheads stepped out from behind a bush at the side of the highway and started spraying lead at us from their AK-47s. Rounds were pinging over our heads, and one or two rounds struck the Snatch Landy.

They did not give a shit. They must have known we would give it back to them both barrels. My right index finger was poised on the trigger of my SA80. My other hand was ready on the L17A2 UGL (Under-slug Grenade Launcher) just in case.

'Floor it, Macca!' I yelled. 'Incoming nine o'clock – 50 metres or so!'

Macca was a true Cockney, born and bred in East London, full of one-liners and always on the look-out for a bargain. But he was also a great driver and didn't need telling twice. His foot slammed on the deck. We must have been touching 60 mph.

I pumped out a couple of rounds, followed up by a couple of bursts. Matt, another lad I was on top cover with, had a stoppage right at the critical moment, so I pinged off one from my grenade launcher instead. It was an easy weapon switch and a seriously good move. The UGL round is effective with a five-metre killing circumference, and the ability to penetrate light-armoured vehicles. It made light work of those two bastards, smashing into the ground directly in front of the insurgents. It totally fragged them. I could not be sure they were dead, but the clatter of the AK-47s stopped as we sped by, and the round landed literally a metre in front of them. If they were goners, they were the first kills of my second tour of Iraq. It was a good job.

We were on Route Irish. We shouldn't have even been there. We knew the rules and when it was dark we weren't supposed to travel on this 12 kilometres of highway from the BIAP (Baghdad International Airport) to the Green Zone. But we thought we would get away with it, because it was only just coming up to dusk. Someone told me the road had got its name from the football team of the Notre Dame University, called the Fighting Irish, following the tradition of naming supply routes after sports teams. I knew nothing about all that Yank bullshit, I just thought you needed the infamous luck of the Irish to get down it unscathed. There was nothing sporting about your chances of survival on Route Irish if you didn't keep your wits about you.

We were taking a risk on this job and we knew it. We had weighed it up and whichever way you looked at it we didn't really have an option. It was either stay at the BIAP with no food or beds, or just get under wire down the road, because it was coming up to dusk and we still had a little bit of time. Our destination was the relative comfort of the Green Zone in Baghdad – the ultimate gated community, due to its numerous armed checkpoints, coils of razor wire, chain-link fences, and reinforced, blast-proof concrete slabs. There we would have bunks and decent scran waiting for us. There was no berth for us at Camp Victory, so we thought, *What the hell!*

We found out when we got back to base that the US patrol that was immediately behind us had stopped and recovered two dead bodies pumped full of shrapnel from the grenade launcher. *Two killers less in our war on terror.*

Further along on the same journey an RPG zapped us, too, just as we were coming to the end of our transit. I heard the old familiar loud swoosh, and shouted to Matt 'RPG!' As I did so I dragged him down the hatch and inside. Who knew where that RPG was going to hit and how much shrapnel would head our way? Our passengers peered out of the back of the Snatch's bulletproof windows to see the RPG skimming along the ground behind us. It impacted on a curb 20 metres or so to our rear, splattering the back of the Snatch with small bits of shrapnel. Whilst Macca was trying to keep control of the vehicle and get out of the area asap, Matt and I jumped up into the hatch again and started laying down rounds into the area where the RPG was fired from. Maybe we should have taken an alternative route. We were clearly pushing our luck that night.

Eventually, we came up to the US checkpoint. The Yanks there looked a bit on edge. I couldn't blame them really, after hearing explosions and gunfire just down the road. We informed them of what had happened and cracked on to our small camp on the far side of the Green Zone. We were in a controlled environment now, so me and Matt unloaded our weapons, checked ourselves off and ducked down back inside the vehicle to see the two worried faces of our passengers looking at us.

'Take it easy lads, calm down,' Macca said.

We pulled into the BSU and parked up the vehicle. The lads got out and automatically looked over the Landy for signs of damage. It was a bit fragged, but it could have been much worse considering the proximity of the attacks.

We all de-kitted and had a late lunch. There was a fancy dress piss-up later on and the Gurkhas were there as well. Some of the lads came dressed as all sorts, and we had a good night looking back at the day's events over a few well-deserved beers. The watch officer was an Army captain, who came and chatted to us as he'd just found out from the Yanks that they had recovered three bodies from the areas of our previous contacts. I knew I'd killed two, but wasn't so sure about the third. I went up to the Ops room just to confirm a few things. It was playing on my mind that the contacts were in a fairly urban area, and I wanted to make sure no civvies had got caught up in it accidentally. It turned out that all of the bodies recovered by the Yanks were found alongside weapons, and all were confirmed as being insurgents. That put my mind at ease, and it was back to the beers!

We could not believe how much of a holiday camp Baghdad was. In the heat of the day we could strip off to our civvies and go for a swim in one of the many swimming pools inside the Green Zone. You could even stroll around out of uniform with just an L9A1 Browning 9 x 19 mm Parabellum semi-automatic pistol on the hip. You could just wander around the souk, buying laptops and Iraqi dollars, and loads of other trinkets and stuff.

We had a fairly laid-back routine of four days on and two days off; and whilst our duties included transportation and close protection for high-ranking officers and officials, there was also the less glamorous task of providing local security to the BSU.

There was one very large outdoor pool in the Green Zone. It was open most days with water slides and diving boards, and was manned by US lifeguards. With the sun shining down and a beer in your hand it felt more like *Baywatch* than Baghdad – only without the birds. Me and the boys were bored one day and got chatting to some US Navy SEALs who reckoned they were well hard. They challenged us to a diving competition. Me and the boys were more than up for it, and the rivalry between the Yanks and us Brits was always there. For our comp, the board was about five metres high, and all the neighbouring slackers at the pool would be our judges. It was decided that the most insane stunt off the top of the board would win! The SEAL lads went up and mostly jumped off backwards. I think a few attempted a back flip or something, but nothing too spectacular. Then it was our turn. First Shorty went up and cracked a double back somersault straight off. I rocked up and did a cartwheel off the side. Eventually it stopped because it was getting a bit silly in the end, with some of the lads managing to give themselves nose bleeds.

'You guys are out of your mind, man!' one SEAL quipped.

'No, mate,' I replied, 'we're just Bootnecks.'

The rear sangar overlooked the river towards the notorious Sadr City. It was probably the most volatile place in Iraq during our tour there, and it made Brixton look like Beverly Hills. There was always something going on to be aware of. There were many times when I would see Delta Force guys going in low and fast in Little Birds, fast and light helicopters that could turn on a sixpence and had mounted six-barrelled 7.62 mm mini-guns and rockets. The Delta guys thought they were real badass, hanging out the aircraft in black gear, with their helmets and body armour and brandishing the latest M4 carbine with all sorts of weapon attachments. I was a little jealous when I looked at them. They had all the good jobs busting around.

These mean Little Birds and on occasion Black Hawks would go in higher and hover above their target areas. They often went on raids, catching suspects or taking out enemy strongholds. You also had the guys from Blackwater, a private security company, who had their own helos carrying out ops in support of regular US forces.

Sometimes the shit you would see going down was mental. It was like one giant Hollywood-style cluster-fuck. One of the lads watched a US patrol go past a roadside bomb, which exploded and took out a Humvee on the other side of the river. IEDs (Improvised Explosive Devices) were becoming a real problem and you heard stories every day of guys being maimed by them. Sometimes some of the lads would spot insurgents planting IEDs, and they were eager as anyone to cut them down, but as it was in such a built-up area, firing our GPMGs was too risky. There was the chance of a lot of collateral damage, and the risk of injuring or killing civilians. Every so often the snipers got to have a pop, although it was more or less at their maximum range for a .338, so their effectiveness was limited. Quite often we'd pass the int up to the Yanks, and then an IED team would go in and clear the area.

The Green Zone was one of the weirdest places in the world. I remember one time sitting on a lilo in a swimming pool, swigging on a beer and rocking out to Nickelback on my iPod and it was ace. Then suddenly the siren went off and mortars started landing nearby. I had to scarper out of the pool, grab my gear, and find the nearest building for some hard cover. This insurgent tactic was pretty unsuccessful, but even though the enemy generally failed to maim anyone, they pissed off just about everyone in the Zone. Wankers.

Although the odd suicide bomber, kidnapping or killing in the Green Zone was rare, it had happened on occasion in the past and we were warned to expect it in the future too.

Unexpectedly, the orders came down that we were to be relocated – and not a moment too soon either. I'd had enough of caning Yanks on the diving board. Our unit was tasked to push up into Maysan province in the east of the country, on the border with Iran. This was real *Mad Max* country, a place teeming with evil bandits and where the insurgency was a big problem. Iranian intelligence agencies, foreign fighters and arms, all were being smuggled over the border into Iraq, and we were sent to do what we could. The whole of Delta Company on our own, carrying out offensive ops again. This was more like it! I had the feeling of TELIC I again, and there were still a fair few lads that I was fighting alongside back then still in the Company. I was well looking forward to it.

Al Amarah, the capital of Maysan province, was located on the banks of the Tigris river, and surrounded by farmland and marshes. It had long been a chokepoint for munitions and militants entering the country from Iran. It was the strong-hold of Muqtada al-Sadr and his lethal Mahdi army. All in all, it was a seriously miserable place.

We deployed up to Al Amarah, where we would do battle prep, kit out our vehicles and get orders with regards to the forthcoming Op. We deployed out into the eastern desert, where a troop from the Black Watch Regiment had set up a Patrol Base and would act as our force protection. Razor wire acted as our perimeter and there were a few 12 x 12 tents with cot-beds in them. It was relatively comfortable compared to what we would usually have in these situations. The Black

Watch had brought with them two Sabre CVRT (Combat Vehicle Reconnaissance Tracked) vehicles to act as local defence. These things were shit-hot and came with 30 mm Rarden cannons. Guys from 539 Assault Squadron joined us in four RIBs to undertake the river and lake patrols of the surrounding area.

There was a Black Watch 2nd Lt who was in charge of the Patrol Base. He was a very well-spoken guy and hadn't been in the Army that long. He loved the fact that he was working with us, and was excited about the various patrols we'd be carrying out. He would never order any of the Marines to go and do something in an officer-ordering type of manner. It was always, 'If it's not too much trouble,' or 'If you don't mind', and we had a lot of respect for him and he for us.

We used to deploy the boats from a nearby re-entrant. We'd go past local fishermen and civilians who used to keep themselves to themselves, cracking the odd smile or wave. We quickly realised that the 2003 war and the ongoing coalition operations happening in their country didn't really affect them, as they were so far out in the boonies. I think we were virtually the only Westerners they had seen. Sometimes we would stop and chat to them and ask them about Iranians in the area. We wanted to know about unfamiliar boats and people they might have seen. They were totally aware that there were suspicious boats about, and they understood they were being used to smuggle weapons and people. The fishermen told us that there was no specific time when these boats would come or go, it was all fairly sporadic.

Our RIBs had twin outboard engines and were able to outrun any boats we came across, so we weren't worried about not being able to catch them. We just had to find them first. We did encounter some problems with the RIBs. Some of the waters we went into were fairly shallow and the props used to drag up reeds, which, if left over time, would over-heat the engines, so we had to keep a close eye on them.

After our first day of patrolling we loaded the RIBs onto the flat back of the four-tonner and went back to the Patrol Base, located only a couple of hundred metres down the road. We de-kitted, cleaned what we needed, got everything ready for the next day and grabbed a solar shower before chilling for the evening. We mingled with the Army lads and their 2nd Lt was never too far away for a chat. We thought it was odd that this guy from quite a posh background and education was in charge of a bunch of Jocks. At one point I was chatting away to him and took the opportunity to ask him about this.

'You don't sound like you're from Scotland, sir?' I said.

'No, I'm from Chelsea.'

'So why'd you join the Black Watch all the way up in Scotland then, sir?'

'My family owns some estate in Scotland and I love it up there.'

'You must have a few bob then, sir? Any chance they can fly a helicopter over and get us out of here?' one of the lads joked. He was a good egg and took it in good spirit. No one suggested he didn't fully deserve to be in command of the Black Watch as he'd done a brilliant job leading us.

A few days went by of doing similar patrols, but still we hadn't been in a contact or had any decent results. We questioned a few people, did the whole hearts-and-minds bit. At least word got out that we were in the area, as int suggested the insurgents and Iranians might hear about our presence and quieten down a bit. Finally, it was decided that we were going to head back to Al Amarah for further tasking.

At Al Amarah Camp we tried to keep ourselves busy until

our next deployment: cleaning weapons, checking kit, playing cards, having a bit of banter, talking about Wrens, the usual stuff. Al Amarah was crap and we couldn't wait to get out on patrol again. A bunch of Bootnecks under the command of an army Sgt Major whilst on his camp didn't work too well.

We didn't have to wait long. Our next task involved us carrying out desert patrols on the eastern borders mounted in vehicles. This was a very heavily mined area of Iraq – a legacy of the Iran–Iraq conflict in the 1980s. Back then both sides would just lay landmines everywhere, and they were still lined up in rows all over the place. Some were obvious, but others were obscured and a lot harder to see, so venturing off the roads was a dangerous business. But we had to do it in order to carry out our patrols effectively along the border.

We made a number of patrols up to border-control bases. We'd rock up in a 14-vehicle patrol, looking from the Iraqi border towards the Iranian border bases. On the Iranian side there were these mini medieval castles. In front of them was a no-man's-land with barbed wire and ordnance. The facades of the castles were still peppered with bullet holes from when the Iraqis had taken a pop at them years and years ago. You could happily go up and take a gander at them through your binos, and there would be an Iranian doing the same straight back at you. I gave one of them a wave, to take the piss, and he gave me a wave back. It was all a bit surreal.

We used to piss ourselves with laughter every time. We'd get the binos out and have great fun watching the Iranians running around like ants, standing to! Every time they must have thought we were getting ready to launch an attack – if only!

We had two Lynx helicopters attached to us, which we

used. So when we had to stop a vehicle one of them would drop down in front as we approached on our Snatch, as the other chopper hovered above. We spotted a brand new Range Rover hoofing it across the desert from Iran and he somehow managed to give the helicopters the slip. That was about as suspect as it got. We also had to report on the number of illegal foreign fighters that were infiltrating the country from Iran. At one checkpoint about 100 Iranians had poured over the border on the previous day. So it was quite frustrating that we had missed them.

The Iranian intelligence services were another key area to monitor. They would be armed with cash and bribe people to take photographs of British troops and come back with intelligence. It was very dangerous doing patrols around the Maysan province on the borders. They were very heavily mined as a deterrent to the Iranians – they didn't want them to just come rolling over the border.

There were rows and rows of minefields. I stepped off the track a couple of times and very nearly trod on landmines. They're obvious when you see them, but when you are just bimbling about they could easily catch you out and rip off your foot or leg.

On one border patrol in our Pinzgauer we came close to crossing onto Iranian land. According to the GPS, we drifted over a little bit too far around a sand dune, and we were faced with a dozen Iranian troops with .50 cal machine guns pointing straight at us.

They must have been shitting themselves thinking we were invading. We were thinking *shit* too. We were only a small patrol of about 20 guys. It was a serious stand-off. Matt, the guy in charge of the patrol, had to weigh up the situation quickly. We decided to do a tactical withdrawal and not to engage. It was the wisest outcome. We withdrew behind some sand dunes and headed west.

It was a blisteringly hot day, but on the face of it no better or worse than any of my time in that country. But my luck was about to run out.

We were on our way back to Shiba Logistic Base from Kuwait on the outskirts of Basra. I was in a soft-skinned Discovery, quite exposed, and something felt not quite right. We were caning it down the gravel tracks going way too fast. I'd been listening to the BBC World Service that morning and they were comparing Iraq to the Vietnam conflict. To be honest I thought they were chalk and cheese. I was having a great laugh in Iraq. The idea that I would get slotted and seriously injured didn't cross my mind. But I was forgetting the reality that no one is invincible.

One minute we were driving down the road, then the next thing I knew there was a blinding white flash and I was face down chewing dust with the worst headache you could imagine. It was like someone was drilling directly into my skull. I could barely open my eyes. My whole body felt numb. For a split second I thought, *I'm browners.*

I fell in and out of consciousness. But all the time I was aware of what was going on around me. I was casevacced out to Shiba and then a few days later I was choppered into Kuwait for an MRI scan. Turns out that we'd hit a roadside bomb and I fractured my skull as a result. I wasn't so bulletproof after all. This wasn't Hollywood, this wasn't Xbox, this was real war – no second lives. The doctor told me I was lucky to escape with my life. I was a lucky man, but it turned out I was even luckier. There was a corking nurse who treated me. It certainly helped me recuperate quicker, and as soon as I was up and about I was using the famous Croucher charm to good effect.

It was a good fling, but I had lots of other crap on my mind. My brush with death had got me thinking about what I was really doing out there. Things had felt different this time in Iraq. On TELIC I I had felt this burning sense of purpose and achievement. Now it felt like we were on the back foot and the bad guys were winning. Everything was messed up. I took the IED incident as a sign. After the second tour, leaving the Marines had seriously crossed my mind. Doubts were beginning to creep into my mind. Was this really all worth it? I honestly didn't know. The more I thought about it the less everything made sense. All this for just £7,000 a year. In the autumn of 2004 I decided enough was enough and I handed in my notice to my Sgt Major.

TWELVE

Karbala
United Nations warehouse
100 km south-west of Baghdad
2005

In 2005 I was still knocking around in Iraq. But now it was my turn to make a killing.

I transferred into the Royal Marines Reserves, which meant I was free to take up lucrative private military contract work. It was big business, with big bucks the reward for undertaking dangerous assignments in the worst areas of Iraq. Going home after my second tour had felt flat. I experienced none of the highs or the lows of my first trip back home after the invasion. I started to think I had to do something different. I'd been a Marine. I'd been whacked. I'd taken part in the biggest invasion and rebuilding job since World War II. Now I wanted to make some dosh.

I was part of 'The Circuit', a new world of professional bodyguards and soldiers hired for hard cash.

Anyone wanting to identify us only had to watch the passengers in Dubai International Airport waiting for flights to Kabul and Baghdad. That would give them an idea what this modern band of brothers looks like. Half are 40-something, a little paunchy, their hair thinning and their faces red. Some of them have not done a pull-up or run an obstacle course in 20 years. Some are divorced and paying alimony, child support, and mortgages on homes they no longer live in.

The other half, like me, are in their twenties, keen as mustard and enticed into leaving military service early in order to quadruple their salaries in the private sector.

Iraq is not exactly a place you would want to call home, but for a daily rate of £400 plus expenses, with a £200 retainer for the month we were back, we were happy as Larry to call this place 'home' for a bit longer yet.

Our job was to protect a United Nations warehouse with a security force of Iraqis about 100 km south-west of Baghdad in Karbala. It's one of the holiest cities in Islam after Mecca, made famous as the place where George Clooney and Mark Wahlberg filmed *Three Kings*. I was effectively doing a Marine's job with Gucci kit for tons more cash. It was safer too, despite the incredibly hostile and tense environment we operated in. We had armoured vehicles tooled up with a serious amount of kit and hardware. We were bombed up with shitloads of ammo, and armed with state-of-the-art weapons systems and the latest communications equipment on the market. As our job was part of a UN contract, we had US back-up too – an armed escort with an Apache as top cover to our area of operation. For the six of us on the team that was a great feeling. It was like unlocking the infinite weapons cheat on *Grand Theft Auto IV*.

For all the gear though, we were permanently on edge. None of us could escape the brutal reality that al-Qaeda had put $1 million bounties on every Westerner's head. We were top targets for these insurgents and we knew it – six of us meant $6 million, plus all the kit we had that the insurgents could use. We were definitely Grade A targets and make no mistake. We had to keep our wits about us at all times.

There was one other ex-Marine in the team, and three ex-Cherry Berries (our name for Paras), so a heavy Brit influence on our team and no bad thing. It was all good fun and we got on fairly well.

Within the first couple of days we were engaged in a couple of sporadic gun battles from the warehouse. We had posted a sentry position on each corner. We were in charge of around 40 Iraqi guards from two different tribes, and this was a bit of a pain as it could get volatile between them. They were a bit trigger-happy too, and tended to fire off their AK-47s for absolutely no reason.

The moment we heard gunfire from outside, the natural reaction was to get armed up and check out the lastest int. It would not take much to turn the Iraqi guards against us. There was a mutual mistrust between us, leaving all of us in the team feeling isolated, exposed and certainly vulnerable to attack. It is a very strange situation to be in – one I had not fully experienced before. I suppose the nearest I came to it was working with the Iraqi police and army on my previous two tours. But this was different.

I took the approach to engage with them. I tried to be friendly and teach them a bit of English. The ex-Para lads were more dismissive. A couple of our lads were quite hostile towards them. They made it clear they didn't want to get involved with them. Instead I tried to befriend them. My reasoning was, if they turned on us and tried to slot us, it would be the Para lads who would cop it, not me.

The money was great and the kit perfect, but something didn't quite sit right with me about this whole set-up. When I was in the Marines I felt part of something special, there was a noble reason for doing stuff, whether that was toppling a brutal dictator or trying to help make part of the country better for its inhabitants. As a PMC (private military company), there was none of that feeling. You could never really forget that you were just a hired gun, a merc (mercenary), no different to the freelance Hessians that the British Army used to employ in the old days. Was this really what I wanted? What I trained for?

We managed to get our warehouse as comfortable as we could. As part of the contract, we had $7,000 to make it spick and span. That sort of money goes quite a long way in Iraq, believe it or not, to the extent that we had a tower constructed outside with wireless Internet. We had Sky TV installed, got things like a deep-fat fryer and a lot of half-decent scran, as opposed to using rations all the time. We did discuss splitting the $7,000 equally each way, but with the amount we were getting paid each day it wasn't worth making ourselves uncomfortable for the duration of our stay.

The first month we were protecting the warehouse where completed referendum votes would be counted during the forthcoming elections. We wanted to let local insurgents know that this place was fortified and if they wanted to try and disrupt the elections they'd have a real fight on their hands. We were then given November off and went back in December. It was a bit strange returning to the warehouse after a month away. It was straight back into work for the elections proper. Our job was to help make sure there was no corruption and to guard key locations and generally make sure everything went as planned. This was the only mission I did as a PMC that gave me a different feeling, because you could see the real benefit of the elections and how much of a difference our presence made.

Afterwards we returned to the warehouse. For some reason the UN paid two tribes to help us with guard duties. We were in charge of these guys, but it was a volatile situation and we didn't trust them much. It was only a matter of time before they fell out with each other, and on one particular day they did and it kicked off big time. A riot broke out outside. They were kicking the shit out of each other, and then suddenly one of them pulled out a small, semi-automatic pistol and shot at one of the guys from the other tribe.

The other lads in the team were watching this from the warehouse compound and thought, *bollocks!* The fuse had been lit. The other guys in the melee were armed with AK-47s, and they were waving them in the air. We stood off, watched, and were debating what to do. Our rifles were cocked, but we didn't want to shoot one of the guys with the AK-47s, because as soon as you do that they can all turn on you. We didn't want to inflame the situation any further.

I thought the best way was to show our authority. We were supposed to be the bosses and I felt obliged to move in and stop this before one of them died. Tooled up with an extendable ASP baton – a 21-inch black stick made from 4040 high-carbon steel – I waded into the thick of it. Swinging the baton, knocking blokes down and all sorts. Within a few seconds, I was at the centre of the riot, ringed by screaming, sweating Arabs. I got to the guy clutching his handgun and smacked him round the side. He refused to let go of his handgun and struggled furiously with me for it, so I gave him a few rapid, sharp digs and managed to wrestle the gun from him in the end. Luckily, it had a stoppage at the critical moment. Otherwise, I might have copped it.

Once I had disarmed this guy, the guards from the other Iraqi tribe literally tried to lynch him. For his own safety, I dragged him into the warehouse. There was a guy behind me trying to wrench my rifle off my back. He fully intended to zap the guy I was dragging. This nob-jockey was pulling at my rifle frantically, trying to get the sling off, and ragging me around a bit.

As soon as I got my balance back I clocked him round the legs with the baton several times. The prick screamed in pain and eventually fell to the floor, grabbing his legs and crying like a baby. I thought I must have busted him up pretty bad. As soon as I had extracted the culprit, the situation started to die down, though. My plan had worked. A short while later everything was back to normal again: no more shouting, no more screaming. They were even getting on with each other as if nothing had happened. Arabs are a strange bunch. I saw the guy I'd whacked round the legs the next day and he apologised profusely, as only an Iraqi can.

'Meester Matt, I am so terribly sorry for my actions. It was so out of character for me. The heat of the moment you see. You understand?'

'Not really, mate. You lost it,' I said. 'You deserved what you got, you nutjob. You were lucky.'

He then showed me his injuries. They were gopping: the biggest bruises I have ever seen on his thighs and legs. I had completely messed him up. I must have winced.

'No, no, Meester Matt, it was my fault. I deserved the beating. You were right,' he added. 'I will never offend you again.'

My iron-fist approach had worked. I am not justifying Saddam's methods, far from it, but it became clear to me that day why he had ruled this screwed-up country with fear. The Iraqis respect power and force, and from my experience when they know who is boss they prefer it and comply.

It was bizarre. Everyone was friends again the next day. Both tribes were sitting and smoking together as if nothing has happened. I could barely believe what I was seeing.

'That guy tried to kill you the other day, now you're friends,' I said with a bemused look on my face.

'I know, Meester Matt,' he replied. 'It was just a misunderstanding.'

'OK, mate,' I responded. 'Do it your way.'

Such is the wacky Iraqi mentality. Maybe the ex-Cherry Berry lads were right, although the loss of comrades had undoubtedly tarnished their views of Iraqis. The longer you worked there the more you questioned if real peace could ever be achieved in a country so bent on infighting and religious division; a country whose differences could increasingly only be settled in blood.

It was a laborious process, but you could not take any chances – even just taking a shower. We had to boil water, then put the kettles in the solar showers located outside. Washing yourself down put you in a vulnerable position, so we would double up and go twos-up on it. It was essential to twos-up for your own safety. One person would watch the other's back when they were in there and vice versa. The guy in the shower would wash with his Glock 9 mm on a shelf. I used to buddy up with Lee on shower protection. You got into a sort of routine. It wasn't ideal, but you couldn't take any chances in a country as desperate as Iraq.

A couple of days later the lads and I were just sitting

around in the warehouse one evening when we suddenly heard shitloads of gunfire. We were used to gunfire, but nothing ever quite like this. It was mental. All hell was let loose and we wondered what the hell was going on. There were tracer rounds flying everywhere. We could see from the warehouse doors and we were thinking, *We're going to get absolutely battered here*. We thought we were under a massive attack, and ran out outside with our weapons cocked and ready to vittel people up.

When you work privately, you can pretty much crack your own detail. I had a Croatian-made AK-47 slung over my shoulder with a magazine on, a semi-automatic M21 assault rifle with an effective range of 300m using 5.56 mm rounds, 30 in the mag. I collected a grab bag with rounds, grenades, and smoke grenades too. We needed all of this kit if it was seriously going to kick off.

However, we soon realised that we were not under attack. Bizarrely, the gunfire was to celebrate Iraq's national football team winning a match. As soon as the final whistle blew, hundreds, maybe more, began firing their AK-47s in the air. I couldn't believe what idiots these guys were – where did they think all the bullets went? They would have to come down somewhere. Me and the lads decided to go back into the warehouse, but they were still firing rounds off and we would hear a big dink on the roof as the rounds fell out of the sky. About three or four rounds actually came through the roof and I stood up and thought, *Bollocks to this*, and went out to sit in one of the armoured vehicles outside, as I didn't fancy any hitting me. I sat in there until all the celebrations had ceased. Again, you can't take any risks.

I had heard a story of the same thing happening at a different compound. A round had come through the roof and lodged in the shoulder of one of the Brit guards. Luckily, his body armour stopped the round from penetrating fully, but a couple of inches over and it would have hit his head and split him in two.

We were all hoping we would be out before the New Year. Christmas Day in the warehouse did not appeal. When the day finally came, the warehouse manager went out and fixed us up with a Christmas tree. It was a nice touch.

We pulled out of the warehouse a day or two before New Year's Eve and spent the actual day in the accommodation area at BIAP waiting to get a flight back. I had a couple of beers and slept through most of it, flying back to Gatwick via Jordan. I was shattered, and surviving in such a hostile environment on a daily basis had clearly taken its toll. I went for a crap in the toilets and checked myself out in the mirror. I looked well rough – great big bags under my eyes, unshaven, hollow-looking. I needed to sort myself out, get a bit of purpose back. After collecting our bags, we all wished each other the best. I didn't know if I'd ever see any of these guys again. With a quick handshake, we were all gone in our different directions.

I came back a far richer man, with enough wonga to buy myself an updated Subaru, as well as a new Suzuki motorbike, a GSXR 750 K4. *Ah, the spoils of war*, I thought. But I felt empty. Was this what it was all about? Had I really almost been killed just for some new wheels? I put the thought to the back of my mind and took my new Suzuki out for a spin. I'd always wanted a top-notch bike, and I couldn't wait to get this baby out on the road a few months later in June. I went down to Aberystwyth with seven other guys. Wales has got some blinding stretches for caning it hardcore.

I was doing 120 mph, maybe more, along this stretch, when

suddenly there was a big dip in the road and as I came out of it there was a 90-degree turn that was unsighted due to the dip. I smashed straight into it and that was the last thing I remembered. Next thing I knew I woke up in hospital surrounded by doctors and machines. I'd had another lucky escape – I hadn't broken anything, but I was still seriously fucked up and out of it for about nine months recuperating. I had all sorts of ligament and joint damage, and even the most basic tasks took double the time.

It's funny when you're stuck in a bed like that and struggling around on crutches, you're forced to think more about stuff. I had plenty of time on my hands, and I was not satisfied with what I'd become. I found myself thinking more and more about the Marines. I wanted to have that feeling again of being part of something special. On the TV I saw more reports about Afghanistan and how that country was going to hell in a hand-cart. Slowly the thought took shape that I could get out there and make a difference. But first I needed to go back to being a real Marine. I would be getting a lot less money as a Lance Corporal reservist than a PMC, but that didn't matter to me. I wanted to get out there and I wanted to do it for Queen and country.

THIRTEEN

Forward Operating Base Inkerman
Sangin Valley, Helmand Province
Operation Herrick VII
September 2007

I didn't have to wait long to get my chance.

Iraq may have been cooling down a bit, but it was seriously hotting up in Afghanistan. I really wanted a piece of the action. Everything about it appealed to me – the danger, the hostile environment, and making a difference. Down the pub my civvy mates thought I was crazy, and told me it was time to get a safer job. But being a Royal Marine Commando is a state of mind.

So I was called up to undertake OPTAG (Operational Training and Advisory Group) training before deployment to Helmand Province as part of Operation Herrick VII under HQ 52 Infantry Brigade. I knew straight away it was going to be a perilous mission. It had been a serious battle for the Cherry Berries on their previous tour. Now it was our turn to step up to the plate and take the war to the Taliban.

We all understood that we would have to hit the ground running, and do a lot of learning out in theatre on our feet. The range packages on OPTAG were well handy for preparation. We had shitloads of range time, and we were able to get to know all the new equipment that had been issued. A lot of the gear we had used before was outdated. I had to familiarise myself with the new anti-tank missile-system upgrade, the Javelin – the fire-and-forget anti-tank missile used for bunker-busting – that we would take with us as the Commando Reconnaissance Force. It was awesome. As was the new grenade machine gun, a Heckler & Koch version of the US Mark 19 system. This would fire high-velocity 40 mm grenades at a rate of 350-plus rounds a minute. It was a barrel of laughs, and I couldn't wait to use it on ops.

On OPTAG I had a royal run when me and the lads bumped into Prince Harry. One of the lads bummed a fag off him.

'No sweat, mate,' the Prince said. 'But can I have some of your Haribos as a swop?'

'Sounds good to me, sir,' my mucker said, and offered up the bag.

Harry gave him a fag, but then my mate looked down at his bag of sweets and frowned.

'Matt, he's taken half my Haribos!'

I had to laugh. Prince Harry, in true soldier fashion, had seen off my mate good and proper. We knew then that he, like us, was getting ready to head off to the most dangerous country in the world. Fair play to him. All that money and he still wanted to serve his country, and his grandmother.

We were deployed from RAF Brize Norton to Kandahar, Afghanistan. From there we got straight on a C130 Hercules for the 60-minute ride to Camp Bastion, the main British military base in the country. It was situated north-west of Lashkar Gah, the capital of the notorious Helmand Province in the south of the country. I had heard from mates that this part of Afghanistan was a shithole. It didn't disappoint.

We arrived in the afternoon, and as we debussed the horrendous heat just hit us. I was sweating hard, and all the kit didn't help. It was Harry von redders. The landscape was as flat as a pancake, basically just a grey desert. The soil was so arid, not even a weed – let alone a poppy – would grow here. Four miles long by two miles wide, Bastion had an airstrip, a field hospital and accommodation for the 2,000-odd service personnel stationed there. We had just enough time to unpack our kit before the RSOI (Reception, Staging and Onwards Integration) began the next morning. Thank Christ there was air conditioning in the RSOI tent, as we had a full day's briefing, going through various packages on intelligence, health, the environment, all the usual stuff.

These packages went on for four days and they were intensive. It was a case of just dotting the i's and crossing the t's as far as I could see. Lectures and briefings, followed by more lectures and more briefings. I didn't take too many notes. In truth, the Ruperts don't really give out too much advice. It is pretty basic stuff that we had learnt as sprogs. Don't play around with unexploded ordinance and stuff like that. *Cheers for that*, I thought, but as an experienced Marine I let the pongo have his moment. I had learned to keep my trap shut.

I had done my homework and read up on why we were there. This place had been invaded so many times I'd given up counting. But clearly it was a tough nut to crack, serving as a buffer between the British and Russian empires, until it won independence from notional British control in 1919. Its fiercely independent people had given both great empires bloody noses too. A brief flirtation with 'democracy' had ended in a 1973 coup, and a 1978 Communist counter-coup. The Soviet Union's Red Army invaded in 1979 to support the tottering Afghan Communist regime, touching off a long and destructive war. The Reds withdrew in 1989, under relentless pressure from internationally supported anti-Communist mujahideen rebels. A series of subsequent civil wars saw Kabul finally fall in 1996 to the Taliban. These guys are a hard-line Pakistani-sponsored movement that first hit our radar in 1994. After the 9/11 terrorist attacks in New York City and the Pentagon in 2001, a US, Allied, and anti-Taliban Northern Alliance military action toppled the Taliban for sheltering Osama bin Laden. Now we were there to build a new Afghanistan – but primarily to protect the people back in the UK from the terrorists being trained there. In 2006 it was decided that more troops were needed for Helmand. An extra 3,300 troops were despatched to the province. It was essential to stop the country falling back into the clutches of the Taliban, the evil regime. They had taken control of the country and wanted to send it back into the Dark Ages. Music was banned, women were stoned, children indoctrinated. The bastards even blinded the lion in the local zoo by chucking a grenade into the enclosure. I had never met a member of the Taliban, but already I hated them more than anyone else on earth.

Presidential elections were held in 2004, and National Assembly elections in 2005. But President Hamid Karzai – the first democratically elected president of Afghanistan – was no more in control than we were. Most of the country looked almost biblical, like something out of Monty Python's *Life of Brian*, minus the laughs. It was a long way short of a stable central government, with little influence out in the provinces where there was practically a total lack of governance anyway. Why? The answer was simple, one word: Taliban. They were the source of continuing provincial instability, particularly in the south. Through campaigns of terror, intimidation and extreme violence the Taliban were determined to take control of the south of the country again. Running Helmand, with its poppy fields, drugs barons, and proximity to the international border, was their number one priority. It was ours too.

Helmand is about half the size of England, the Helmand river flowing through the mainly desert region, providing water for irrigation. The main crop is poppies, making it the largest opium-producing region, responsible for nearly half the world's total production. It was big business for the Taliban, and they were prepared to fight to the death for it. The message was clear from the briefings: our enemy may be decked out in dishdashas, wear sandals and sport long beards, but we were left in no doubt that we underestimated them at our peril. It was a point that was repeatedly rammed home to us in the briefings. My ears pricked up at this bit. I wanted to know who I would be facing in the field of combat.

'Gentlemen, do not be influenced by appearances. They often deceive, and they most definitely do in the case of the Taliban. They are a professional fighting force, very professional,' the Rupert went on with an air of drama, but he had got us hooked. 'They are sharp, too, and above all bloody brave. These men will keep coming, and, gentlemen they don't mind dying.'

They don't mind dying! I thought that was hilarious. If that was the case I had no intention of disappointing them. If they tried to drop me or my mates, I would slot the hell out of them.

Icers! From the deserts of
Iraq to the Novice Cold
Weather Warfare course
in freezing Norway.

Me and Cyclops in our snow
hole on the same course.

Amidst all the violence,
the Green Zone could
be a surreal place.
Here me and Woody
chill out in one of the
many swimming pools.

Me getting carried off a Puma Helicopter after returning from my MRI scan in Kuwait following an incident where I was hit by a roadside bomb on Op Telic IV.

With the Bagdad Support Unit in Iraq in the autumn of 2004. I'm carrying an M4 Carbine – weapon of choice for the Yanks. (*Inset*) Me on Christmas day 2004 in Basra Palace after a food fight. An hour or so later and we were in contact.

Getting some practise in on the ranges outside Camp Bastion in Afghanistan, Oct 2007. You need to keep yourself sharp because the threat of Taliban attack is always there.

Me on the Heckler & Koch 40mm Grenade Machine Gun. This is a truly awesome weapon.

A team of 40 Commando mortars firing away during the siege of FOB Inkerman. We had to fight wave after wave of attacks from a relentless enemy.

Our home for three months whilst stationed at FOB Inkerman. Not exactly the Hilton but it did the job.

The wooden cross that stands proud in the centre of FOB Inkerman, a constant reminder of the risks we faced and why we were there.

Suspected Taliban 'dicker' watched closely by a CRF sniper through the sights of an AI .338 Long Range Rifle LRR.

Defensive bed spaces at FOB Inkerman. Nothing much changed since the beginning of the last century, except the porn!

My bed space at Inkerman, starting at the top: Javelin Command Launch Unit (CLU), 5.56mm SA80 A2 assault rifle with underslung grenade launcher (UGL), HE grenades, smoke grenades, 40mm grenades, night vision, Harris radio, Browning 9mm pistol. Typical fighting order for a patrol, discounting, food, water, clothing, medical gear and extra ammo.

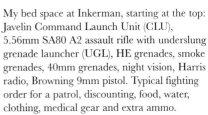

HM the Queen awarding me the George Cross at Buckingham Palace.

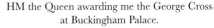

Myself and Steve Hands, another former Bootneck, outside Downing Street with my Pride of Britain award, October 2008.

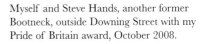

Myself and Ross Kemp at the *News of the World* Children's Champions Awards in December 2008.

Steve, Dom Lovett and me in Florida. Taking injured troops on a diving rehab programme run by Deptherapy and sponsored by Help for Heroes. Guys like Dom are incredibly brave and the sacrifices they have made should never be forgotten.

My daysack and helmet from the grenade incident.

Once we were acclimatised, we went on a series of range packages, driving it out into the desert in WMIK rovers to the various ranges. Now it was time to step it up a bit – as we were outside the UK. It always helps to go to ranges like that. Out there the instructors have a lot more trust in the skills of the individual, whereas back home we are slowed up by rules and regulations. These do not apply in Afghanistan.

In the field you can do a lot more realistic training, rather than just lying there shooting at wooden targets. This time we could do compound clearances, throwing grenades and going in after them. Firing the 66 mm rockets and the 84 mm LAW (Light Anti-Armour Weapon) we got some good rounds down. We set off high explosives, getting the .50 cals firing and also rocking with the GMG (Grenade Machine Gun).

We were part of the Commando Reconnaissance Force (CRF), and our job was to disrupt and destroy the Taliban. The idea was that we would move from FOB to FOB as back-up and extra manpower for missions, as well as recon. We would move by helicopter when we could, although we had our own vehicles out there, mainly Landys, WMIKs and Pinzgauers. So we were fairly mobile and carrying a lot of firepower with us. We got a proper wash maybe every two or three days, but we didn't care.

Our first mission as CRF was to act as sniper cover for an assault. The guys we were covering disappeared in a Lynx helicopter and our snipers provided cordons, along with a Pongo unit that were used as dog hands, similar to a local security protection force. Effectively we took out targets for the assault guys as they were coming in and doing a raid. It went down well. Next stop for us was the Sangin Valley and FOB Inkerman.

Now we were ready – well, as ready as we could be.

*

The Taliban made sure to give me and the lads a traditional welcome to Inkerman. A few 'Afghan Wasps' – Marine slang for enemy AK rounds – snapped over my head as I ran down the back ramp. 'Go, go, go!' the loadmaster screamed, as one by one all 44 of us crammed inside.

We didn't need the loadie to prompt us. Half the lads were already running off the back outside into thick clouds of choking dust whipped up by the chopper's downdraft. It engulfed you as, head bowed, you dashed for cover 20 metres straight ahead of you. It was like having the contents of a vacuum cleaner emptied into your lungs. One of the lads even got a nosebleed caused by this filthy crap. Dotted around the LZ (landing zone) were collapsible HESCO Bastion containers packed full of rubble designed to protect us from any small-arms fire that might be headed in our direction. This was a pretty dangerous area, and we didn't want to give Taliban fighters the chance to slot us before we'd even settled in. Overhead an Apache roared, circling, keeping eyes out for advancing Taliban and potential threats against the helicopter.

The Chinook pilot was taking no chances. His blades were already rotating faster and faster to take-off speed. All he wanted to do was get in and the hell out of there as quickly as possible. Around here it was only a matter of time before some Taliban arsehole started popping mortar rounds at us, and the pilot knew that if he hung around the LZ too long he would be a sitting target. Anxious to avoid enemy hits, he was nearly about to pull several feet off the deck before all the lads had debussed. The helo stated to shake and the engines were speeding up. One of the sprogs had to leap off the back in double-quick time.

'Give us a chance, mate!' he screamed out, as he rolled over in the dust. He was wasting his breath. The loadie couldn't hear a thing, and didn't give a toss anyway. He was out of there. In the blink of an eye the Chinook that had taken us to the front line was pulling away 30 or 40 feet in the air already. His job was done, his arse covered, his cargo of Marines delivered on time and fighting fit. Our destination was Inkerman in the upper Sangin Valley, a commando camp right at the sharp end of the battle against the Taliban, and arguably the most dangerous place to be at during our tour.

We had been in theatre for just a few weeks. It was red pigs out there, a filthy shithole of a place. I hadn't expected anything else, but I was combat-hardened. I was one of the guys who would keep an eye out for the lads on their first tour. All the guys were top blokes. All of them had made it through the 32-week Royal Marines training, acknowledged as the hardest specialist infantry course in the world. But anyone who reckons they don't get scared in combat is a gobshite. Experience helps, but you still crap yourself every time. Experience had taught me one thing: you're only as good as the guys alongside you. War-fighting is about team-work, not individuals. You and your muckers are all that count in combat.

Conditions were spartan in the camp. Fresh water was at a premium and at night it was lit by candles. The only exception was the night lights in the galley area and in the makeshift medical centre. We were sleeping near the firing positions and mortar pits. Inkerman got its name from a British and French victory in the Crimean War, when the British and French armies had whipped the Imperial Russian Army in 1854. Happy days! Here, though, the lads had dubbed it FOB Incoming, on account of all the Taliban fire it attracted. And while I was there it never failed to live up to its name. Just a couple of weeks before we arrived an Army officer had been picked off by a Taliban sniper, the round penetrating his skull and killing him instantly.

Virtually every single day the place would get hit. At one point we were in contacts ten days in a row, from morning until dusk. It was very exciting, but it took a while to find my feet in combat again. In this austere home for around 200 soldiers, fear lived in every man. Dealing with that gut-wrenching feeling is part and parcel of combat soldiering. It's a cold courage that every one of the lads displayed every time they stepped outside on patrol, and you couldn't help admiring it. The place was sombre most of the time. During the summer months temperatures could exceed 45 Celsius. In the winter it could dip as low as −15 Celsius. It was tough going, even for the experienced lads. When we first turned up it was T-shirt weather during the day and night. We had to wash our own kit and ourselves in the exposed solar showers. This was new to a lot of the lads, but I had plenty experience of it from my time in the Corps, and I was used to it even down to the freezing-cold water.

The toilets – the heads as we call them – were a line of open-air pits in the ground, and even made the area 'private' up to a point by using Hessian. The heads absolutely stank of ammonia, and human waste was burnt every night in a pit not 100 feet from where we slept. It was gash grim. In fact, the biggest threat in the first couple of days was not mortar fire but diarrhoea. It happens, and when it does it can go through the entire camp. If a bug strikes it can take out everyone, so we took precautions like using an alcohol gel to keep our hands sanitised.

We arrived towards the end of summer. Living conditions were very basic with the soldiers sleeping out in the open on cot-beds with only a mozzie net to protect them from the elements. The rain, when it came later in the tour, was torrential. It caused flash floods, and it meant we sometimes had to wade through water just so we could get about. Just bliss!

We did have simple luxuries, such as running water, pumped up from a well bored by Royal Engineers, and electricity from generators. We could make calls, too, using satellite phones, and we could exercise using makeshift free-weights and anything else we could find to maintain our fitness levels.

At the heart of the camp stood a simple wooden cross. It served as a stark reminder that many of those who had been there before us never made it back. Men like Captain Dave Hicks from 1st Battalion the Royal Anglian Regiment (The Vikings), who earned his posthumous Military Cross for his actions in trying to defend the base from being overrun by the Taliban. There were many now-silent heroes of war. I always felt very humble every time I walked past that cross. For our tomorrows, they gave their todays.

In this place the war was measured in metres, as we pushed the Taliban back across the Helmand river. Some of us were lucky enough to bag in an open-ended shed made from HESCO sacks and corrugated iron. This is where they slept in their damp camp beds and doss bags. There was no lighting or heating inside, but it was the best accommodation in the camp. The rest of us would have killed for it. Everyone slept in small, HESCO Bastion protective areas, which are like giant sandbags that protected us while we were being mortared or rocketed by the Taliban.

It took me a while to get back into the swing of things. In Iraq I had got used to rounds flying about, it almost became second nature. Straight away we had bullets snapping over our heads, and instinctively you hit the deck and stay down, not getting back up for a while. It took a bit of time to become accustomed to it again. After a while, you would just duck and then move and go somewhere else, as opposed to over-reacting and chewing the dust.

From the outset we were constantly up the line on patrols. These were designed to unsettle the enemy and to ensure the Taliban didn't have free rein in the area. You had to keep your wits about you at all times, not just for your own personal safety – stepping on a landmine was one of our biggest fears – but for intelligence gathering too. We would be sent out for close observation in places that had been identified by observation posts. Patrolling outside the FOB was central to the Helmand strategy. We had to show the Taliban and the local people that we could and would go anywhere we wanted, that we – not the Taliban – were in control.

The first time I went out on patrol I was well keen. You never know exactly how long you'll be out there in the field before setting off, so you do your best to prepare for every eventuality. It varies from patrol to patrol. What is planned for a three- to four-hour hearts-and-minds patrol a few miles outside the FOB might end up taking 15 hours, involving serious enemy contact. On my first time out I soon got into the swing of it, but I took too much kit.

Each man is responsible for his own kit, provided you are fit enough to take the load for hours on end. So it's your downfall if you take too much, because you are the one who has to carry it, usually over 100 lb. Each Marine carries around 16 magazines, a dozen or so in pouches and the other four in his day sack. I took three phosphorous grenades, the same again in HE (High Explosive) grenades, support weapons ammo, 66s (which are shoulder-launched rockets), night-vision equipment, maps and bags of water. Of course you had to pack food, too, in case you were out for a while, but nothing too exotic, biscuits or boil-in-a-bag scran, just enough to keep you going. Also, water – and buckets of it – is vital on any patrol. At the very least I always took three litres of the stuff in my camel-back. In winter it was icers, especially early morning and late at night, so we would have to wear extra kit like cold-weather layers that bog you down.

Every Marine had a specific role on patrol. Commanders carried Bowman radios, the rest of us carried a PRR (Personal Role Radio) and spare batteries that enabled us to stay in touch with each other. The patrol medic had to pack enough equipment for the task. I was on the GPMG, and took 800 7.62 mm rounds. Grenade-launcher gunners and the lads in charge of the Minimis would take extra ammo. Each section would carry ECM (Electronic Counter Measures) gear for jamming all comms frequencies used by the Taliban, blocking mobile phones, and disrupting the infra-red signals on IEDs, and these would load you down even more. The equipment was heavy, but mostly necessary. Maybe on the first time out I took just a bit too much though.

I soon got used to the physical exhaustion. The more you went out the fitter you became. Patrol requires extreme mental strength too. Overcoming fear means you have to stay headstrong. The last thing any of us needed was a flapping Bootneck at our side. Not that that happens. Of course, the fear of not coming back weighed on every Marine's mind. But we all knew we had a job to do. Disrupting the Taliban and showing the local people we meant business, and also that we could offer them real security and push their violent oppressors out. It was a big ask, but one we needed to meet. It was always going to be a tough job, especially in Helmand. When the officers decided to hold a shura (consultation or meeting with Arab tribal elders) in the desert or villages, everyone present knew the Taliban would be there, too, always lurking in the background, sizing up and eyeballing their enemy. Before going on patrol we would all be sweating. Would this be our last one? Would this be the one where some raghead zapped me or took out the oppo next to me? You would do these hearts-and-minds patrols, chat to a bloke who would offer up decent scran, some chai and flat bread. But this is Helmand, where the man offering you tea in the morning would gladly take up arms against you in the afternoon, or tip off the local Taliban that you were coming. You could never be certain what side anyone was on, unless they were your muckers and wearing the same desert rig.

We painstakingly searched the area for landmines and IEDs. This area was one of the most heavily mined countries in the world, with mines planted indiscriminately over most of the country. Agricultural farms, grazing areas, irrigation canals, residential areas, roads and footpaths, both in urban and in rural areas, were contaminated. They were a major obstacle to repatriation and relief. They had to be cleared. On patrol we would also search compounds, and search for weapons and signs of enemy activity. Every time we discovered a munitions dump it would seriously piss off the local Taliban commanders. Each find would save lives – our lads' lives.

The first patrol was planned to last four, maybe five hours.

It went on for 15 hours, after which I was absolutely knackered. My stamina and general fitness were up to a decent standard. At least that's what I thought. The difference between being fit when you can run and run with full kit on, and being patrol fit is stark. Patrol fit means you can walk five or six miles with all your kit on your back, maybe 100 lb, and then have the stamina and be mentally alert enough for a serious firefight. I suppose it's like a footballer who has been out and just training and one who is match fit, only off the scale. It is a different level of endurance that takes time to achieve. With each patrol, with each contact, the sharpness returns.

I didn't beat myself up about it. After all, it was my first patrol and I expected to be a little rusty. I wasn't the only one suffering. A few of the lads were hanging out by the time we got back. It was a learning curve for the lot of us, and for the next time I went up the line. We were under no illusions. We had to take the war to them. We had to retain the initiative. Our presence would draw them out of their ratholes and into contacts – contacts that, with our air support, we felt confident we could win.

FOURTEEN

Patrol
Green Zone
Sangin Valley

The ninth of November 2007 is a date that will live long in the memories of everyone out there. It was to be our 9/11. We were all absolutely knackered, returning from a 12-hour foot patrol in the Green Zone in the Sangin Valley. Comms flagged up that the ICOM chatter had increased significantly. The enemy had spotted our patrol. The only godsend is that they didn't know we were hacking into their conversations on their hand-held VHF, using specialist equipment. They were discussing a pending attack, and we were their prey. Worryingly, their spotters were accurate. There was talk of a single section moving forward. They were targeting us and we could expect a strike at any minute. If the enemy did know we were listening to their chatter, there was a chance they were feeding us false int, but none of us wanted to take that chance, and it seemed like the real McCoy.

I scanned the area, desperately looking for cover. If it kicked off we were completely exposed to sniper fire in open ground. They would just cut us down. There were several man-made irrigation ditches running away from a sprawling, vittled-up compound a few hundred metres way at ten o'clock. Some of them were no deeper than kerbstones, others were deeper and full of Taliban shit, because they used them as latrines. Neither looked like good cover. The compound was the best bet, but we could not be sure there were not more of the raghead bastards inside, waiting to leap out and cut us down with AK rounds. But we had no choice. All of us simultaneously made a dash for it. This was a Taliban ambush and we were sitting ducks out there in the open.

The enemy were well dug in. They knew the terrain and they were well up for the fight. One of my muckers called Ryan spotted a couple of Taliban moving swiftly across a field 200 metres straight ahead of us. He screamed out, telling all those in earshot of the enemy's movements. They were tooled up to the nines, their RPGs clearly visible. They meant business. By now we already had a load of incoming rounds to contend with, snapping over our heads and churning up the dust around our legs. The lads took cover in nearby ditches and compounds.

All of a sudden there was a massive explosion 20 metres to my right. I felt a huge shockwave as an RPG round slammed into this compound wall I had been standing next to.

The earth shook and it put me on my arse. I was peppered with dust and shrapnel and debris and shit, covered in bruises and cuts. It took a few seconds for me to get my composure back. We returned with huge volleys of firepower, but it didn't seem to have the desired effect. We'd walked into their killing zone, on their terms, and they had total control of the contact. It was the situation every Marine fears the most: you're half-cocked and caught in an ambush.

No pissing around, we'd been hit hard, good and proper, and it was as clear as daylight that we were up against a formidable Taliban force.

'Get 3 Zero on comms now!' Ryan responded.

'We've got to get to cover now!' I screamed.

This was going to be a tasty contact. They had waited until we were hanging out, dead on our feet, and then struck when they knew we were at our most vulnerable. Every Marine present knew we would be lucky to get out of this one alive. We would all be tested to the limit of our endurance, mentally and physically, by what was about to unfold.

Ever since we arrived a few weeks earlier, we had been pushing patrols out deeper and deeper into Taliban territory in order to limit their movement. Well, that was the thinking anyway. Our objective was to carry out fighting patrols around various villages to flush out the enemy and engage. Our forays into their territory were like a red rag to a bull. We would provoke enemy activity. Well, it sure as hell worked this time.

Within seconds, more RPGs crashed into our positions with their distinctive woosh and bang. The RPG fire was coming in from multiple areas. Within seconds of the onslaught up went the dreaded cry: 'Medic!' Now one of their machine gunners started putting serious rounds down and pinned down the troop.

'Fuckin' 'ell! . . . Incoming! . . . Keep your heads down! Cover!'

'Lads take cover, that was bloody close!'

'Zero 3 Zero, this is 32 . . . tell the lads to keep looking out to the left!'

'Machine-gun fire coming down, mate!'

The situation was now critical. Some of the patrol troop had made it back to the dusty, bullet-riddled compound, but there was limited safety or security in that. Both the entrance and the roof were now being raked by enemy fire. Our TACP (Tactical Air Control Party) Captain Paul Britton co-ordinated artillery, mortars, Apaches and air strikes. He was doing his best, but he was pinned. AK rounds were snapping into the doorway of the compound, and all around him and from my position I simply could not understand why they were not hitting him. He had frantically been calling in Apaches. But that could take time, and time was not on our side. It would not be long before daylight would start to fade. If we were overrun, which looked a distinct possibility, there would be very little time left for a successful rescue op. We would be sitting ducks.

When I heard the blood-curdling cry of 'Medic!' and the pain in the voice of the poor sod calling out, I was convinced an RPG has slammed directly into one of the lads. If that was the case, there was little hope for him.

'Medic, medic!' Again the same cry went up. It was a different voice this time, but his pain was evident from his scream. I was a trained patrol medic with essential supplies such as IV, tourniquets, chest seals, saline, morphine, HemCon (Haemorrhage Control dressing, manufactured from chitosan, a natural product that is found in the shells of shrimp). I was nowhere near as experienced as a company medic, but had done my courses and could handle myself in the field. I knew how to patch up injured guys in an emergency. This was an emergency. But I couldn't make it to the compound where the cries were coming from, as the incoming rounds were too intense.

Our company medic, a hoofing lad, Marine Gary ('Oggy') Ogden, was pinned down by enemy fire. He was being zapped from all sides and there was no way he could get to the injured Marines. In times like this you cannot worry about your personal security. If you did, you would never get out of your doss bag in the morning. I knew it was up to me to fight my way back to the compound and administer what medical assistance I could. I, too, was being zapped from all sides now – only a racing snake would make it back alive, but this was no time to flap, I had to get my head down and just go for it. Instinctively, I turned and sprayed rounds from my SA80 back towards the enemy, at the same time running backwards towards the cover of the compound, where the majority of the lads, including the injured ones, were holed up.

There was only one way into this compound – a medieval-looking mud shack – so that made the entrance a prime target. A spray of bullets whizzed across the doorway, peppering it and embedding into the thick mud-like walls behind as I darted through. My heart was in my mouth. Somehow I had made it without a scratch. The old Croucher luck had returned. I was the lucky one. In front of me my oppo Corporal Simon 'Sy' Greening was not so fortunate. He had been shot clean through the chest with a 7.62 mm round. That same burst of ammo that had been aimed at me and the compound had also targeted Sy, and unfortunately found its mark. As it struck, he stumbled back before collapsing against the compound wall. Blood was pumping out of his chest and seeping through his body armour. The bullet had missed his ceramic plate body armour and penetrated in and then straight out his back, embedding itself in the wall behind. It didn't look good.

We were getting seriously vittled up. Seconds after Sy had

been hit another bullet zapped me. But miraculously the bullet struck my rifle and ricocheted off. As I looked down I just couldn't believe my luck. I was just one seriously lucky bastard. I was at least five lives down by now. I could see a few of the other lads dropped down on one knee, giving as good as they were getting. There were no wrap-hands in this unit. If we were going to go down, we were taking as many of them with us as we could. My rifle was now pretty much wrecked after being struck by the machine gunner's round, but luckily the UGL was still in good working nick, and I had 14 40 mm rounds to cause some serious damage to whatever Taliban bastard wanted it.

First, I surveyed the compound for casualties that I could help. There were two people on the roof that had been hit by an RPG. One of them, Marine David Fletcher, 'Fletch' to the lads, was in a critical state. He was what we call a T1 casualty. Most of the muscle mass on both thighs had been sliced from shrapnel wounds. He had almost lost both of his legs. Fenners, the other guy, had some of the shrapnel in his foot. Even though he was seriously injured, he was only a T3 casualty: walking wounded – not critical. There was a T2 casualty inside. He could not walk, because he had also been hit by shrapnel and shot through the backside.

I went to help Sy, with another couple of lads to assist. Propping him up on the floor, I helped him remove his body armour. He wanted to see the extent of his wound. Once he'd seen it for himself his face dropped. He could see straight away how bad it was and he slumped against the wall. I checked for the exit wound, first exposing it and then sealing it front and back with a chest seal. The entrance and exit wounds were small. His Kevlar armour had, at least, slowed the round down to a subsonic speed. Normally you'd get a much larger exit from supersonic rounds, which produces a cone effect on exit and tears the shit out of your insides. So it could have been worse for Sy. He was pale, but doing his best to hold on. For the next 20 minutes, whilst the company medical assistant was still pinned down by enemy fire, I applied life-saving first aid with two other lads helping out in a bid to stabilise Sy. If he was going to survive, he needed to be extracted and fast. I could see that this had sapped Sy's morale, and who could blame him?

'Sy!' I shouted. I got his attention, but he couldn't really focus, he was faint. 'I'm not going to lie, mate,' I continued, 'you've been shot in the chest. But it's not as bad as you think.' I told him about the small entrance and exit wounds.

I was bullshitting, of course. I had seen that the round had entered right by Sy's heart and I was worried it had struck against it. We inspected the wound further and decided that although it looked like a direct hit, the round had probably missed his heart. But there was still a load of blood, and we all thought Sy would rapidly go downhill. The only positive sign was that his condition hadn't deteriorated in the three or four minutes since he'd been hit.

The chest seals were a pain in the arse, blood was gushing from Sy's wounds and the sticky seals kept falling off. I was conscious about using up more and more seals, as we were in the middle of a heavy contact and I was sure we'd have other casualties to deal with before the day was out. Still, the seals were essential to keep Sy stable, especially as the round had punctured his lung on the way out. Without the seal his lung would have collapsed and caused a potentially fatal tension haemothorax.

Five minutes had now passed since Sy was struck. He was drifting in and out of consciousness and looked rough. We had to get him out of there quick, but we were a good few miles from FOB Inkerman, with no vehicle access and a load of Taliban giving as good as they got. I looked around at Fletch as his body was lowered down from the roof to the compound floor. If you didn't know better you'd have thought he was dead. He looked lifeless. There was blood absolutely everywhere, like someone had thrown buckets of red paint around the compound.

I got Sy's attention again, remembering from my trauma-aid training that if you survived the first five minutes of an injury you had a 70 to 80 per cent chance of survival.

We were still massively on the back foot. We had two T1 casualties, one T2 and one T3. T1 casualties need to be evacuated within an hour or their life is in danger. T2 and T3 are lower priority, although T2s can progress to T1 critical status if they don't receive proper medical attention asap. Apaches had been called in, but they were 30 minutes away, and in the meantime we called for mortar and artillery fire on the Taliban. But there were so many of them that even a sustained fire on their positions didn't seem to have much effect.

If Sy and Fletch were going to have the best chances of survival they needed to be extracted – and fast. As I was checking on Sy, an RPG streaked over and arced down into the compound, hitting the wall I was facing. That was a one in a million shot. It landed just two metres away from me, and the only reason I wasn't hit was because three of the TACP guys standing right next to me took the force of the impact. Then I saw two more bodies drop, signaller Corporal Dave Watts and Captain Paul Britton, both with shrapnel wounds.

Eventually, Oggy, the designated professional medic, managed to make it over to us. He showed exceptional bravery just getting there under enemy fire, and he had his work cut out by now with at least four lads down. Without flapping, he just got on with it. It was touch-and-go for Fletch, and his life was certainly in the balance. He had lost a huge amount of blood and needed two tourniquets to cut off the circulation, as he had severed his arteries on both legs. Oggy stabilised the casualty as bullets zapped through the open door, thumping into the walls around him. He was really going to town on him, as well as checking up on Sy too. I had put a line in Sy and checked his chest seals to keep his lung inflated. The pressure would be so intense he would not be able to breathe, and he would then suffocate. If he started coughing up frothy red blood there was a good chance he would be browners and I would have failed him.

Captain Britton was lying behind a mud bank. He had defied the odds and done a great job calling in air support. At this point, we had three Apaches up there, circling, laying down covering fire, along with the lads in the ditches just in front of the building laying down rounds. But for once it didn't seem to make a blind bit of difference. We loved the Apaches. They were fitted with Rolls-Royce Turbomeca RTM322 engines, which meant they could carry heavier loads than their US and European counterparts. It also meant they could take their fire-control radar systems into battle, giving the pilot the capability for terrain profiling. This helped them hunt out the enemy hiding in the dips and hollows on the deck. They were also equipped with Longbow radars on the top of the rotors, which enabled them to distinguish between enemy and friendly vehicles.

Not surprisingly, the Taliban were shit-scared of these birds, with their precision and manoeuvrability. Once the enemy is in the pilot's sights and the target acquired, the

BULLETPROOF

Apache has everything on-board to blow him off the face of the earth. The firepower on these things is just awesome. The 30 mm automatic Boeing M230 chain gun located under the fuselage can pump out 625 rounds a minute and can carry double that in ammunition. It is armed with the Lockheed Martin/Boeing AGM-114D Longbow Hellfire air-to-surface missiles, which has a millimetre wave seeker allowing the missile to perform in full fire-and-forget mode with a range of 8 to 12 km. These bunker-busters can blast open thick walls behind which the enemy might be cowering.

'They're sprinting towards us now!' I could hear the tension in the first-timer's voice, but he was true Marine and he wasn't flapping. He was doing a sterling job keeping it together as he watched other Marines, experienced lads, too, keel over in pools of blood.

'What direction?' I shouted back, as much to engage him. To make him feel and know he was not alone out there.

'Straight at us, Royal,' he chipped back.

I could see them straight ahead. They didn't seem to give a toss about the Apaches up in the air making mincemeat out of their mates. They just got up and started sprinting towards us, firing off automatic fire on their AK-47s. It was true this enemy was not afraid to die, and that made him a seriously dangerous foe. Suddenly, an RPG landed smack inside our mini-fortress. A couple more lads went down with fragmentation wounds. The situation was now critical.

We had two, maybe three T1 casualties, the rest T2s or T3s. We couldn't use the front door of the compound, because when anyone went near it a flurry of Taliban rounds would be dished out in their direction. The Taliban sensed a sensational victory and they just kept coming. I was still trying to patch up Sy, but I knew the lads in the firefight needed as many guns as they could get. I glanced down at my weapon. The only part of the SA80 that was useful was my UGL. The rest was useless after being vittled up. I had about nine 40 mm grenades left on me, so I thought I might as well make use of them. There was nothing more I could do for Sy, he was on Oggy's radar now, and Oggy knew exactly what he was doing. It was time to take this fight to the enemy.

I snurgled around the corner from the door of the compound and peered around, then I kept popping 40 mm grenades off into the enemy compounds that were about 300 metres away. The Apaches kept laying down covering fire from the M230 chain gun, and by now the 30 mm shells were having the desired affect. It was an awesome sight, but this was no time to stand and watch. As the rounds smashed in at least it got the Taliban running for cover, and gave the injured lads in the compound some respite. For the rest of us it was the impetus we needed to start taking the fight back to the enemy.

Oggy knew we had to casevac our injured out and fast. Every second would count in this rescue op. We were never going to win this contact: fact. We were outnumbered and the Taliban were relentless. It felt like there were millions of them. They just kept coming and coming. It was like the film *Zulu* with waves and waves of them. They didn't seem to give a shit about being shot. If we didn't get the casualties back and treated in hospital they would soon be fatalities. For a long time, a twin-bladed Chinook MERT (Medical Emergency Response Team) rescue helicopter had been circling around, waiting to land. I had spotted it and so had the enemy. The pilot was holding off, because it just looked like a storm of rounds going in and out. Mortars were going down and artillery was smashing up the place. The Apaches were waiting to come in.

It was up to the helo pilots to help us out. We needed to make an aerial evacuation of the injured. This meant the pilots would have to land in a hot LZ (Landing Zone), with enemy fighters blazing away at them. The Taliban fighters were not stupid. Far from it. They knew the Chinooks would be coming in, so they set up shop and just waited. They were ready to have a pop at them on the way in and on the way out, and if they spent any more than 30 to 60 seconds on the deck, then they could expect to get mortared. A Chinook is a 99 ft-long helicopter, and while it's not that slow – it will top out at 140 to 150 mph – it's a big and relatively easy target. Though it has one of the best defensive-aid suites on British helicopters for missiles, they wouldn't go anywhere without Apache top cover, keeping the pilot and crew alive as they go into the killing zone.

The only available landing site was directly adjacent to the compound that had just been attacked. Alpha Company had already gone south through the cornfields and irrigation ditches in a bid to secure an LZ for the MERT helicopter. But as the Chinook approached, it found itself engaged from numerous firing points. Daylight was fading fast and time was running out for the rescue operation. As the Chinook finally dived down to land, its three Apache escorts swerved ahead and rocketed the treelines. For the Chinook, the continuing gun battle made it a hot landing zone, a helicopter pilot's worst fear. The Apaches asked if the landing zone was secure. Our response was no, but as secure as it could be.

With AK-47 rounds peppering the front of the compound there was no way we could exit and reach the MERT helicopter. We had to extract – and quickly – so it was up to the Gurkha Assault Engineers we had with us to come up with a plan. The only way out was to blow a hole in the rear of the compound. But the walls were extremely thick – hard to believe it's just mud. It would be impossible to shoot through them with .50 cal rounds or even Apache 30 mm cannon rounds. We soon realised that the only way to punch a hole was to put a massive breaching charge on the wall. The shaped charge includes an annular liner located centrally between the ends of a cylindrical container filled with explosive. It is placed in a pilot hole in the wall and is detonated simultaneously at the ends. The charge creates an annular, radically expanding jet of explosive gases and fragments directed into the wall, providing a man-sized opening.

The Gurkha chap was having none of it. He argued that the device could end up causing more casualties. The rest of us didn't see it like that. It was something we had to gamble on. We had to take that chance to save people's lives – we had the T2 and T3 casualties to consider. We were just sitting ducks and could get overrun at any time. It was do or die.

The Gurkha managed to fill a gap with plastic explosives and blew it. When the smoke cleared, we saw the breaching charge hadn't created a big enough hole for a man to squeeze through, but it was something to work on. As we continued to take the battle to the enemy the Gurkhas put their backs into it. They got to work with the hooligan tool, a big crowbar to hack away the rubble, and got a decent hole for everyone to escape through.

Inside I knew this was a time for mental strength, a moment in your life journey to show what you are really made of. I knew we were on the back foot. You only had to look up to see the number of Apaches above us to appreciate that we were really in the shit.

There was no point in flapping. I knew I had to keep a cool head. It was blatantly obvious we were losing the contact. The lack of what we were achieving in the ground battle was testament to that. We were totally hemmed in, and there was nothing we could do about it.

We could not counter-attack. To do so would be suicide. It was time to extract and live to fight another day. My assessment was that our priority was evacuating the remaining casualties. The Taliban aren't daft. They must have known it, and would have watched our casevac with glee. It would only be a matter of time before the bastards were all over this compound like flies round shit. There was no way I wanted them taking pleasure in our pain.

As the lads, one by one, retreated through our man-made hole, passing the casualties through on stretchers, I did my best to clear up as much of the mess inside as possible. I was determined not to give the Taliban any sense of victory. They were going to push forward, and the last thing we wanted was them being buoyed up by the sight of the blood from our boys. I made sure I didn't leave the wrappings behind or any of the medical equipment. That would have given them a clear idea of the scale and the severity of casualties they had inflicted upon us.

Blood was splattered everywhere, but I wanted to leave the impression that the blood could have come from one individual as opposed to six or seven of our blokes, which was a truer picture. My mop-up op would leave them with the impression that no matter what they threw at us, their fight was futile. We were better soldiers, better equipped, better trained and resilient. It was just a mental game, but sometimes mind games are just as important in war as blood and bullets.

I glanced up as the Chinook pulled itself skywards, its twin engines whining furiously as it made a desperate escape. Within seconds it was hovering precariously right above our position. We knew it was a prized target for the enemy, and Royal Navy pilot Lt Nichol James Emslie Benzie needed to show nerves of steel to evade RPGs and small-arms fire and get our injured lads out safely.

Lt Benzie RN played a blinder. He must have been either crazy or overloading on adrenalin, flying by the seat of his pants. I'm not sure if he fully realised what he was doing, or was fully aware of how bad the situation was. To land that close with a Chinook bordered on the suicidal. I could see bullets bouncing off his Chinook as he approached. He showed exceptional courage and ability just to reach us. He flew in about 100 metres from the front line. With close air support, he demonstrated exceptional skill by landing his aircraft in a small area between crops, while avoiding enemy positions. Inside the Chinook were doctors ready to tend to our wounded mates. They knew the urgency of the situation and one of them came running down the ramp of the helicopter. He suddenly found enemy rounds pinging all around him, and he had to be dragged into cover as bullets streaked by.

'Quick, guys, the shit has hit the fan here, mate!' he said out loud, as if talking to himself. We loaded as many on as we could, but in the end there were too many casualties for the space. The Captain took the brave decision to stay and fight rather than be evacuated, along with a couple of other casualties – there were seven or eight casualties and only space for four on the Chinook. The Chinook was held off by heavy enemy machine-gun and anti-aircraft fire, but eventually Lt Benzie just went for it despite coming under ferocious fire. Against all the odds, our casualties had been successfully extracted.

Within a couple of minutes it was clear that the casevac had been a success. All the T1 casualties made it out of the killing zone alive – well, barely alive. We had pulled together as a unit at the decisive moment, but those left fighting on the ground could do no more for their fallen comrades now. Their lives depended on the skill and professionalism of the emergency staff at the field hospital at Camp Bastion.

It was no time for reflection. This ferocious battle had a few more hours in it yet, unless we were lucky. It was up to the rest of us still on the ground to save our skins. The Apaches circled high above us. They had acted as top cover for the casevac and fired relentlessly into Taliban positions, causing mayhem. Enemy small-arms fire was returned with huge volleys of firepower from us, too. They kept moving every two or three minutes, evading our rapid machine-gun fire and mortars as well. These tossers were like the zombies in *28 Days Later* – millions of the bastards.

We began our fightback. We had ID'd their original grid position and our mortars went to work. One shot – it was a direct hit: yes! – and the machine gunner that had been keeping us pinned down was just a pile of shit. That was one less of them to concern us. Despite the fact that they had been under attack for two, maybe three hours they were still able to fire RPGs at our positions. They were a tenacious bunch. The Taliban were pretty mobile for a rag-tag gang of fanatics. They just kept moving, so good int on their positions was hard to come by during the battle.

It was now our turn to withdraw. If we didn't get out of there soon, I thought the rest of us would be going home tagged up in body bags.

FIFTEEN

Under fire
Compound, somewhere in the Sangin Valley

We patrolled back towards FOB Inkerman. It felt like a long slog. My head was ringing and my heart didn't stop pounding the whole journey. Until that moment, the ambush I had experienced on my first tour in Iraq had been the hairiest moment of my life, but this came a close second. There were times when I seriously thought my number was up.

I never thought that ramshackle shithole would look so welcoming. The lads at Inkerman were shocked at the state we were in. We looked like shit, and were covered in dust and blood and crap. We stank. You could understand why the lads all looked like they'd seen a ghost. For them to see the CRF, about 40-strong, in this state and with two men down – one with extremely life-threatening injuries – was shocking.

'Jesus, lads, what happened out there?'

'Some serious shit, Royal,' I said. 'It was a really hard fight.'

Then I said, 'What's the gen on Fletch and Sy? Any news?'

He looked away. 'No buzz, mate,' he said.

Bollocks, I thought. I hoped the Devil Dodger hadn't been called in. They were good Bootnecks.

I was totally knackered and needed to yaffel some serious scran down. The first thing I did was unload my kit and gulp some water from my water bottle. The CRF lads that didn't go on the ground helped us out, cooked us scran, helped with kit and stuff like that. It was welcomed. Marine lads are like that – they help each other out – there's no fake camaraderie.

Word came back from the sickbay that Sy would be back in the UK with the gunshot wound to his chest within 24 hours. Fletch was to be kept in Afghanistan for an extra day. That got our hopes up, but it was false hope. We all thought he was being kept in Afghanistan because they might be thinking about treating him here. But the situation was that he was just too ill to fly. He had been touch-and-go because he had lost so much blood. The medical staff at the sickbay only managed to stabilise him after two days, just enough so he would survive the flight home for further treatment.

Fletch was taken to Selly Oak Hospital in Birmingham, where there is a single NHS-dedicated, military-managed ward with uniformed military nurses, but only 14 beds are set aside for military personnel. Civilians with no under-standing of the terrors of war only set that up after some of the lads had come back from Iraq and Afghanistan to find themselves on ordinary wards, isolated from their comrades. Fletch was one of the lucky ones. The doctor said he was the only patient he had ever seen come so close to death without actually dying. Later, when I saw Fletch I said to him, 'You've finally got something to boast about!'

After that big contact, the Taliban kept coming, swarming

around the FOB, sensing blood and victory. If they could overthrow us it would be a major coup. Inkerman's strategic position at the head of the Sangin Valley meant that it was a bulwark against Taliban attacks, allowing efforts to improve the political and economic infrastructure to take hold in towns like Sangin. We knew they were out in big numbers, because usually when an Apache is in the sky, it tends to put the fear of God into the Taliban fighters on the ground and they disperse whenever one of them is about.

What was worrying was that despite the Apache presence, they kept on coming. Obviously they were about in such numbers that even an Apache or three didn't shit them up this time. Suicidal bastards. There must have been hundreds in the area and they were making a consolidated effort to overrun Inkerman. The Apache fire would suppress them for a while. Sometimes they would only come out and fight for a bit, but they would always be back for more. We estimated the numbers on the ground must have been high, because if there are a lot of them they are more willing to stay and fight. When three Apaches were in the air it showed just how many there were. They were still sticking to their ground fighting.

The assault was relentless and by the next afternoon the enemy were as close as 100 metres from the compound's HESCO Bastion protective walls. At that distance there was a series of sprawling, interconnected compounds and dwellings inhabited by locals, but now being overtaken by Taliban fighters to put rounds down on us from. This was a seriously shit-hot strategic position, providing them cover, and it increased the urgency of our situation.

We just kept on whacking these ragheads. And they just kept taking it. We worked our way through a mountain of ammo, including our heavy machine-gun systems and grenade machine guns, whilst teams of two fired off Javelin missiles at around 60k a pop. The Javelin was a massive improvement on the wire-guided MILAN system I used in Iraq. It was literally a fire-and-forget missile with lock-on before launch and automatic self-guidance. Equipped with an imaging infrared seeker, the warhead has two shaped charges. They smacked ferociously into the buildings 600 metres away, opposite Inkerman's outer perimeter, where Taliban fighters were stashed. It was a good job.

For 11 days it was the same pattern: attack, whack, attack, whack. I couldn't believe they were still coming. It was like the Alamo. We used enough firepower to kick off World War III. And slowly but surely the waves became less frequent. Maybe these bastards began to lose heart after seeing so many of their Muslim brothers maimed, killed or injured.

To live and work there, constantly under threat from Taliban attack, took a certain kind of physical and mental toughness. Flanked by bleak hills and distant mountains, the perimeter surrounded by razor wire and HESCO Bastion walls it was like the Wild West.

The enemy never missed a trick. They shot at us from little holes in the compound's walls.

What impressed me most about the lads I served with was their ability to be warriors one minute and playing the hearts-and-minds game the next, chatting to locals like friends, but knowing that they might shoot you in the back given half the chance. One minute you can be talking politely to local people, and then again, in an instant, you can be in a firefight or combat situation.

We all knew the Taliban were a daily threat. The real possibility of suicide-bomb attacks focuses the mind. It is a lot for young men to process, especially sprogs on their first tour. Although we would receive parcels from home, letters and Help for Heroes packages, it is hard to gauge what people back home really knew about the sacrifices being made by servicemen.

One morning, during a brief lull in the gunfire, I found myself staring again at the wooden cross at the top of a pile of stones inside the compound. I noticed now that a few brass plates were inscribed with the names of the fallen. Their lives were lost a long way from home in this bleak, unforgiving land, against an uncompromising enemy. I couldn't help thinking of those lads kicking the shit out of that bus shelter. They were just a few years younger than some of the servicemen and servicewomen who had perished in Afghanistan. Tossers. They cannot have any comprehension of what we have been through – or care, for that matter.

Our mission was not counter-terrorism, but a concerted effort to stop this country falling into the hands of the Taliban. History showed us that this was a land in which ordinary people were constantly at the mercy of warlords, bloodthirsty dictators and tribes. They had been crushed underfoot time and again. But their people knew how to fight against powerful invaders. The might of the Red Army had come unstuck here, driven back by determined tribal fighters funded by American dollars. About 150 years or so earlier, experienced soldiers from the British Empire had been humiliated, when more than 16,000 officers and men died as they retreated from Kabul, the Afghan capital.

By the end of day 11 it was calming down a bit, but the Taliban still hadn't pissed off into their ratholes, and we now had another problem. We'd spunked a shitload of ammo on these ragheads and our munition supplies were low. We desperately needed more bullets and grenades and missiles and mortar and artillery rounds in order to keep on slotting these bastards. Problem was, it was still too dangerous for resupply by helicopter. As soon as the Chinook hovered over Inkerman, the Taliban would start spitting out RPGs left, right and centre.

The only way we could get resupplied was a C130 supply drop in the middle of the desert. The C130 could fly much higher, out of RPG range. My CRF was tasked with securing the perimeter of what we call 'intimate security' for the landing on a desert strip a few miles from our camp. The mission was on a need-to-know basis for security, but it was pretty routine stuff. We loaded up on a WMIKs and I was on top cover as we hoofed it out to the proposed landing site at midnight. It was rough terrain and our driver, Brenty, had his work cut out. We were in Taliban territory now, even though those fuckers hate coming out at night. We couldn't take any chances.

I was on top cover, peering through my NVGs. Visibility wasn't great, even with the goggles on. We started to crest a mound, expecting there to be flat desert on the other side of it. Instead we found a sheer vertical drop of about six feet, followed by a further drop of equal depth. The WMIK nose-dived towards the desert floor and I flew out like a rag doll. I distinctly remember looking down as the vehicle dipped into the drop. I could see the heads of my two muckers. They were wondering where the hell I'd gone!

I smashed back down onto the top of the WMIK and was thrown off about ten feet onto the ground.

I opened my eyes to see my trashed NVGs lying next to me. For a moment I was stunned, and then my second thought was, *Fuck!* It hurt everywhere: my legs, my back, my head, it was all shit.

Bollocks, I thought, *not again!* The pain was excruciating. I couldn't move my neck, and my left leg was swelling up, much the same as it had when I came off my motorbike. It was the same damn leg! The lads could see it was serious. They were on the radio immediately calling for a Chinook to casevac me out of there.

I couldn't hear very well. Their voices were muffled. My thoughts were also confused. I was concussed as well as being in a right mess physically.

I just made out the words of one of the lads: 'T2 casualty . . . Cannot tell if his neck and leg are broken or not. His left leg is swelling in a bad way. We need to casevac him out of here.'

There was a pause and then I heard another lad shout: 'Are you mad? If his neck is broken he might never walk again!'

Within thirty minutes I was on a Chinook on my way to the medical centre at Camp Bastion. I had a brace for my neck and my leg was strapped up. When I arrived at Bastion I was put in the back of an ambulance and rushed to the trauma room. I was already high on morphine. I was in utter agony, and the doc dosed me up on ketamine to sedate me. This stuff is really strong and all of a sudden there were clowns everywhere. The doc was dressed as a clown, the nurses were on unicycles, the anaesthetists were juggling, the lot! I was hallucinating. It was insane.

I couldn't move my head as the doctor directed. This went on for a couple of days, and I became genuinely concerned that I may have done some serious damage. The doc was worried because the X-rays had shown up something 'dodgy' regarding my neck, which wasn't exactly great for morale. On the third day I thanked my lucky stars. I could move my head. After about eight days I was flown back to the UK for intensive phys on my injured leg. Amazingly, it wasn't actually broken, just some ligament and muscle damage. *My leg must be indestructible*, I thought. I was a lucky guy. One of the lads joked that he should ask me for six numbers for the lottery!

I was determined to get back on the front line, especially when I heard about the push for Musa Qala in early December 2007. Some 2,000-odd Taliban had occupied the town, and coalition forces had launched Operation Mar Karadad. Just north of Helmand Province, Musa Qala was a major Taliban drug-trafficking hub and it was of central importance to their ability to operate in Helmand. Hence the big push by the coalition to take it back. I heard that Afghan National Army troops played a significant role in the assault. Those guys aren't the best soldiers ever, but they're pretty fearless and they're always mad up for a fight.

So I was mustard keen to get back and do my duty, and back up my mates. Other guys were dying. I remember reading about Sergeant Lee Johnson from the 2nd Battalion Yorkshire Regiment being killed during the Musa Qala assault. He'd stepped on a landmine. It focused my mind on the need to get back into the field and do my bit.

There was only one way forward: I had to blag it.

'How's that leg now, Lance Corporal Croucher?' the doctor asked me. 'Any repercussions? Are you moving well?'

With a straight face and my fingers crossed, I replied, 'It feels fine, sir. I am fit to return.'

He signed my chit and within days I was heading back to Helmand Province, Afghanistan, to rejoin the lads. I managed to get on the tail end of the Musa Qala op, which was a winner. I couldn't stand it back home knowing that they were having all that fun without me.

SIXTEEN

FOB Robinson
Sangin Valley, Helmand Province
February 2008

In 2008 our mission also involved supporting international efforts to counter the narcotics trade, which poisoned the Afghanistan economy. After all, 90 per cent of the heroin on British streets originated from Helmand's poppy fields. We were there, too, to train the Afghan National Army to ensure they could one day take care of their own security. In the end, there is no long-term role for a foreign military force. However, training the local army and police was no easy task, especially as many of them had switched sides. Some of them were stoned half the time, caning it on hashish whenever they could. When I was there, we were still giving the orders and fighting the fight, even if they were hoisting the Afghan National flags for victory for the cameras. It was all part of the political bullshit that is Afghanistan, and we had to just live with it.

Like any op for any commando you don't expect five-star luxury, penthouse suites or chilled-out nights sipping champagne on the Algarve. You sign up for dirty, tough, demanding missions in gruelling environments and you don't complain. You take what you're given and just get on with it. We were four months into our six-month tour and a few of us, rightly or wrongly, had an eye on getting out of there with our limbs still attached to our bodies. We had certainly broken the back of our stint, but battle fatigue and frustration were beginning to set in. We needed a significant victory to lift our spirits and make us feel we were really making a difference. One thing that they had drummed into us during commando training and throughout our Marine service was the need to keep sharp. It is essential to keep on top of the moment. Day-dreaming or thinking about what comes next could literally cost you your life. It is a tough task, though, especially in a place like Afghanistan, where hours, days, weeks and months all merge into one. Personal focus is crucial to survival on the front line in any war.

I wasn't the only one finding it tough. The enormity and complexity of our job in this war-ravaged country was taking its toll on the whole of the CRF. There were always a couple of jokers in the troop, you always get them. They tried to keep spirits up with their banter and pranks, although there was the odd occasion or two when their jokes tested someone's patience. It was good to try to break the tension, but in the back of all our minds was the burning question: could there ever be a real victory in a place like this, a place where the natives who are on your side rarely give any active support for fear of reprisals, if their line in the sand happens to fall under Taliban control? The stripeys and PIGS did their best to keep you on your toes, but ultimately it was down to the individual to stay focused on the daily duties. Preparing for a patrol is down to you. If you forget a vital bit of kit, ultimately it could cost your life, and the life of the lad next to you – simple as!

Our new home from home was FOB Robinson – or FOB Rob as the lads called it. Situated on the edge of the Helmand Province Green Zone, this was right at the sharp end. With its big outer perimeter and tighter, more compact inner one, it was right smack in the middle of Taliban supply routes and movement corridors, so it was about as kinetic as it gets.

We called it the Green Zone because it was predominantly green. And it was best to keep it simple for the Gravs! There was a two-, maybe three-kilometre-wide stretch either side of the Helmand river, peppered with irrigation ditches, ploughed fields, and thick vegetation. It was also littered with little compounds, perfect for the Taliban to hole up in. It was a frustrating landscape and a place that the Taliban, with good reason, believed was their turf. It was our job to show them that for the British soldier there were no 'no-go' areas. The Green Zone stood out a mile from the barren desert all around it, like a long winding oasis – at least from a distance. Close up the ditches were festering, full of human shit. But it was fertile and the Afghans grew poppies, the lifeblood of the Taliban's evil empire, which provided vital funds to their reign of terror. From these bright, even beautiful red flowers the Taliban produced at least a third of the world's heroin. The elected President Hamid Karzai declared a 'jihad' on drugs. But many people in this area are locked into the evil trade. It is big business, and none of them were about to hand over what they saw as hard-earned cash from drugs. The smuggling kingpins who control the £1.5 bn trade have become rich, powerful and apparently untouchable. Until

Karzai arrests and jails one big dealer, people will not listen to the central government. The Taliban and the drug smugglers are still in bed together.

The natural environment of the Green Zone made open combat a nightmare. We called it Ambush Territory Central. You never knew when someone would pop up brandishing his AK and let off a volley of rounds, so everyone's straining into the darkness. For some reason, it has long been a Taliban stronghold, too. Though that's not easy to prove. They blend in, threatening the locals to deny their existence. Often, they are the locals. Up to 95 per cent of the population of Helmand lives around the Green Zone, so it's easier for the Taliban to operate there in the shadows. Sometimes you just know. But you can never be 100 per cent sure – so you take what you're being told with a pinch of salt and keep your finger on the trigger. Sometimes you'll be patrolling through an area and they'll suddenly pull AK-47s from haystacks and start hosing you down. We've pushed them out of this area time and time again. Plenty of British blood has been spilt here. But they keep coming back . . . so we'll keep going after them.

The Taliban, with good reason, believed the land around FOB Robinson was their turf, and they fought to the death to keep every inch they could, not least because of the vast income it generated to fund their cause. As far as they were concerned they had full freedom of movement there. It gave them great cover from which to launch ambushes against our daily patrols. We knew once inside it was never easy to get back out again unscathed.

This region is to opium what Florida is to oranges. It's part of the 'Devil's Triangle' in the Sangin area, along with two other FOBs around the Sangin district, Inkerman and Gibraltar. Heroin with a street value of billions helps prop up the Taliban military machine. Their commanders were pre-pared to commit young, fanatical men to the slaughter to protect this lucrative trade. They were not about to let us march in there and destroy their trade routes and vital illicit income stream. If we were to have any chance of destroying the Taliban's influence, cutting off the cash supply was crucial.

Most Taliban there were armed poppy growers, ferocious fighters who would put their necks on the line to protect their drug crop. We always knew when the professionals – outside fighters brought in to school these guys in the way of war – were teaming up with them, because the mortar fire became more accurate. In Helmand it seemed like the silent majority definitely wanted us here to quell the violent reign of terror of the Taliban, but this was no cushy peacekeeping role. Without doubt it was one of the most dangerous places on earth, a place where life is cheap and bloody violence is par for the course.

Here, almost daily, the threat to the lives of British servicemen and women was palpable. The Taliban would regularly hurl 107 mm Chinese-made drab olive rockets – incorporating a high-explosive fragmentation warhead containing white phosphorous, or HE – in at our camp from their multi-barrel rocket launchers. Just to make it interesting, they would shake it up with 102 mm mortars. If the firing stopped for a while, it was just as unsettling. We would wonder what else they were cooking up. The first we knew about a pending attack was the terrible shrieking sound as the rocket hurtled in towards us. Just the sound of it would strike trepidation in all our hearts, as it was the signal for everyone inside the inner compound to take cover. Each time you heard the shout, 'Incoming! Take cover!' you would dive for cover, clutching your bone-dome and praying that it wouldn't frag you. You could never be totally sure that that screeching sound wasn't the last you'd hear on this earth. Then came the distinctive thud and crump as it impacted, followed by a massive explosion.

FOB Robinson looked like something out of the film *Apocalypse Now* – a favourite DVD among the lads to watch during our rare downtime. Four miles south of Sangin, adjacent to the Helmand river close to the town of Heydarabad. Even FOB Rob's name was a constant reminder of our mortality. The camp was named after 36-year-old Special Forces Communications Sergeant Christopher L. Robinson, from Brandon, Mississippi. The poor sod had died defending this place. He was awarded a posthumous Bronze Star Medal for Valor, Meritorious Service Medal, Purple Heart and Combat Infantryman Badge for his troubles – and, of course, a sprawling collection of tents, sangars and metal containers, surrounded by HESCO block walls, sandbags and razor wire bore his name as a memorial.

Living conditions at FOB Rob were gash grim, among the worst I have ever experienced. When we arrived in early February it was the height of the bitingly cold Afghan winter, so it was icers and we had little, if any, protection from the elements. The temperature plunged well below freezing at night. Washing was impossible before mid-morning in winter, as the water remained frozen. Later in the day, you could grab a cold shower using hanging bags, and limited hot water was available from the 'Puffing Billy' boiler. Most of the time we simply kept clean by just washing with bottled water, but that was in short supply. There was also a pump rigged to a well. We had electricity of sorts from a giant generator, but it was never that reliable.

To be an effective soldier it was essential that we grabbed a few zeds whenever we could. Nobody knew when the next

16-hour patrol or extended contact would come, and when it did you would be useless if your eyes were out on stalks. Someone somewhere always had their head down, night and day. Staying alive is, after all, a 24/7 operation, and the camp was always manned and guarded in case of an attack. FOB Rob, in winter at least, resembled old footage from World War I. Only with this enemy there would be no friendly Christmas Day truce and a kick about in no-man's-land. We shared no common culture or ideals. These guys might as well have come from another planet. They were ideological warriors – men prepared to die for a belief, a concept. I believe in my country, and just being in that godforsaken place I knew I was risking my life. But I wasn't prepared to throw it away. I would always do my best to stay alive. For me, what was important was protecting my oppos, and I was soon to discover just how far I would go to do it.

We slept in ISO containers – the big metal ones that go on the backs of trucks – surrounded by HESCO Bastion walls for protection. The containers were freezing inside. Filthy too, and needed scrubbing out regularly just to maintain a basic level of sanitation. But you got used to it. After a while we were oblivious to the sound of incoming small-arms or mortar fire.

The urinals were metal tubes hammered into the sand. All of us had lost weight since arriving in theatre. D and V – dysentery and vomiting – were, thankfully, not so common during the winter, because the bugs die off. Rations consisted of rice, mainly, maybe with some chicken, and pasta, which meant it was almost impossible to bulk-up. The galley served up hamburgers, beans and treacle pudding, too. It wasn't exactly up to Jamie Oliver standards, but it did the trick.

FOB Rob was a testament to the international make-up of

the NATO force in Afghanistan. It was well situated and fairly easy to defend from our perspective, as the Yanks built it on a dusty hilltop. Columns of heavily armed US Special Forces, Dutch and United Arab Emirates peacekeepers, Afghan National Army troops and Royal Marines patrolled in and out. We were one big and mostly happy family. The Brits and the Yanks grudgingly respected one another. 'Fucking Americans,' was often heard, but the truth was the Brits got on well with the Yanks most of the time. They were good guys, tough as nails, and straight from central casting for Mercs R Us: moustaches, Gucci kit, complete with wrap-around shades. They had more weapons than anyone else, and made sure we knew it. They operated differently, too. Maybe some of them had watched too many war movies – or maybe the war movies had just captured the Yanks spot on. Their approach was to blow the crap out of everything and ask questions later. On reflection, perhaps it was not such a bad policy.

I remember the ground shuddered as we arrived. Canadian and American artillery were pounding Taliban positions five miles away. In between dropping 155 mm howitzer shells, two Canadian artillery teams bitched about each other. In a small enclosure near the front gate, young Afghan soldiers were smoking charras. One of them looked as high as a kite, but nobody seemed to care. What was the point? Half these local guys were more of a hindrance than a help as we tried to bring some semblance of peace and stability to this lawless land. None of us could ever be sure of the allegiance of the local police and troops. Spies were everywhere, including inside the ANA and ANP. We would be naïve to think otherwise.

Some senior members of the ANP had been Taliban

sympathisers and switched sides. Why wouldn't they switch back if the Taliban started getting the upper hand? The natives, too, were about as non-committal as you could get. In this area where villages had been won and lost in the past – changing hands between our control and the Taliban's – it was best not to be seen to be too co-operative for fear of reprisals if the Taliban took over again. You couldn't blame them, but it made our job harder.

The Taliban were everywhere – even in hideouts just a stone's throw from our front gate, amongst a sprawling ragbag of houses and compounds. The whole place reeked. It stank like a sewer, but that was par for the course in Afghanistan. Open drains and stagnant irrigation ditches ran between compounds, and rubbish piled up all around. Sanitation was extremely basic, too. It was the first thing that hit me when I deployed there. The natives had started to move back, which was a good thing, our OC said, because it proved we were winning their 'hearts and minds'. They had more confidence in their own security, because we were here, he reminded us.

I wasn't convinced. To me, though, it was never easy to differentiate between friend and foe, and you were never all that confident you had got it right either. They all wore long flowing cloaks, the dishdasha, and keffiyeh (headscarves) of varying colours. It wasn't that I was paranoid, but I didn't want to take any chances. The risks were real. Two months before we arrived on Christmas Eve, one of the 40 Commando lads, Marine Mark Ormrod, lost both legs and an arm when a Taliban landmine strapped to a Chinese-made rocket blew him up during a routine foot patrol. It was a miracle that he survived his terrible injuries, and, frankly, he nearly didn't. It took 28 pints of blood and brilliant emergency surgery to save his life. We knew we were not there to win hearts and minds, but to kill the Taliban before they maimed and killed us. Other guys have been killed and seriously hurt by mines and IEDs – a couple of lads just round the corner from FOB Rob itself.

A few days into our posting we discovered a shedload of ordnance – six anti-tank mines dug into ground near where we were patrolling in vehicles.

'Jesus,' one of the lads chipped in as the engineers uncovered a deadly cache. 'Check out these bastards for size!'

They were about the size of a dinner plate, but as thick as your arm. Six of them would create one hell of a blast. We destroyed them in a controlled explosion. But it was a thankless task. There were literally millions more left over in the so-called legacy minefields of the 1970s – all sorts of ordnance buried all over the place, and worse than anything I'd seen on the Iran–Iraq border. There was enough bomb-making gear there to keep these bastards going for years – if they were nuts enough to crawl around an unmarked minefield surrounded by tons of unstable high explosives to get it. And they were nuts enough. The Taliban would dig them up, disarm them, then re-use them wherever they thought they could cause the most damage: on roadsides, in villages, anywhere our lads patrolled, really.

Casualties caused by roadside bombings were consistently high throughout Helmand Province. The injuries they inflicted on our lads were terrible and sapped morale. It reminds you that the whole point of landmines and bombs isn't to kill – it's to destroy the morale of the enemy. As far as the Taliban was concerned, the more Brits and Yanks they sent home minus a leg or an arm the better. In my view this was a really cowardly, evil way of fighting a war, but then again the Taliban are pure evil. They're bastards. I noticed as time went on that the use of roadside bombs by the enemy became more and more commonplace, and this was because of our total success against the Taliban fighters in toe-to-toe, manly contacts, when your skills as a professional soldier really count.

We were determined to get our own back, and the top brass jumped at the chance when the Americans offered us the gig. In one gun battle we fought through for five miles, chasing the Taliban on foot, then patrolled back another five miles. That's ten miles carrying all the kit.

'You guys are nuts!' this Yank said to me. 'You should just be doing all that in vehicles instead.'

'Yeah, maybe,' I said, shrugging.

Without doubt it would have been easier, but it is not in the Marine code, although there were times when the idea of jumping on a Viking all-protective vehicle and chucking your kit on the back certainly appealed – especially after ten gruelling hours in the field. In contrast, there were contacts where all of a sudden the Americans would knock it on the head because they'd want to get back for scran! That's not the commando way. We never do a job half-cocked and we always carry on until that job is done. Absolutely no bullshit and no moaning – just get on with it.

Back at FOB Rob I was kicking my heels, getting bored with doing weights and cleaning kit, when suddenly the buzz came down the line that our four-man team was in line for a big gig. We were led by Corporal Les, who was sharp as shit and a top bloke to work with. Everyone on his team trusted him. They knew that if the shit hit the fan he would be there for every one of us. That counted in my book. Apart from me, there was also a burly South African bloke called Dave. He was shaven-headed and looked like he should have been working the doors at a night-club. He used to go round the camp making shit all the time to make people's lives easier: camp fireplaces, clothes lines, he was always trying to domesticate our living quarters. Then there was Scot, Reconnaissance Operator and a great bloke to boot.

Turns out we had nabbed a plum job for that night as part of a wider mission involving 40 lads in total in four teams. Ads came back from the early evening briefing with a huge grin on his face.

'It's a biggie tonight, lads. We're CTR-ing a probable Taliban bomb factory. It'll be a quick in and out, quiet as you like, right under their noses too, while the other lads provide cover.'

He pulled us all together and mapped out the plan. We were the guys who would be going directly inside a live Taliban compound. The buzz at the time was that the Taliban were cooking up something really big. Wankers. We had to get in to this compound and stop it before they could launch a serious offensive. The compound was rumoured to be a bomb-making factory, but we needed firm int. So our mission was not seek and destroy but, rather, to gather vital int, the evidence we needed to nail these bastards before they killed anyone else. It was our chance to regain the upper hand in this war of attrition, and to seriously disrupt the terrorists in their own backyard. Our instructions were clear, though: if we stumbled across any sleeping Taliban, we should let sleeping dogs lie.

Once we had completed our reconnoitring of the com-pound we would radio it in to HQ, then get the hell out of there as quick as we could without being detected with evidence in hand. It would require every ounce of commando tactical awareness and expertise, and we had been selected for it. I felt proud that I had been picked, but soon told myself not to be a dickhead. It could have been any of us. We were all shit-hot commandos, and it was the luck of the draw. Ads said out loud exactly what we were all thinking.

'Yes, lads, I know,' he said. 'It will be tempting to shoot them in their sleep and drop them there and then, but we must hold back. Their time will come soon enough.' *The sooner the better*, I thought.

This was about as good as it got. As a member of a Commando Reconnaissance Force CTR team (Close Target Reconnaissance), I had to crawl around in the middle of the night, surrounded by probable Taliban fanatic diehards, right in among them. At any moment they could stir and you'd be right bang in the middle of a firefight, outgunned and outnumbered, with only your soldiering skills to get you and your muckers out of there alive. It's funny, but to an outsider, from our response to Ad's briefing, he could have been telling us the football results. We all must have looked pretty blaze about it. But that's the way commandos are. It's our job. Putting our lives on the line is just what we do 'at the office'. Inside, we were all raring to go. Ads, me and the other lads in our team, Scot and Dave, went through the SOPs (Standard Operating Procedures). We prepared for every eventuality. What would we do if someone turned an ankle in the dark, for example, right through to our patrol being compromised by the enemy. Ultimately, we had the other teams close by as protection, ready to arrest any terrorist suspects and act as a Quick Reaction Force to extricate us if the situation turned bad. But we were also prepared for a fighting withdrawal back to friendly forces. If we had to blaze our way out of the compound then we would. After that we would regroup with the other teams and either launch a counter-attack or call in air support.

Whatever happened, we knew were going to be razors that night.

SEVENTEEN

Recce mission
Near FOB Robinson

My captain was not one for bullshit. He didn't have time for it. He called a spade a spade and said what he needed to say – no more, no less. He didn't take prisoners either. If you had messed up he told you straight and you took it on the chin. If you had done well, he told you that too – both with equal inflection. There was no need to ham it up. There was enough shit flying around on the front line without the officers flapping too. Above all, he respected the lads and we respected him.

H-hour – the moment when a combat operation is initiated – was fast approaching. It was around 1 a.m. and we were freezing our bollocks off waiting to get the nod to go. The temperature was well below zero and the patches of snow lying around had turned to a shitty brown slush. We waited to move out from the staging area, away from the relative safety inside Robinson's perimeter. My team huddled around the boss as he gave a final briefing. Down on one knee, holding a map in his right hand, the Captain's expression was stern and serious. The three other lads and I were crouched beside him in a tight circle. This was private chat, for our team only. After all, we were the ones going inside the compound to gather the int, and he wanted to be sure we knew exactly how he wanted to play it.

'Listen up, lads. Do not, repeat, *do not* – take any stupid risks. You got that?' he said. We all nodded our agreement in unison. 'Just get in and out as fast as you like. Find the evidence, and we'll leave it up to intelligence to decide what we do next. If, for whatever reason, the mission is compromised, you know the drill. Make a fighting retreat back to the LUP [Lying Up Position] where we'll be supporting you. No heroics, lads. OK?'

Heroics was the last thing on our minds. After all, being a hero is about the shortest-lived profession on earth, and none of us wanted to join the ranks of the Dead Heroes Society. I for one intended to live long enough to bore my mates back home in Solihull with a shitload of war stories, and so did the other lads on the team. I hadn't survived being shot at, bombed and mortared just to cop it sneaking around some supposed Taliban bomb factory. We only had a couple of months to go out there. None of us wanted our bollocks blown off at the last hurdle. We were focused. The boss needn't have worried.

I checked my watch again. February 9, 2008 didn't mean a lot to me back then. About 30 of us were waiting outside. It was dead quiet and dark, and any light – as was the SOP on all patrols – was kept to an absolute minimum. We didn't want to light the place up like a candle. If we did it would become an easy aiming-marker for the Taliban to launch rockets and mortars.

As we readied ourselves to step outside, all we could hope for was that this patrol wasn't dicked by Taliban spotters or sympathisers. Your stomach was in your mouth every time you stepped outside on a mission like this. The first few seconds were crucial. That night a half-moon lit up the surrounding terrain, so there wasn't a lot of ambient light. Not ideal for a dangerous recce like this. It was tense that night as we checked and rechecked our kit, and prepared to leave the relative safety of the base. Some of the lads at the staging area still managed a whispered laugh and joke – a bit of the old 'Ging Gang Gooley' or just letting off a bit of steam. A bit of banter is a good way to deal with stress. Some of the lads smoked a last fag, others checked their equipment again, and some just kept themselves to themselves.

We had been on dozens of these patrols, maybe hundreds. Your friends and family are thousands of miles away, but none of us could afford to think about them getting threaders about you and waiting for bad news. You always have to focus on the job in front of you. In combat or on patrol one thing you learn is to go for it 100 miles an hour and sod the consequences. The lad next to you in combat is all the family you can handle, and it is your job to keep him safe, then he will return the compliment. My best mate there was Dave. I didn't need to, but, as the lads gathered their kit, I patted my webbing anyway from force of habit.

At night you can forget a lot of things. So I made sure I had everything ready before last light – that way I knew as soon as I woke up I would be ready for the go signal. The VIPIR thermal-imaging scope was fixed to my rifle, and we had much larger SOPHIE thermal-imaging equipment too. This was real Gucci kit. The imaging equipment identified body heat and helped us get dabs on the enemy when it was pitch black. My NVG intensified the available light, too, giving the impression that everything was bathed in a green glow. It always took a few seconds to acclimatise, but it was essential kit in this war and meant the Taliban as a rule hated fighting at night, because they were seriously disadvantaged. As this was an overnight reconnaissance mission, I had also packed warmers – heavily quilted trousers, jacket and gloves. In Helmand the temperature often fell to below freezing. It was weird coming across snow in the middle of the desert, but when the sun went down it was bitingly cold. You could often get laid up for hours on end just watching and waiting for something to happen.

Strapped to the breastplate of my body armour I had a Gucci knife that I had exchanged with a US Special Forces guy for a Commando dagger. I got a $200 knife that was razor-sharp. I definitely had the better deal. The Yank was a sucker, although the RM Commando is a classic and a war memento.

'Where'd you get that from, Croucher?' the boss asked me.

'Swapped it with the Yanks for a Commando, sir,' I said.

He raised his eyebrows. He was clearly impressed with my trading skills. Point is, everyone carries a knife. If someone gets injured, you use it to cut off their clothing to get to the wounds – although even a small nick can result in a bleed-out and someone dying in front of you. At the back of your mind, you know that your knife is your weapon of last resort in a close fight. You'd stab the shit out of someone if you had to. Messy, undoubtedly, and maybe not what people back home want to hear. But I never said war was all fun and games.

I also had three or four fragmentation grenades stuffed in pouches, and a Browning 9 mm pistol for close combat. In the confines of a small compound, or an alleyway, it's sometimes better to patrol with a 9 mm instead of a rifle. To be effective, you need to be within 20 metres of your target. But the damage a 9 mm can cause is awesome, it's a real man-stopper. You soon get through 13 rounds on semi-automatic, but it rocks. Pumping away with it on the firing range, you feel like James Bond. Mine's cleaned and oiled, ready for action.

Slung over one shoulder I've also got my standard SA80 assault rifle, a brilliant weapon as long as you keep her clean, and I'm carrying my day sack over the other, so I can drop it in a second if we hit a contact. My day sack's heavy, because as well as the morphine, field dressing, tourniquets and spare socks, I'm carrying an extra lithium battery for the patrol's ECM system – it weighs a ton, but it could help save lives by jamming bomb signals sent remotely by mobile phone. Let's just hope we don't need it tonight. I've also got 500 rounds of ammunition stashed in other pouches, as well as chocolate, chewing gum and about three litres of water in a camel pack, so I can suck it through a straw without stopping to think.

Some lads will carry everything and the kitchen sink, but you get to know what you really need. You cut it to the bone the more times you go out. On a foot patrol, it's best to travel as light as possible, because there's never time to mess about. It's balls dangerous fighting at night, and you need to keep absolutely razor-sharp because a single mistake, no matter how slight, could cost your life or, even worse, that of the man next to you. You need a lot of command and control, because there could be guys running around all over the place – and through your night-vision goggles any man with a gun could quite easily be Taliban, or one of your mates. No one wants a blue-on-blue (friendly fire) incident on their conscience. A couple of the lads had UGLs, too – great for clearing compounds and the tight little rat runs between what passes for homes out here – and GPS systems for greater accuracy. We would also be backed by a couple of GPMGs in case the shit really hit the fan, but, in all honesty, we were not expecting trouble that night.

Basically, we were kitted out like mean machines, and ready to rock and roll. I pitied the poor bastard who dared to cross us.

Outside, the desert was cold and still. Noise travels a long way at night, that's one of the first things you learn in basic training, and rural Afghanistan, with its wide open spaces, is no exception.

You notice without noticing, when you're trying to see in the dark and hear the enemy moving at 50 metres in the pitch black, so you can drop him before he drops you.

The buzz was we would be moving out beyond Robinson and towards the target area in five minutes.

'Hell yes,' said one of the lads. 'Can't wait.'

Me too.

We had done it often enough, walked out into the desert terrain. It wasn't anything new. But for some reason this mission felt different. I was more focused than at any time before. My nerve ends were tingling. Maybe it was the cold. The breeze was icers as it whipped in across the desert, but inexplicably I was supremely conscious of everything around me. Then, with a quick nod from the lads manning the defensive sangars with the .50 cals, we had the signal to go.

Without a word we moved out as one, patrolling out, then boxing around the perimeter. On patrol, each man left enough distance to the next, around 15 metres, so we were not a group target, so if one guy was taken down the others wouldn't get fragged by the same fire. Yet we were still close enough to cover each other's backs should a sudden enemy contact ensue, or, God forbid, the lad in front stepped on a landmine.

We headed off in the opposite direction to our intended target. Deceptions like this were vital. The Taliban knew how to set an ambush, especially if you didn't shake it up a bit and got complacent. We'd heard stories of the Taliban booby-trapping routes, so that when the lads used them again, they blew up. We would drop off forces along the route, too, to cover our rear as we went. The Taliban know this terrain like the back of their hands, so in a guerrilla war of attrition like Afghanistan it is essential to keep them guessing for as long as possible. No matter how good the plan looks on paper, you have to keep your wits sharp in practice out in the field, where you are exposed.

Landmines were never far from our thoughts. In the back of your mind you're always wondering what's under your feet. No one wants to lose a limb. But there's almost nothing you can do. If you step on a mine, you're pretty much fucked. Many are as small as a coffee-cup saucer. Some leap into the air, exploding into a thousand metal splinters and maiming everyone within a 25-metre radius. A few are small enough to hide in a fag packet.

They are designed to maim, not to kill. When some unlucky bastard treads on one and loses a leg, the other lads want to go and retrieve him. That draws two or three lads into the killing zone. Suddenly, you're facing a massacre and morale's screwed along with everything else. It happened to the Cherry Berries in September 2006, a few miles up country in the Kajaki Dam area of Helmand. Seven blokes were injured and trapped in a minefield, three having lost legs – absolute carnage.

You can never be certain what's in front of you. Sometimes you see a path with fresh soil that looks like someone might have been digging. You don't always have time to check it, but you'll avoid it and warn the lads behind you. Equally, there might be no sign at all that a few inches below the surface a precision-tooled, spring-loaded pressure plate attached to several pounds of high-ex is waiting for your footfall.

It stank of rotten eggs underfoot. The ground was sodden and sticky as we bimbled through the fields. My mind was racing. It had been a pretty quiet period in the previous month or two, compared to when we first got there in the autumn. Back then we were engaging in daily firefights pretty much from dusk until dawn. We had fired off thousands of rounds every week, keeping our QM busy resupplying us. It gave us all a kick, a sense of achievement. We were sending the message to the Taliban that we were the real deal, and to the ordinary Afghan we were hopefully instilling confidence that we wouldn't just up sticks and leave them to the Taliban. Since I got back in situ in January the number of enemy had slowed considerably. Yes, they would still throw in rockets and mortars and there was always the buzz of Afghan Wasps whizzing about, but serious contacts were down to about once, maybe twice a week. We were all a bit frustrated. Commandos, after all, pride themselves on taking the fight to the enemy. This mission was at least a chance for us to regain the upper hand.

I knew what the other guys were thinking: the same as me, the same as all the Marines out tonight scouting around in the dark of a foreign country more than 7,000 miles away from home. *Just don't mess up*. At night we were a little bit closer together, because it's easy to lose track of your mates in the darkness, even with the night goggles. We tended to keep relatively close to the bloke in front, but far enough away so that if someone does trip over a grenade or mine you don't catch the shrapnel too. The killing zone can stretch up to ten metres away. As we snurgled forward, I was the third in the team behind Ads. It took us just over an hour to travel barely two miles, and despite the intense cold I was dripping with sweat when we reached the laying-up point about 400 metres from the target compound for final instructions from the boss. I slumped down, shouldering my rifle into a prone firing position. I spotted our target through the green of my NVGs. It looked dead calm. There was no sign of life inside or outside the compound. Maybe the int was wrong. Maybe the Taliban fighters had been tipped off and had left.

That would be just like them.

EIGHTEEN

Taliban compound
Sangin Valley
9 February 2008

As we headed in there we could see two buildings inside the compound and a stable. Once we had sneaked in undetected we split into two teams. Two lads went one way, me and Dave checked out the stable. We didn't have to look far.

It was a mud-walled construction that wouldn't have looked out of place 2,000 years ago. We thought the Taliban, or the guys they had guarding this stuff, were upstairs sleeping. They hadn't put anyone on nightwatch. But we were not there for a firefight. It was crucial, as the boss said, not to wake anyone. We carefully explored the ground-floor rooms instead. Still, if anyone moved, I was poised, finger on trigger, to cut them down.

Through the green haze of my NVGs I identified six large sacks of heavy-duty fertiliser, maybe as much as 200 kilos of the shit. Next to it was a load of electrical gear – batteries, circuitry, wires – and you didn't have to be a genius to put two and two together. Fertiliser plus electrical equipment meant only one thing: homemade explosives. The Taliban were using it to make a devastating explosive compound. There was plenty enough for a really big bang, and it was all still in white plastic sacks bearing the Arabic name of the supplier. It was precisely the evidence we needed to blow that place to kingdom come.

Dave and I stared at each other for a moment.

I thought, *Shit, this is the big one*. Dave gave me the thumbs up, as we were on silent signals. We'd cracked it.

Dave, still grinning with the success of the find, scooped out a couple of samples and took some of the circuitry with him as well – that was all the evidence we needed. Within seconds we were outside again, looking to meet up with the other two lads.

Ads appeared out of the gloom and gestured for us to form up. Incredibly, we had been inside for 40 minutes, but it had just whizzed by. It was now time to get the hell out and go home with our spoils. We'd got what we came for. I took point position this time.

A minute later, Scottie's earlier false alarm came horribly true – for me.

My shin brushed against a wire, just below my knee. I felt it go taut under my leg and I desperately tried to pull back, but it was too late. Suddenly the tension was released and my heart skipped a beat.

I looked down through the green haze at the object I had brushed against.

It was a four-metre tripwire. I couldn't believe my luck. We were so close to getting out, and I just walked straight into this bastard. Some devious raghead bastard had wired an old pineapple-style Russian grenade round a stake and driven it into the ground, then tied wire through the pin and wrapped it round a nearby tree. It was a deadly surprise. I was the prey snared in their crude trap.

The tension of the spring was released in a loud and unmistakeable metallic ping that sent a chill up my spine. The handle ejected, arming the grenade, which fell from the stake and rolled ominously towards me.

Everything seemed to go into slow motion.

Ads was now directly behind me, just feet away. He was followed by Scottie and Dave. If I didn't take decisive action – and fast – all four of us were within the five-metre killing zone. We'd all be browners.

I screamed at the top of my voice: 'Tripwire! . . . Grenade!'

Ads hit the deck behind me, while Dave, last in the patrol, darted back behind the building wall for cover and Scottie took cover in the doorway of the building. There was no time to lose.

I flipped the day sack from my shoulder and onto the grenade, dropping down with it, my back to the ugly little oval-shaped pineapple. Then, pulling my legs up into the foetal position, I tucked my head back so my body armour and helmet would make a shield against the inevitable blast.

Nuts I know, but I hoped by doing this I would prevent shrapnel taking a chunk out of my brain or spine or even slicing my head clean off. What I did know was that if I didn't smother the blast with my body I was certain one or more of my oppos would have been browners. I reckoned it would be wrong for them to cop it because of my balls-up. I could see them from where I was on the ground, desperately trying to shield themselves from the inevitable blast. I remember thinking, they're not very far away at all, only a couple of feet.

I gritted my teeth, waiting for the explosion. Deep down, I thought I was going to get really fucked up, but I was ready to make the ultimate sacrifice.

After seven agonising seconds there was the loudest noise I could imagine, like someone firing up a jet engine inside my head. Next thing I knew I'd been flung through the air and I was lying face down in the shit, chewing dirt as warm blood poured from my nose and down my face. I was covered in dust.

I immediately smelt the cordite from the grenade. It was like someone had shoved a load of fireworks up my nose. I could feel something burning. I wasn't sure who it was, but I could feel someone frantically patting me down. Later Scottie and Dave told me they had run their hands under my armour to check for injuries, searching for holes in my combats that would signify a shrapnel entry point. My eyes and face were caked in dust and I struggled to breathe. It felt like every ounce of oxygen had been forced from my lungs. I was coughing and choking like an elderly chain-smoker.

I was dazed, but I could see Ads. He had blood streaming down his nose from a slight fragmentation wound. I heard him calling in on the radio. His voice was urgent. 'Man down – grenade!'

Dave and Scottie were shouting to each other, checking that they weren't seriously injured and covering the corners of the compound ready for the inevitable Taliban reaction. None of the lads flapped, though. The training just kicked in and the adrenalin was pumping. As I opened my eyes, my muckers clawed at me, pulling me off the ground. My SA80 was still slung on my arm, but my day sack had been blown a good ten metres away, the strap sliced away by shrapnel. It had saved my life.

Most of the fragmentation was contained under my body. Miraculously my equipment and protective clothing had prevented lethal shards from hitting me. Somehow I had suffered only minor injuries. My body armour and helmet were peppered with grenade fragments.

The next thing we knew the lithium battery from my day sack exploded and we hit the deck again. I remember thinking it was a secondary device or another grenade. The heavy, metal-coated battery had borne the brunt of the blast along with my armour. It saved me once, but if I had still been attached to it, I would have probably burnt to death within a couple of seconds, because it flamed up like a welder's torch, only 50 times stronger.

Suddenly, the whole compound was lit up. Scottie and Dave grabbed my arms and marched me out of there.

'My God! I can't believe what I've just seen!' said Ads.

'I had to do something, mate. It was my fuck-up and I didn't want you guys to get fragged,' I replied in a haze.

'Croucher, you're one lucky sod! Nine out of ten people would have died back there.'

'I think that's all my lives used up now, mate,' I said.

He was almost laughing at the sheer madness of the situation. Disorientated and gobsmacked, I couldn't believe I hadn't lost a leg or an arm or anything.

'You're in once piece,' whispered Scottie in disbelief. 'Cheers, mate,' he said. He knew he would have been browners otherwise.

We patrolled back carefully to the LUP (Laying-Up Point), then fell back to a ditch, which gave us more cover. The boss – in between telling me what a lucky bastard I was – decided to exploit the situation.

He set an ambush and waited to see who turned up to investigate the blast, reckoning that the Taliban would come to see what poor bastard they had nailed this time. They were going to get a nasty surprise. The back-up team, ready to extract, sat tight. There was movement around the compound, I could see out of the corner of my eye as a medic checked me over again. He wanted to call in a chopper to casevac me out of there, but I was having none of it.

'I'm fine, mate. Never been better!'

I felt like shit, but I was determined to see this through with my mates. I was desperate to engage the enemy.

Out of nowhere seven suspected Taliban turned up at the compound. Our unit quickly subdued and arrested them, and kept them all separate, so that they didn't have the chance to cook up a bullshit story before int arrived to quiz them. As the lads mopped up, someone found bits of my fragged kit all over the compound, and in the neighbouring one too. A glove was found somewhere else.

There were also shedloads of Pakistani rupees there, proving this mob were Taliban terrorists.

It was bright now. Dawn breaks quickly in Afghanistan. We had been out several gruelling hours. It felt like a lifetime. My head was aching, and the bruised areas of my back and shoulders were burning with pain. Basically, I felt roughers, but I didn't show it.

Another hour passed and we were getting ready to pull back to FOB Robinson. One of the lads claimed he had seen a lone Taliban fighter down by the river. We took it with a pinch of salt. No one believed anyone would be mad enough to come forward in broad daylight with a major Brit op taking place. Not even the Taliban were that bonkers.

'No honestly, lads, there's a guy with an AK,' he said.

So I rolled round, still prone and brought my rifle up to bear. It was pressed firmly into my shoulder. I had a perfect view down my sight onto the riverbank some 300 to 400 metres away. I scoped the area. I couldn't see anything. And then, just like that, there was a movement. I trained my sights on the target. He was decked out in a black dishdasha and carrying an AK-47. The dickhead had popped his head up for a quick scan round. It looked like the bomb-maker had come to see who he'd caught. That or it was another curious fighter being nosy. I glanced over to the boss.

'Can I engage, boss?'

'If he points his gun at us, Croucher, you can shoot,' he said.

The bearded Taliban brought the weapon to bear. His luck had run out. Now I could neutralise him. I let rip. The other lads from E Company started putting rounds down on this bloke as well, and there was a sharp crack as the rounds passed him. He gave a start and I trained my sights on him again as he started to move. My SA80 was on single shot, which is more accurate, rather than just hosing someone down. Automatic kicks up; the first couple of rounds might be on target, then it goes all over the place.

I depressed my finger on the trigger.

I saw the round strike.

He fell to the ground and all I could think was: *Take that, you bastard!* Other lads followed up with fire, putting a few in the direction he fell to make sure he couldn't crawl away.

It was a waz end to a mad patrol.

Later that day, I jumped on the back of a Chinook to get properly checked out at Camp Bastion. I did have mild concussion and my hearing was gone, plus all the minor cuts and bruises. None of it bothered. I'd saved my mates and done my duty. The medic even reckoned I would be back on the line in a couple of days. It began to sink in just how close I'd come this time to meeting my Maker.

Apparently, while I was gone, Ads told the boss: 'We should put Croucher forward for something, sir.'

The boss, with a wry smile, agreed: 'Yeah, we should buy him a pint when we get back to the UK.'

'With respect sir – bollocks,' Ads replied.

I'm pretty sure the boss was joking!

A week later, while I was still recuperating at Bastion, the news came in that Corporal Damian 'Dee' Mulvihill, who was also in 40 Commando, had been killed up the road near Sangin. He'd been on a clearance patrol when an IED had detonated, killing him instantly. I knew Dee, though not that well. He was a giant of a man, always cheerful, and no one had a bad word to say about him. The guy loved his boxing and his rugby, just like me. And he was even planning to get married to his fiancée. It was a devastating blow for all the lads in 40 Commando. After all, we are just one big family and we felt his loss strongly.

More than ever I now understood the fine line between life and death, which every Marine and soldier walks in the line of duty. That could easily have been me – or one of the other lads. It could have been our families that were getting the knock on the door and the letter of condolence from the OC.

War is not about gongs and trinkets and glory.

It's not even about winning or the thrill of victory.

Bottom line, it is about survival, sacrifice and real loss for those we leave behind, as well as their grieving families at home.

We shipped out between March and April. Our thoughts

were with our fellow Marines and other servicemen and servicewomen who had fallen and died for their country in foreign fields.

NINETEEN

The Ballroom
Buckingham Palace
Thursday, 30 October 2008

I stood to attention at the west door to the Ballroom at Buckingham Palace, decked out in my Blues, my arms locked down my sides. I could see Her Majesty the Queen, my Sovereign and Commander in Chief, out of the corner of my eye. She was the picture of regal elegance, immaculate in a salmon dress and pearls. It was only for a split second, but thankfully our eyes did not meet, her head was bowed with her glasses perched on her nose. Obviously she knew the drill better than anyone. I consciously averted my eyes and stared straight ahead. This, after all, was the most important kit muster of my life by the ultimate Boss Lady.

She had been escorted into the room by the Lord Steward and after the national anthem was played, he stood to her right in his black tails. It was his job to announce the names of each recipient, and the achievement for which he or she was being decorated. As the orchestra from one of the bands of the Household Division played I was as nervous as a nod on his first day and desperate not to show it. As a Royal Marine recruit I had sworn my allegiance to the Queen and her heirs and successors on my first day at Lympstone all those years ago.

Now, incredibly, I was about to meet her face to face, and be presented with the joint-highest honour for gallantry – the George Cross. The room, apparently the largest one in the palace, was stunning and opulent – just how you would expect it to be. One of the flunkies had told me it dated back to Queen Victoria's time. It had a deep-red carpet, there was gilt everywhere, and above was this huge ceiling. Facing the throne dais down the length of the ballroom was the Musicians' Gallery at the east end, the great organ's gilded pipes set against a crimson background. What was a boy from Solihull doing here? It was a surreal, yet magical moment that I will never forget.

The Queen had entered the Ballroom attended by two Gurkha Orderly Officers, which was a tradition begun in 1876 by Queen Victoria. On duty on the dais were five members of the Queen's Body Guard of the Yeomen of the Guard, which was created in 1485 by Henry VII, the oldest military corps in the United Kingdom. Four Gentlemen Ushers were also on duty to help look after the recipients and their guests. I was one of 100 or so recipients. Usually, each person is able to invite three guests to witness the ceremony. I had been allowed five, so I brought along my mum, dad, sister and nan Mary and grandad Les. They were made-up and proud, but their unbridled excitement made me nervous.

I was up first.

The reason I was standing there was down to the other lads on Spartacus One Zero, the recce mission on the Taliban bomb-making factory. Ads couldn't believe what I had done. He knew my actions had saved their lives. He and the lads were determined my actions should be recognised. So when I was being checked over at the sickbay in Camp Bastion and without my knowledge they had put me forward for an honour. When I heard, I was honoured. I was a bit embarrassed, to be honest. So many heroic acts on the battlefield go unnoticed, I didn't understand why they tried to single me out. I tried to play it down. I thought it had been blown out of all proportion. I knew the lads that had been there with me would understand. When the story started to get out there was a wave of stories in the media. I rang my mum and told her I might be meeting the Queen. She just laughed. She thought I was kidding.

Soon the story started gathering pace, and the buzz was that I could be up for a Victoria Cross. The truth is that nobody can put anyone forward for a particular medal. The system doesn't work like that. The citation is sent off and it is up to the top brass to decide which medal is fitting for a specific action. A guy called Michael Ashcroft, an expert on the Victoria Cross, wrote that I should get one. Apparently, one of the criteria is that a serviceman needs to show astonishing courage, and nine times out of ten he would die carrying out the action. He wrote: 'If that is the case, Lance Corporal Matthew Croucher is absolutely entitled to be awarded Britain's most prestigious bravery award.' To me it seemed daft. I never really saw myself as a hero. I was just there and had to make a split-second decision to save my muckers, that was all.

The first I knew about it was when I got a call from a

reporter who told me I was getting a George Cross. I was chuffed to bits. A few hours later my CO confirmed it. It was quite a shock. It is a higher medal than I expected to get for that situation. I've been in lots of contacts throughout my military career, and I've seen enough to know that there are plenty of unsung heroes out there. So I was truly humbled by this honour. I was lucky that I got picked up for mine, I suppose, but there are other guys who haven't been picked up for theirs.

When I got back from Afghanistan I was feted in the national media. They were looking for a hero, I guess, and I suppose I fitted the bill. Loads of people were writing letters to me, giving me a pat on the back. I hadn't expected any of this, or any of the media interviews I was doing. I liked it, but I also felt a little awkward. One by one, I was bestowed with various honours. I was given the freedom of Solihull, which made my schoolmates smile. I won a Pride of Britain award; I was made Englishman of the Year by the St George's Day Society at a siap-up do in London; I was given an honorary membership of the Naval and Military Club, where the Duke of Edinburgh is the president and Prince Andrew is a member; I was even given two season tickets to my beloved team Birmingham City FC. I started doing TV appearances and mixing with the stars. I presented the Hero of the Year category at the *News of the World*'s Children's Champions Awards, televised on Sky TV. I was standing on stage next to Ross Kemp, the BAFTA award-winner. He was a top bloke. Kemp's father was a soldier with the Royal Norfolk Regiment, and I really respected him for all he had done to raise awareness about our boys in Afghanistan with his front-line documentaries. He showed a side of Afghanistan that people had not really seen before, and that took real guts. I got a standing ovation, which was a bit embarrassing. I just said I was not a hero, but just doing my job.

The greatest accolade of all was being awarded the George Cross. When I arrived at the palace it began to sink in just how big a deal this was going to be.

For more than three minutes I waited there as the Lord Steward read out loud the citation in his clear, distinctive voice:

'In the darkness, moving silently through the compound, he felt a wire tighten against his legs below knee-height. It was a tripwire . . .'

As he spoke, the memory of the moment when I should have died came flooding back.

'Approximately five metres away, the team commander and another marine; the fourth team member, was a short distance behind them. Reacting with extraordinary clarity of thought and remarkable composure he shouted, "Grenade and tripwire" in an attempt to warn his comrades and enable them to find cover before the grenade exploded.

'In the dark he was unable to determine the type of grenade, and therefore unable to determine how long the fuse would take to function. With his comrades so vulnerable and time running out, in an act of self sacrifice . . . He made the decision to shield the other members of his team from the impending explosion . . .'

Now I finally understood what all the fuss was about. For a second or two I was back there again. Reliving the moment.

'He threw himself on his back on top of the grenade, pinning it between his ruck sack and the ground. He then braced himself for the explosion, quite prepared to make the ultimate sacrifice for his fellow marines . . .'

Now, for a split second, I sensed Her Majesty looking over

at me. I stared straight ahead, not wanting to catch her eye.

The Lord Steward went on: 'Without question, Lance Corporal Croucher's courageous and utterly selfless action has prevented death or serious injury to at least two members of his team . . .'

I got the nod to move forward, and took a few steps until I was right opposite Her Majesty, then bowed my head and stepped forward. She flashed me a wonderful, disarming smile, and immediately I relaxed too. She had this down to a fine art. I had expected somebody sterner, but she was very warm. We chatted for a bit. She asked me whether I had sustained any other lasting injuries, and I said that I still suffer hearing difficulties and have occasional memory loss too. I mentioned Prince Harry, too, saying I was sure he had told her all about Afghanistan.

As she was talking, she pinned on my chest the silver George Cross, inscribed with the words *For Gallantry*, and suspended from a dark blue ribbon.

I told her that I was sure if any of my Marines comrades had been in the same position their training and well-honed instinct to save their muckers would have kicked in. She smiled knowingly. After all, her husband, the Duke of Edinburgh, is the Captain General of the Royal Marines. I bowed again, and the moment was over.

Afterwards, I was asked by the Ladies in Waiting to the Queen to join them for a glass of champagne. I raised a glass to Ads and the other lads who put me up for this.

Outside in the quadrangle the Press were waiting for me. From now on nothing was going to be the same again. I knew what to say; I was well rehearsed by now.

'It was a great honour to receive my award from the Queen today,' I told them. 'I feel very proud to be part of the Royal

Marines, and it was very special to be awarded the George Cross.'

My mum got in on the act too.

'I am a very happy mum today,' she said. 'I am hugely proud of my son and all he has achieved. It has been a fantastic day.'

It sure had been.

EPILOGUE

Since being awarded the George Cross I have been privileged to be involved with the charity Help for Heroes, working on fundraising events and with injured troops. Recently, we took some lads over to the US for rehabilitation run by Deptherapy. One of the guys I helped was a former Royal Marine, Dom, who was paralysed from the neck down after an accident in Norway. His enthusiasm and courage were humbling, and I thought, *That could have been me.*

People always ask me, 'Do you think you're really lucky to be alive and in one piece?' To be honest, not really. Yeah, I think back every once in a blue moon, and I do thank my lucky stars. Maybe once or twice I've had the odd flashback about certain events, but in reality I spend very little time dwelling on them. I don't understand people who waste half their lives dwelling on aspects of the past that you can't change anyway. There's no point, and I always look to the future. I'm a glass half-full type of lad. Always have been, always will be.

Since events in Afghanistan, I have been fortunate enough to meet a lot of influential people, and I'm not into being lauded for my actions. But the George Cross has given me access to the highest levels, and I intend to use this to help people I regard as the real heroes. One of the guys I served with, Fletch, has got his legs in rag order. He has no thighs, basically, and lads like him and Dom have got to live with their injuries for the rest of their lives. Their tour of duty will last a lifetime. Other muckers I've served alongside have been more fortunate, thank God. Sy, the lad who took a round clean through the chest in Helmand, made a full recovery and he is still a serving Bootneck to this day.

Being on the front line, everyone knows you can cop it, but none of the lads really thinks or talks about it. It's sad when you lose one of the lads or see someone you've served with suffer serious injuries, but we've all got a job to do, and if we think too hard about what 'could' happen to us personally, the chances are our minds won't be on the job, and then it probably will happen. So it's just better to crack on.

Everyone's mortal. The best of lads get injured or killed. A lot of the time it's just down to luck. Maybe your truck goes over an IED, or your WMIK gets slammed by an RPG and it explodes rather than fizzing out. Maybe you turn that corner and that Taliban with the AK-47 is writing your name on his next bullet.

Although I help run a security company, Pinnacle Risk Management, I'm still a Royal Marine, although now I'm in the reserves, but I'm still ready to serve Queen and country at a moment's notice. I wouldn't think twice. I realise that if I keep doing tours of duty in Afghanistan or anywhere else, my luck might run out one day, and I might need Help for Heroes. But that's the reality. It's something every combat soldier has to mentally overcome each time they deploy. Everyone's thoughts are different, but I know from the groups of Royal Marines I've had the pleasure of serving with that they're always willing to make the ultimate sacrifice for what they believe in, and for the lads they fight alongside. I think that's what makes the Corps what it is.

APPENDIX 1

The George Cross

The George Cross ranks alongside the Victoria Cross as the highest British and Commonwealth medal for valour. It is awarded for the same level of gallantry expected of a VC, but when no enemy is present.

It was announced on 24 July 2008 that Royal Marine Lance Corporal Matt Croucher would be awarded the George Cross for his actions in Afghanistan.

Her Majesty Queen Elizabeth II presented him with the medal, which bears the name of her father, King George VI, on 30 October 2008 at Buckingham Palace.

He was 24 years old when he received it, and is one of only 20 living recipients of the George Cross.

APPENDIX 2

*Tributes to Matt Croucher on the Announcement of His
Receiving the George Cross:*

'His exemplary behaviour and supreme heroism are fully
deserving of the highest recognition.'
——Chief of the Defence Staff Air Chief Marshal Sir Jock
Stirrup GCB AFC ADC DSc FRAeS FCMI RAF

'His action epitomises the ethos of selfless devotion to duty,
courage and comradeship in the Marines.'
——First Sea Lord and Chief of Naval Staff Admiral Sir
Jonathon Band GCB ADC

'This magnificent act absolutely typified the highest
traditions of commando service.'
——Lt Col. Stuart Birrell DSO, Commanding Officer of 40
Commando Royal Marines

APPENDIX 3

Royal Marine Lance Corporal Matt Croucher's Full Citation for the George Cross:

'Throughout December 2007 and January 2008, Forward Operating Base Robinson, an International Security Assistance Force/Afghanistan National Army location situated 10 km to the south of Sangin, had been targeted relentlessly by an enemy seeking to inflict death and grievous injury on Coalition Forces.

'Complex and highly effective improvised explosive devices had been deployed by the Taliban throughout the Forward Operating Base's area of responsibility with deadly success. Movement around the Forward Operating Base location was fraught with danger and exceptionally high risk for troops, whether vehicle borne or operating on foot.

'Tasked with conducting both overt and covert patrolling to disrupt and interdict enemy forces, 40 Commando Battle Group was determined to regain the initiative.

'Lance Corporal Croucher was deployed to Helmand

Province, Afghanistan, as a reconnaissance operator in 40 Commando Group's Commando Reconnaissance Force, elements of which were operating from Forward Operating Base Robinson.

'On 9 February 2008, the Commando Reconnaissance Force was tasked to conduct reconnaissance of a compound in which it was suspected that Taliban fighters manufactured Improvised Explosive Devices.

'Lance Corporal Croucher's section was deployed on this highly dangerous and challenging operation. In the early hours, utilising night-vision devices and under constant threat of attack from Improvised Explosive Devices or enemy ambush, the Commando Reconnaissance Force successfully negotiated the complex and varied terrain between the Forward Operating Base and the suspect compound, and established an over-watch position to observe for any sign of activity.

'In order to determine conclusively that the compound was an Improvised Explosive Device-manufacturing site, the decision was made to send a small four-man team, which included Lance Corporal Croucher, forward to conduct a very high-risk "close-target reconnaissance".

'This required the team to enter the compound. It was believed to be occupied. The team moved forward with extreme caution and stealth, and successfully gained entry into the compound without incident.

'After 30 minutes on-task, and having identified numerous items that could be used by insurgents to manufacture Improvised Explosive Devices, the team commander gave the order for the team to extract back to their prearranged rendezvous point with the remainder of Commando Reconnaissance Force.

'Lance Corporal Croucher was at the head of the group as they commenced the extraction; behind him, approximately five metres away, the Team Commander and another Marine were in the open and fully exposed, with the fourth team member a short distance behind them.

'As the team moved silently through the still-darkened compound, Lance Corporal Croucher felt a wire go tight against his legs, just below knee-height. This was a tripwire connected to a grenade booby trap, positioned to kill or maim intruders in the compound. He heard the fly-off lever eject and the grenade, now armed, fell onto the ground immediately beside him.

'Instantly realising what had occurred, Lance Corporal Croucher made a crucial and incredibly rapid assessment of the situation. With extraordinary clarity of thought and remarkable composure, he shouted "Grenade", then "Tripwire" in an attempt to warn his comrades to find cover before the grenade exploded. It was clear to him that given the lack of cover in the immediate vicinity, he and the other team members were in extreme danger.

'Due to low light levels, he was unable to determine the type of grenade and therefore had no way of knowing how long the device's fuse would take to function. With his comrades totally exposed and time running out, Lance Corporal Croucher made the decision not to seek cover or protection for himself, but to attempt to shield the other members of his team from the impending explosion.

'In an act of great courage, and demonstrating a complete disregard for his own safety, he threw himself on top of the grenade, pinning it between his day sack, containing his essential team stores, and the ground. Quite prepared to make the ultimate sacrifice for his fellow Marines, Lance Corporal

Croucher lay on the grenade and braced himself for the explosion.

'Meanwhile, the Team Commander, upon hearing the initial shouted warning, dived to the ground. The rear man in the team was able to take cover by stepping back around the corner of a building; the other team member was unable to react quickly enough and was still upright, fully exposed within the lethal range of the grenade.

' "I was just gritting my teeth waiting for the explosion and I had that deep gut feeling of this is going to hurt, or I'm in serious trouble now."

'As it detonated, the blast effect of the grenade was absorbed by Lance Corporal Croucher and the majority of the fragmentation was contained under his body.

'Miraculously, his equipment and protective clothing prevented any lethal shards hitting his body and he suffered only minor injury and disorientation from the effects of the blast. Lance Corporal Croucher's day sack was ripped from his back and was completely destroyed; his body armour and helmet were pitted by grenade fragments.

'A large battery being carried in the side pouch of his day sack, for his team's Electronic Counter-Measures equipment, also exploded and was burning like a flare as a result of the grenade fragments breaching the outer case. Incredibly, the only other injury was a slight fragmentation wound to the Team Commander's face.

'The others escaped unscathed. Without question, Lance Corporal Croucher's courageous and utterly selfless action had prevented death or serious injury to at least two members of his team. Immediately following the explosion they manoeuvred tactically back to their rendezvous location.

'After confirming with the Troop Commander that no

significant casualties had been sustained, the decision was made to interdict enemy forces attempting to conduct a follow-up to the incident. As anticipated, enemy activity was observed by Commando Reconnaissance Force and Lance Corporal Croucher, having refused to be evacuated, along with other members of his team, engaged and neutralised one enemy fighter.

'Throughout his service in Afghanistan, Lance Corporal Croucher has served with the utmost distinction. His actions on 9 February 2008, when he willingly risked his own life in a most deliberate act of self-sacrifice to save his comrades from death or serious injury, were wholly typical of the man.

'During a previous engagement at Forward Operating Base Inkerman on 9 November 2007, Lance Corporal Croucher helped save the life of a fallen comrade who had received a serious gunshot wound to the chest during a ferocious firefight with the enemy.

'For 20 minutes, whilst the company medical assistant was pinned down by enemy fire, he applied life-saving first aid, which stabilised the wounded man until medical assistance arrived and the casualty could be extracted.

'Meanwhile, on 16 November 2007, whilst providing intimate security to a night airdrop in the desert near Forward Operating Base Inkerman, Lance Corporal Croucher was injured in a road traffic accident.

'Evacuated to the UK with a suspected broken leg, he was determined to return to theatre and, following intense physiotherapy, he returned within a matter of weeks to resume his duties with Commando Reconnaissance Force.

'That he was willing to risk all in order to save the lives of his comrades is indisputable; that he possesses an indomitable fighting spirit is abundantly clear.

'Lance Corporal Croucher is an exceptional and inspirational individual. His magnificent displays of selflessness and gallantry are truly humbling and are the embodiment of the finest traditions of the Service.'

NOTE: Lieutenant Nichol James Emslie Benzie, 34, a member of the Joint Helicopter Force in Afghanistan, was subsequently awarded the Distinguished Flying Cross (DFC). His citation read: 'In recovering seriously injured casualties on successive days in the most demanding environmental conditions, and in the face of such intense enemy activity, Lt Benzie showed exceptional courage, inspirational leadership and flying ability of the highest order.' He received his DFC from HM the Queen at Buckingham Palace on 30 October 2008. It is awarded to all ranks of the Royal Navy, Royal Marines, Army, and RAF in recognition of exemplary gallantry during active operations against the enemy in the air. His gallant actions undoubtedly saved lives and deserve recognition.

APPENDIX 4

List of Living Recipients of the George Cross

1941 Stuart Archer (b. 1915)
Acting Lieutenant (later Colonel), Corps of Royal Engineers.
   Bomb disposal.

1942 Charles Walker (b. 1914)
Petty Officer Cook, Royal Navy. Malta convoy rescue.

1943 John Gregson (b. 1924)
Apprentice, Merchant Navy. Shipboard rescue.

1944 Henry Flintoff (b. 1930)
13-year-old schoolboy. Stopped runaway bull.

1945 Ernest Wooding (b. 1918)
Warrant Electrician, Royal Canadian Naval Volunteer Reserve.
   Rescued people from boat.

1948 Kevin Walton (b. 1918)
Temporary Lieutenant, Royal Navy, Falkland Islands
   Dependencies Survey. Ice crevasse rescue.

1948 Arthur (Dick) Butson (b. 1922)
Doctor (later Colonel), Falkland Islands Dependencies Survey.
   Glacial crevasse rescue.

1949 Alfred Raymond Lowe (b. 1931)
Boy 1st Class (later Petty Officer), Royal Navy. Sea rescue.

1949 Margaret Vaughan (b. 1934)
14-year-old schoolgirl. Tidal rescue.

1951 Awang anak Rawang (b. 1925)
Iban tracker, Johore, Federation of Malaya. Guarding wounded
    soldiers.

1952 John Bamford (b. 1937)
Colliery worker. Fire rescue.

1954 Derek Kinne (b. 1930)
Fusilier, Royal Northumberland Fusiliers. Fortitude as PoW.

1958 Henry Stevens (b. 1928)
Constable (later Chief Inspector), Metropolitan Police. Captured
    armed criminal.

1967 Anthony Gledhill (b. 1938)
Constable (later Detective Sergeant), Metropolitan Police Force.
    Arresting armed suspect.

1972 Carl Walker (b. 1934)
Constable (later Inspector), Lancashire Constabulary. Foiled
    armed robbery.

1974 James Beaton (b. 1943)
Inspector (later Chief Superintendent), Metropolitan Police
    (Royal Bodyguard). Foiled kidnap attempt.

1978 Michael Pratt (b. 1954)
Constable, Victoria Police, Melbourne, Australia. Arresting
    armed criminals.

1990 Barry Johnson (b. 1952)
Warrant Officer Class 1, Royal Army Ordnance Corps. Bomb
    disposal.

2003 Christopher Finney (b. 1984)
Trooper, Blues & Royals, Household Cavalry. Rescuing fellow
    soldiers.

2006 Peter Allen Norton (b. 1962)
Captain, Royal Logistic Corps. Outstanding bravery in Iraq.

2007 Matthew Croucher (b. 1983)
L/Cpl, Royal Marines. Prevented death and injury to others.

Glossary of Royal Marines Slang

ABC: All Been Changed
ABCBA: All Been Changed Back Again
ATS: Anti Trapping Squad i.e. a mate can see you off by thinning a girl out, you were trying to trap
bag off: to have sex
bag rat: packed lunch, invariably containing salt and vinegar crisps and a rotten Cornish pasty
banjo: A fried-egg sandwich
battle bowl: combat helmet
basha: improvised low-mounted shelter in the field, mainly used by **Pongos**
beasting, beast: give someone a hard time; serious physical training
bezzy: best, as in 'bezzy oppo'
bimble: to walk at a casual pace
bit of kit: someone who is **honking** in everything he does
bite: to fool somebody into doing or believing something stupid
bivvy: tactical camping positions – from 'bivouac'
black maskers: thick black masking tape that is the all-in-one answer to service DIY
Blues: Royal Marines Number 1 (Dress Blue) uniform
bone: a stupid thing to do or a stupid person
bone dome: helmet
boogie: (pronounced *boo-jee*): similar to **dhobi**, but applied to equipment, e.g., a **nod** might be **pinged** to give the **heads** a quick **boogie** as a (very mild) punishment

Bootie, Bootneck: Royal Marine

bottom field: the assault course at CTC where the recruits spend most of their time being **beasted**

bowser: a large container of water; also refers to a **gronk**, as in a 'spunk bowser'

browners: dead

buzz: a rumour, sometimes true, though usually not

cabin: one's room or accommodation

casevac: short for 'casualty evacuation'; US forces use 'medevac'

Chad: something that is considered 'cheesy' or low quality

Chad Valley: a piece of equipment that is prone to failure (most **pusser**'s kit)

Cherry Berry: a member of the Parachute Regiment, from their red berets

chit: a request form

chuck up: to receive praise

civvy: a civilian

cloggie: a Dutchman

club swinger: a Physical Training Instructor

cluster-fuck: very badly organised

colours, colour stripey: colour sergeant

commondog: common sense

Corps pissed: to be totally intoxicated by the Royal Marines

crab: a member of the RAF – from 'crabfat', the nickname for a blue-grey grease used by sailors, since RAF uniforms are that colour. The RAF as a whole is known as 'crab air'

crabby: dirty

cream in: collide

CTCRM: the Commando Training Centre Royal Marines at Lympstone, Devon, where all ranks of the Royal Marines undergo their basic training. Usually abbreviated to **CTC**

debus: to get off a vehicle

Devil Dodger: a chaplain or padre

dhobi, dhoby: to wash or washing – from Hindi

dhobi dust: washing powder

dhobi run: a trip to the launderette

dhobi waller: a person who gets pinged to do the dhobi

dig out/dig out blind: to make an all-out effort

dip: to come up short or suffer a misfortune

dip out: to lose out on something

dit: a story

DL: Drill Leader – a Marine who has specialised as a drill instructor

Dog and Basket: the Lion and Crown insignia

dossed up: asleep

drip: complain

DS: Directing Staff

Dutchy's: a vendor of burgers at **CTCRM**. Arguably the greatest burger van on the planet

endex: the order given to end an exercise or end it early; also used to halt a conversation, lesson or activity

essence: a vision of beauty (mostly female)

eyebrows: offering something as genuine, and offering to have your eyebrows shaved off if you are found to be lying

flapping: panicking

flash: to lose one's temper

foofoo powder: **pusser**s' footpowder

galley: the Junior Ranks Dining Hall

gash: sub-standard or rubbish; also rubbish as a noun, e.g., the 'gash bag' is the rubbish bag

gash hand: a Marine with no particular job or **SQ**, e.g., 'get a couple of **gash hands** and clean the **heads**'

geeps, jeeps: Royal Marine term for the L7 General-Purpose Machine Gun (the famous Belgian 7.62 belt-fed FN-MAG)

gen: the truth (genuine)

gen dit: the genuine story

gimp, gimpy: see **geeps, jeeps**

girl's time: a Cadet Officer's or Apprentice Marine's (16–18 years old) service, since they are forbidden to go on Active Service.

Globe & Buster: (1) the Corps crest, (2) the journal of the Royal Marines, *The Globe & Laurel*

go outside: to leave the Corps

gob off: see **gobshite**

gobshite: someone who is vocal and often speaks out of turn with little knowledge on the given subject

goffers: (1) cold fizzy drinks, (2) a big wave, (3) big punches

gong: medal

gopping: something that is really horrible, e.g., 'That kebab was **gopping** – it made me ill!'

grav, gravel belly: derogatory name for a Marine from a rifle company

green lid: Green Beret
Grey Funnel Line: the Royal Navy
grip: a kit bag with two carrying handles
gronk: a female who likes to be around Bootnecks
Gucci: a piece of kit that is really good and new
gulpers: a quantity of drink somewhere between **sippers** and Sandy Bottoms
Guz: Plymouth, from the World War I radio ID letters for the port: GUZ
hanging out: mental or physical tiredness, exhausted
Harry von...: used before certain words to increase their magnitude, e.g., 'Harry von icers', 'Harry von roughers'
heads: a naval term for latrines
heartbreak lane: the lane leading back into CTC that forms the final part of the endurance course and nine-mile speed march Commando Tests
Hertz Van Rental: mythical Dutch officer
honking: very dirty or smelly
hoofing: good, e.g., 'hoofing scran'
horse box: the **stripeys**' mess
icers: cold weather, e.g., 'It was icers on sentry last night'
inserted: to get into bed
in theatre: in an operational area of war
jack: a member of the Royal Navy
jack up: to arrange or organise something
joker: see **twat**
jollies: the junior ranks bar at **CTCRM**
jolly: a free outing
junglies: Royal Navy helicopter pilots who fly Marines to their insertion point
KFS: knife, fork, spoon
kit muster: a personal kit inspection
Landy: Land Rover
lash up: to treat someone; also describes a cock-up
limers: lime or lemonade drink
loafing: hanging around aimlessly; to leave something out that should be put away
Lovats: Royal Marines Number 2 (Dress Green) uniform
make and mend: early finish on Wednesday or Friday afternoons
matelot: a sailor

mince, mincing: to achieve nothing whilst looking relatively busy: 'to **mince**'

minging: very drunk

mucker: very good mate: better than **oppo**

Naafi: a canteen or shop run by the NAAFI (Navy, Army, and Air Force Institutes)

neaters: undiluted **pusser**'s rum, aka 'Navy Neaters'

Nelson's blood: rum

Neptune's bodyguard: Ship's Marines

ninja: something that is very difficult or hard, e.g., 'a **ninja** PT session'

nod: a Royal Marines recruit before passing commando course, so called because they are so knackered they're always nodding off

nutty: chocolate (or more generally, any confection), devoured avidly by Marines requiring an energy fix

oppo: best mate

oggin: the sea ('he fell into the **oggin**'), also water in general ('get some **oggin** down your neck'). Comes from the code name for the English Channel during World War II: Oscar Golf 11 November.

pass out: graduate from Royal Marine Commando training; receive your **green lid**

Percy Pongo, Perce: a member of the British Army (from their supposed smell)

phot: a photograph or photographer

PIG: officer; an acronym for 'Polite Intelligent Gentleman', used with heavy irony

ping, pinged: found out, or 'volunteered', e.g., '**pinged** for a **Dutchy run**', '**pinged** for cigs'

pipe: to broadcast a message, usually via the public address system on board ship or in barracks

pips: found on rank slides of officers

pit: bed, bed space or bunk

plums: someone who hasn't **bagged off** in a while, e.g., 'Blackwell is major **plums**'

Pompey: Portsmouth

pongo: see **Percy Pongo**

proffed: goods acquired by dubious methods from the establishment rather than another Marine

PTI: Physical Training Instructor

pusser: (1) the Royal Navy, Royal Marines, (2) official issue, (3) an instructor, (4) Royal Navy Logistics Officer

pusser's apple: onion

pusser's charger: service-issue bike

pusser's gold: rust

pusser's ice cream: lard

pusser's planks: service-issue skis

PW: Platoon Weapon or Platoon Weapons Instructor

QRs: Queen's Regulations

Queens: used to convince someone that you are not getting them on a **bite**

racing snake: someone who runs fast

ragheads: a term used to describe locals/Taliban

recce: generally used throughout British forces for 'reconnaissance'; US forces use 'recon'

red pigs: hot weather

redders: hot weather (the opposite of icers)

rock ape: a member of the RAF Regiment

rover: Land Rover

Rupert: officer

run ashore: short leave with clear naval connection, ideally to involve large amounts of drinking, fighting and 'getting to know the local female population'

sadders, sad on: upset or annoyed

sance: short for 'essence', e.g., 'she is **sance** mate' (originated from the ranks of Air Defence Troop Royal Marines)

scran: food or a meal

scran bag: a collection point for loose bits of kit on a ship. A small fine is paid before retrieval

Sea Daddy: an experienced Royal Marine who looks after the **sprogs**

shiny arse: someone in an administrative position

ship: shipmate. A mate, pal, close friend

shiters: very drunk

sickbay: medical centre

sickbay ranger: someone who spends a lot of time off sick

sippers: a sip of a drink

SITREP: Situation Report

skeg: a quick look

slot: to kill

slotted: killed

slug: sleeping bag

snurgle: to sneak or creep in, or out of sight

spin a dit: to tell a story

sprog: a new and inexperienced Marine

SQ: Specialist Qualification. Royal Marines can specialise after basic training in a large number of skills, earning them extra responsibilities and pay. Each qualification is usually denoted by an acronym and their level of qualification. As an example, three levels of the Assault Engineers SQ are AE3, AE2, AE1 from lowest to highest

stacked: a muscular individual

standeasy: a tea break taken during the morning and the afternoon

stripey: sergeant

swamp: to urinate – 'go for a **swamp**', '**swamp** the bed', etc.

sweating neaters: to be worried (see **neaters**)

tankie: a member of the Heavy Weapons branch

thin out: disappear, disperse or go away quickly

thrashed, thrashing: the same as **beasting**

threaders: fed up, likely to be **dripping**

TQ: Technical Qualification

trap: to engage or chat up females, e.g., 'let's **thin out** now for a **run ashore**, have a few **wets** and then go out on the **trap**'

troop bible: a book containing all the relevant details of the individuals in a sub-unit

turn to: to parade or begin work

twat: someone who likes to be the centre of attention and will do things to amuse others (esp. when the ladies are around)

twat camp: a trip or vacation with more than one **twat**, each vying for Twat No.1 position

twos-up: to take a turn at or with something

ulu: jungle (from Malay '*hulu*' – literally, 'upriver', used to refer to backwater areas

up the line: to travel away from base, originally referring to a train journey

vittled: to be shot at or to shoot at, e.g., 'we vittled them up'

waz: slightly better than **hoofing**

wet, whet: a warm beverage such as a cup of tea or coffee or an alcoholic drink

wrap: to give up
wrap hand: somebody who gives up easily
woolly pully: green issue jumper
yaffel: to eat
yaffeling spanners: see **KFS**
yeti: a spectacular crash while skiing
yomp: move with heavy packs and weapons across country; the Army equivalent is 'tab' (note: 'tabbing' is a much slower version of 'yomping', carrying smaller loads)
zap: to shoot or be shot
zeds: to get some sleep, e.g, 'Let's get heads to **zeds**'

Turn over for an exciting preview of
Matt Croucher's blistering debut novel
available from Arrow, October 2010.

FLASH POINT
MATT
CROUCHER
GC

PROLOGUE

'**G**O! GO! GO!' Coldrain shouted.

There were three two-main lock points on the door. Two were at waist height, the other higher up, which Coldrain figured was a sliding-lock mechanism. Kymor Haydarov, the stripey in charge of Uzbekistan's elite counter-terrorists, took the top lock first because it was always quicker to raise a weapon from a lowered stance rather than an elevated one. With the bitch aimed at the top right corner Haydarov depressed the trigger. There was a short, sharp flash accompanied by a thunderous bang as the Hatton round's metal powder and wax combo tore into the lock structure and the whole frame of the door shuddered. In one smooth move the Stripey pointed the gun down at the main locks and fired a second breaching round. The locks were blown clean off, and the force of the round saw the door swing open back into the hallway.

As soon as the door was free of its hinges, Coldrain pulled

the pin from the flashbang and tossed it into the hallway. Two seconds later the grenade detonated, creating a deafening sound like a clap of thunder striking on top of them. Their ears were cushioned by the walls. Whoever was inside would not be so lucky.

Taking advantage of the small window of diversion afforded by the flashbang, Coldrain was first in, MP5 raised at shoulder level, eyes darting from left to right as he scanned for targets. He was quickly shadowed by Haydarov at his five o'clock.

The hallway was narrow and sparsely decorated with hardwood flooring, glossed and covered in burgundy and gold stencil patterns. To the immediate left was a room with a white door frame. At the opposite end of the hallway from Coldrain and Haydarov were doors to the left, centre and right, all closed. On their left, past the white door, was a narrow staircase leading upstairs to a landing that was out of his line of vision. There was nobody in sight.

Coldrain surged forward and shouted, 'Clear left!' as he turned towards the white door. He gave it a kick and it flew open. Haydarov tossed another flashbang into the room. This time the bang was louder. Coldrain's ears were ringing, but he shook his head as he entered the room and swiftly hooked his MP5 from left to right, ready to slot any lethal threat.

The room was empty. No problem, guys.

He shouted, 'room clear' and ducked back out to the hallway just in time to see Steve Waterford and the rest of Bravo team storm past and head directly for the staircase. Coldrain wasn't a hundred per cent sure, but he could swear that Waterford had been sporting a wide, manic grin as he bounded towards the carpeted steps.

Alpha still had three more rooms to clear on the ground floor. Coldrain directed Haydarov to the room at the rear centre of the hallway, a pair of frosted glass doors flanked by tacky panelling in the same style. Haydarov didn't mess about; he swung the bitch down against the handle and followed through with a solid kick. They were out of BFGs so Coldrain rushed straight in and found himself in a dimly-lit dining room, an imposing, long dinner table in the middle, stretching back to the rear.

Coldrain saw movement. One, no two shapes, at the far end of the room, and coming towards him. He brought his Heckler & Koch MP5Ks (PDW type variant) to bear and locked on to his first target.

He was poised to let rip when he heard a voice scream, 'Orange! *Orange!*'

Coldrain understood the term instantly because he'd taught it himself. It was the warning to make clear they were friendly forces. NATO strapped orange panels onto their vehicles to alert trigger-happy F-16 pilots to the presence of friendlies. It didn't stop blue-on-blue incidents but right now it worked just fine.

He eased his finger off the trigger and watched as the two shapes came forward into the fluorescent light seeping into the dining room from the hallway, and finally identified the shapes as Temur Denisov and Ahmed Soliev. There were glass shards around their feet and resting on their shoulders like sharp, glistening chunks of ice. Behind them he saw a hollow sliding door, the glass punched wide open into a man-sized oval hole.

'All clear,' Soliev said.

Coldrain frowned. This didn't make any sense. Where the hell was everyone? According to Waterford's mark one eyeball there should be six X-rays inside the house – the two guests, Uzbekistan's most notorious drug barons, codenamed Vegas and Rio, their drivers, and the two men waiting to greet them in the safe house. And all of a sudden the ground floor was empty. No more than three seconds had elapsed between Haydarov breaching the door and Coldrain making his entry. They would have to be quicker than Usain Bolt to all flee upstairs in that short space of time. Suddenly he felt nauseous. He had a bad feeling about the whole set-up.

His sense of unease just kept growing. Coldrain knew even as they went through the motions of clearing the rooms to the left and the right that no one was lying in wait inside them. Just an empty living room adorned with a plasma TV hanging from the west wall, well-worn armchairs and the thick stench of Arab cigarettes in the air, and to the right a kitchen caked in dust.

He wondered what Bravo team had discovered upstairs. No gunshots so far. He found Soliev at the foot of the staircase.

'Anything?'

'Nothing.'

Coldrain turned to Haydarov.

'I'm going up. Secure the perimeter.'

Coldrain started to climb the stairs. He could see a door to the left at the top of the staircase, and from the boot mark embedded into its centre he knew that the room had already been cleared. He also saw that the landing panned off to the right, leading in the opposite direction and parallel to the stairs. Coldrain could hear multiple voices. One sounded like it belonged to Waterford, aspiring alcoholic, working-class Clapton operator and former Cherry Berry in 2 Para. Waterford didn't trust the Uzbeks an inch.

He was screaming at something. It sounded like he was swearing. There were other voices too, hectic, rushed, foreign. The other guys in Bravo, he guessed. *Or the targets.* The shouting became more frantic as he neared the top of the stairs. Someone screamed at the top of their voice, a high-pitched yell.

Then he heard two sharp gunshots.

Crack, crack.

Coldrain was almost at the landing. His MP5 swung by his right side. It was a knock-off Pakistani model, not the trusty original, which didn't actually fill him with confidence in the submachine gun. The mags were also chad, held together by black maskers tape to stop them from splitting open and the rounds falling out.

The view across towards the far end was blocked by the ornamental black railings that tapered off above the stairs and ran parallel to the landing.

Just three more steps to go.

He kept his head turned to the right.

As the landing came into view, clear of the railing, he stopped dead in his tracks.

A pair of boots were lying on the floor.

Bates Defenders.

Attached to a body smeared in blood across a khaki shirt and jeans.

Coldrain leapt the final step and charged down the landing, shouting, 'Man down! *Man fucking down!*'

He reached the body in three sprinting strides. He knew it was Waterford, even before he had a confirmed visual on the face. The big man was lying face down and the pool of blood covered the whole area beneath his torso and legs. Blood trails were splashed down the beige wall. Coldrain saw two exit wounds. One was on the left side of his neck; the second at the rear of his right tricep. They were the size and shape of walnuts, the tissue-torn back exposing a deep tunnel of shredded membrane, burst blood vessels and distressed muscle tissue.

Coldrain felt around Waterford's neck and legs. Nothing. Then he ran his hands up and down the obliques, and his fingers hit a sticky, thick substance, like mercury-red glue. Coldrain saw the entry wounds. They had penetrated to the right of Waterford's abdomen and crashed through the body, their course deflected as they smashed into bone and vital organs, and finally tore out of his body. He must have been shot from the side, with two well aimed rounds. That was the only way to inflict a chest wound when someone was packing a ballistics vest.

Whoever shot him knew he was tooled up with body armour.

It was obvious the guy was wasted. He could hear further shouts and shots. Rising to his feet, his bloodied hand firm on the MP5 trigger, Coldrain moved down the landing. There was a white door at the far end, ten metres away. The voices were muffled, coming from behind the door. Bravo and the targets must be in there, Coldrain thought. He kept his MP5 trained on the door as he closed in. He was six metres away now. The shouts grew louder, interrupted by the crack of rounds being put down, a three shot burst then a two shot and a single crack. Some serious shit was going down in there. Behind him he heard footsteps bounding up the stairs. One of the Uzbek lads trying to get in on the action. Coldrain cursed them for disobeying orders. He'd told them to secure the perimeter.

He turned around to face the stairs.

And felt something hot brush against his back.

The next thing he knew he was being banged out against the rear wall, his face smashed into the plaster. He felt a couple of teeth loosen with the impact. There was no sound for a moment, and then the silence was replaced by a roaring, violent wind that sucked the air out of his lungs. He felt his stomach compress, as though a pair of giant hands were squeezing his sides. The world turned pitch black. He could feel ash in his mouth. He tried to breathe through his nostrils but it felt like he was snorting lava.

Coldrain was laid out on the floor, facing the stairs. His vision was blurred. He blinked and rubbed his eyes and things became a little clearer. He looked at his hands. They were pockmarked with cuts, bits of glass and wood and metal. Tiny shards of shrapnel lined both of his legs, leaving small dark red patches along his combats. He could taste blood in his mouth. His left shoulder badly stung.

The next thing he knew Haydarov was kneeling down next to him. Coldrain couldn't move. Everything ached and throbbed with pain. His muscles shook from the vibrations caused by the explosion. Haydarov grabbed Coldrain's head and looked into his eyes. Coldrain coughed violently and spat blood onto the floor. He was in a bad state, and the Bars guys were only packing limited trauma. They would have to rush him to a hospital, and fast.

Then he blinked again and focused on Haydarov's face.

He was smiling.

Haydarov released Coldrain's head and his skull hit the ground with a thud. He could barely believe what was happening. At the end of the landing he saw Bravo team stroll coolly out of the room.

Escorting Rio and Vegas out of the room. The smug bastards beamed triumphantly. They were followed by their drivers and the two hosts. They stepped carefully around Waterford's bloody corpse, which was now slumped against the western wall, opposite the railings. His neck had been lacerated in the blast, and blood oozed out of his perforated throat and gushed down his body armour.

Coldrain doubled over, clutching his guts and coughing up more blood. Breathing was a tremendous effort. He recalled training courses in the Alps, deep cave explorations, finding small pockets of air to survive on; holding his breath underwater for minutes at a time. This was harder. He hurt all over.

Haydarov stood over Coldrain's struggling, prostrate figure, lit a Lucky Strike and took a swig from a hip flask.

'It's funny, I was just thinking, you know, the grenade should have killed you. If this had been any other day I would say you were a very lucky man. But today, as it happens, you are not so lucky.'

Coldrain wiped his mouth. His lips were so dry, his throat so scorched he couldn't speak.

'If you weren't dying, you would ask me what happened. What can I say? This is nothing personal, just business. We all have money to make. These people,' he continued, nodding to Rio and Vegas, 'pay more than those bureaucratic pieces of shit in government. That's all.'

The pain in Coldrain's shoulder returned with a vengeance, a sharp electric shock that coarsed across his back and neck. He arched his head to the left to get a better look at it, and his eyes widened when he saw a large, triangular-shaped piece of sharpnel buried deep in his shoulder blade. The tip was still pretty wide at the entry point, almost two inches. Coldrain started to panic. He could visualize the shrapnel tip now, glistening hard and sharp, pressing against his lungs like a knife point resting on a balloon. He was seriously fucked.

Denisov came back upstairs clutching a gasoline can. He started tossing the liquid over the landing, making sure Waterford's body was dripping head to toe. He let the gasoline trickle onto the floorboards and trailed it back down the stairs. The kid was whistling all the way.

'No hard feelings,' Haydarov said.

Then he stepped back, heading down the stairs.

With a casual flick of his fingers, Haydarov tossed the tab high into the air. It fell onto the floor slap bang next to Waterford and ignited the petrol. The fire quickly swallowed up Waterford's corpse and spread across the landing. Flames licked the walls and doors. The heat singed Coldrain's eyebrows and scaled his arms and face.

He watched Haydarov's lanky frame disappear. Saw the flames crawl closer towards him. The same words rattled around his numbed skull.

No hard feelings.

It's nothing personal.

Only business.

PART ONE

ONE

It was gone 3 p.m. when Coldrain rolled up at the red brick semi-detached at the end of a quiet residential road in Colchester. It was grey and cloudy, as though the sky was covered in crabby blankets. He eased his lime green Kawasaki Ninja ZX-7RR into the narrow driveway and slipped it into first gear, kept his balance dead on straight so he wasn't leaning and employed his rear brake. Placing his left foot down on the ground as he hit the clutch, in one smooth move he jumped off and kicked up the foot stand, leaning the bike onto it. The Ninja was awesome and well worth the cash he'd laid down on it, although he'd just had to shell out for a shit ton of repairs after a recent collision. He'd been cruising it at ninety on a dual carriageway when a BMW M3 had pulled out in front of him without looking. Not for the first time in his life, or in the last six months, Coldrain was lucky not to be browners. The motorist claimed Smidsy after the crash – 'Sorry Mate I Didn't See You'.

The only thing that distinguished this house from any other on the drive was the number on the letter box. That, and the dark memories lurking inside. Coldrain stepped up to the porch and rang the doorbell. Through the patterned glass he saw a gloomy figure slowly shuffle forwards and waited a seeming eternity while the multiple locks were undone. Finally the door creaked open.

'Hey, Mr Reese,' he said in his best cheery voice. The girls in Hooters sounded less fake.

'You're back.'

The old man looked like crap. The beer gut was so prominent he looked as though he'd shoved a pillow down his shirt. His face was pale and waxy. Clutching his can of Heineken he looked like he truly couldn't give a toss about anything. His breath reeked of cheap booze.

The old man didn't invite him in but he stepped inside anyway. The house was a mess. Days' old post lay scattered across the doormat and reception. The carpet was covered in crumbs and dark stains. A stale, milky smell lingered in the air.

Coldrain walked through into the living room. There were two tattered beige leather sofas that were older than Coldrain, the material worn down to the nub. They faced a TV that was permanently switched on, tuned in to Sky News. A faux Victorian mantelpiece was lined with cards. They all looked basically the same. Pictures of flowers, blue skies and clouds with shafts of light, with messages in tacky fonts like 'May Memories Comfort You', 'In Sympathy' and 'He Will Be

Remembered'. Along a window ledge next to the TV were several vases of flowers, some dead, some dying. None of the bunches looked as bright and vibrant as the flowers on the cards.

Mrs Reese was slumped on the sofa closest to the TV, her dim eyes fixated on the screen while she chained a twenty pack of Bensons. The sombre news report was about some kid from the Sappers who'd been zapped in Helmand. Roadside bomb, the weapon of choice for today's courageous martyr.

Coldrain took up a seat next to her on the sofa.

'He was nineteen,' she said in her raspy voice, eyes still fixed in front of her. On the report they were showing a photograph of the dead kid. Coldrain almost felt sorry for him, but they all knew the risks when they shipped out. No one was under the impression they were heading to Disneyworld.

'Shame' was all Coldrain could bring himself to say.

'Our Jamie was the same age.'

Coldrain suddenly felt like joining the old man on the Dutch piss. Inwardly he sighed. Outwardly he gritted his teeth. Not this shit again, he thought. Every time he paid a visit, Jamie's mum found some way of digging up the past. It was this, or the fact that Jamie looked like another kid who was browners, or another corps-pissed sprog fresh out of CTC, Commando Training Centre. It was like the woman was actively seeking out signs. And she was so caught up in this crap now, he didn't even recognise her any more. Before the incident she'd been happy and outgoing. Always had a smile on her face. But now, this. Coldrain realised that coming here was depressing the hell out of him. All it did was open up a can of worms that he'd spent the past three years trying to keep closed with a combination of freelance work, booze and uber-cool bikes. He couldn't take much more of this.

'Where are you going?' Mrs Reese asked as he stood up. It was the first time she'd looked at him since he'd arrived.

'To Jamie's room,' he replied.

It had once been as much his as Jamie's. As kids they spent every minute playing football, chasing each other round building sites and having a laugh. At weekends, when Jamie's parents were out, Coldrain would come over and they would find an 18-rated horror or action movie and watch it in Jamie's room with the lights turned off. They were best mates, had been since the day they were lumped together in primary school. Since Jamie's death, however, it had been turned into a sort of shrine to his younger brother. The room was frozen in time, untouched since the moment Jamie had shipped out to Afghan. Stacks of books on the Marines and a DVD of *Black Hawk Down* were still lying on the bottom bunk. It was all just as Jamie had left it, except that the desk where the Xbox used to sit had been cleared to make way for a display of photographs and cards. His pass-out snap was prominent among them.

He found himself staring at the other item that had been changed in the room. The Union Jack, neatly folded into a square, upon which lay the Dog and Basket, or to those on civvy street, the Lion and Crown, badge of the Royal Marine Commandos. Kind of ironic that Jamie's insignia was so perfectly preserved, Coldrain mused, seeing as he'd trashed his own in disgust shortly after things went pear-shaped.

Memories came flooding back. Bad memories. The type you'd sink a quart of Johnnie Walker straight to get rid of. Images that had been seared into his consciousness, no matter how hard he tried to forget.

He needed a drink. The old man was a beer drinker, but Coldrain had the thirst for something a bit stronger than that.

He sodded out of Jamie's room and went back downstairs to the kitchen. Found the cupboard he was looking for, and behind the vinegars and other condiments located the bottle of Nelson's blood he was looking for. He tore the cap off the rum and took a long neaters swig. It warmed him up and made him shiver at the same time. Then he opened the back door and stepped into the garden, overrun with weeds and grass longer than Terry Waite's beard. Once upon a time the old man had taken great pride in his vegetable plots and fruit trees and gnomes, but now it was merely a testament to long-term neglect.

He took another gulp of the rum.

Three years, but sometimes it felt longer than that, and sometimes it felt more like three days. At least he didn't immerse himself in misery and self-loathing like Jamie's parents, but he'd be lying if he said it wasn't at the back of his mind most, if not all, of the time. After all, when you stripped away the pain, it was Coldrain who'd seen Jamie die. He'd been there.

TWO

They had been based at Forward Operating Base Sangin, in Helmand Province, along with the rest of Charlie Company, 40 Commando. Dispatched there on a wave of gung-ho euphoria in September 2007, the lads had become embittered by the tedium and slow nature of life in-country. Life in those first few months had settled into a depressing monotony of mortar attacks and skirmishes with the Taliban in the few kilometres surrounding the base. The weather was icers and protection from the freezing cold nights was non-existent. Despite the hardships of life in Afganistan, the lads were well looked after. They had cooked meals, centrally sourced, and access to clean water and showers. For some of the other boys in Afghanistan it was not so cosy, and Coldrain was thankful for these small luxuries. Still, having a hot shower and some decent scran didn't make the time pass any quicker.

Jamie was still uber corps-pissed when they rolled into Sangin. Just nine months after pass-out, he'd been a stand-out candidate over the course of the selection process at the Commando Training Centre (CTC). On the legendary Commando Tests, Jamie had completed the nine-mile speed march down Heartbreak Lane with a fractured metatarsal, the sort of nails performance that put English footballers to shame.

That was Jamie all over. He wasn't the most stacked Marine, but he had the biggest heart. He was always looking out for his oppos and doing his best to maintain morale with a good joke about the Scots or which Wrens the lads fancied the most. On nights out on the piss he'd defend any Royal if a fight broke out. He was an all-round good guy, smarter than the rest and Coldrain was proud as punch the day Jamie was sworn in as a proper Bootneck.

'Morning Royal,' Coldrain said, gently kicking Jamie. 'Fancy some scran?'

'Yeah, mate.'

'Then get it yourself.'

'Bastard.'

'I aim to please.'

Jamie rubbed his eyes.

'Let me guess what's on the menu for today,' he said. 'It's either a sixteen-hour patrol with about five seconds of zeds, followed by an all-night barrage of mortar fire from those Taliban wankers. Or it's another day of sitting on our arses doing fuck all except taking the piss out of the Cloggies and Poles and choosing from either *Hamburger Hill* or *Saving Private Ryan*. Again.'

'Welcome to the world of war, lad.'

'I wouldn't mind if it wasn't so bloody cold.'

'Got sore toes again, have we?'

'I'd be a lot less cold if I had a nice warm wet inside me.'

'Put the kettle on then, young 'un.'

'*Bastard.*'

As the winter thawed, word got back to the media in Britain that the Taliban were proving hard to break down. They were using words like 'resurgence' and 'Vietnam' to describe the current state of affairs. Predictably the ruperts all of a sudden passed down the message that forces at FOB Sangin should take the fight to the enemy. They forgot that was what the lads had been doing from the moment they arrived. Still, anything for a decent photo-op and a good piece on the evening news.

Operation Solvent would see 40 Commando, alongside US Marines, breaking the Taliban stranglehold on Kandahar, which was at that time tighter than a Randy Couture headlock. The objective was to launch an assault on the village of Ghorak in Kandahar province, located in the south-eastern corner of Afghanistan. The Taliban were using Ghorak as a weapons cache for launching attacks deeper into Helmand Province. Lads from Charlie Company would carry out the raid. If they were lucky they would find a stash of weapons and High Explosives that would put a severe dent in any attempts to cause mayhem.

Kandahar was the poster child for the giant cluster fuck that Afghanistan had become in the years following the 2001 invasion. On the one hand it was a province of breathtaking beauty. Coldrain wasn't the type of guy who wrote poetry and admired the sunset, but even he was stunned by the natural landscape. Pomegranate trees blossomed in between the purple rock faces and along the verdant green basin of the Arghandab Valley, the horizon dominated by the valley mountains, above which an ultramarine sky seemed to stretch into infinity. The air carried a scent of orange and at night you could see the most incredible star constellations. Unlike London, where light pollution made even the moon all but invisible, here the Milky Way was so clear it cast shadows on the ground. The air was so pure that sound would carry for miles, but the darkness was so absolute you couldn't see your oppo, even though he was right next to you.

Way back in the day, before the Soviets rocked up, Kandahar had been the breadbasket of Afghanistan. The Russian invasion, civil war and drought had changed all that and the place was now a thin collection of settlements that tried to get by on their wheat crops and fruit orchards, a little water and the occasional internecine conflict, when they weren't busy trying to plant IEDs and sniper pongoes on patrol. The atmosphere was one of pure fear. The locals were terrified of the Taliban and lived in a state of constant anxiety about reprisals if they were discovered to be cooperating with the coalition forces. About the only thing different from Iraq was that the Afghan National Army and Afghan National Police could be trusted, which represented a step up from the insurgent-infested Iraqi Security forces. The ANA and ANP were good blokes and willing soldiers, fighting to give their country some kind of a future and not drag it back into the dark ages, where the Taliban wanted it to be.

Everything that could have turned shitty in Kandahar had. The beauty hid a nightmarish reality that was playing itself out in front of Coldrain's eyes.

'We're rolling out at 0200 hours,' sergeant Charlie Wheater, the resident off, said, addressing the lads. 'Moving nice and early, so we minimize the chances of the Taliban assaulting us along the way. For the next eight hours we will move slowly but surely forward, checking for tampering and being especially vigilant against IED attacks. At 0100 hours we will group up at the Forming Up Point, on this rocky rise to the northwest of Ghorak. The FUP codename is Stamford Bridge. Once there, we will prepare for our assault.'

'Finally,' Jamie said. 'A bit of action.'

'Just watch your back,' Coldrain replied. 'No funny business out there.'

'I'll be fine. Still, can't wait to get stuck in. A chance to take the fight to the enemy for a change, awesome.'

'Charlie Company will split into two teams,' Wheater continued. '5 Troop will enter and storm the village from the west, carrying out house-to-house searches rapidly before any locals sympathetic to the enemy have the chance to hide the arms stash.

'Or before the dickers themselves pepper pot out of the village and up into the mountains,' Jamie cracked.

'I heard that, Marine Reese. Quieten it down back there or I shall set your brother on you. Now, the second team, 6 Troop, will make an eastern approach, securing the perimeter whilst Team Alpha clears the buildings, looking out for possible Taliban scouts or snipers and making sure none of the villagers got any dumb ideas.'

'Anyone tries any shit with me, they're browners.'

'Any questions? Apart from who gets to slap Private Coldrain first?'

The boys laughed and displaced, but beneath the jokes, everyone was deadly serious. This was it. And they wanted in. Back home the press and general public had the barmy notion that soldiers didn't like fighting in wars. Bullshit. Coldrain, his brother, the rest of the Royals, they wanted to get some. A war without fighting wasn't really a war.

The equipment they had for the operation was top-of-the-range stuff. A troop of Viking All-terrain vehicles (ATVs) fully equipped with .50 cal Browning heavy machineguns and capable of operating in enviroments from below minus forty degrees to almost fifty degree heat and came fitted with hardcore bolt-on armour plating to protect *it* against anti-personnel mines. It was part of a Troop, and each ATV would transport eight Marines to the RV point. If all went to plan, the lads would seize the cache, gather the village elders around a table and give them a good bollocking, and the dickers would be down on guns, ammo and explosives. Result.

Ghorak was a small village even by the threadbare

standards of war-torn Afghanistan. Population 122, it was essentially a loose arrangement of mudbrick houses built from water, mud sand and clay and mixed with rice husks, and connected via a series of plain low arcs and narrow paths strewn with rocks, straw and the occasional rotting dog corpse. Everything was sandy brown, even down to the weather-beaten wooden doors on each house and the flat roofs covered in layers of branches and woven mats. The only object breaking up the monotony was a large bank of poppies growing to the north of the village with their distinctive pink buds turning rose red atop long green stalks. Branches hung overheard, loose rags hanging limply from these makeshift clothes lines.

Ghorak was considered hot. Recent int suggested that Taliban forces had been seen in the area recently and to emphasize the level of threat Charlie Company was also packing some heavy firepower backup in the shape of grenade machineguns mounted on the Vikings. And just in case the shit was well and truly flung against the fan, they would also be able to call in an airstrike courtesy of an AH-64 Apache attack helicopter kitted out with AGM-114 Hellfire anti-tank missiles, 70 mm Hydra rockets and a 30 mm M230 chain gun to teach the Taliban a lesson or two. If they did have to call in a strike, filling in the insurgents was going to cost a couple of million quid in munitions. Taliban dickers, it seemed, were worth more than gold. Coldrain was of the opinion they were worth considerably less.

Charlie Company moved on from the FUP at 1305 hours and made their approach to the village, Coldrain riding in the Viking.

'Bloody hell, I thought Bootle was crap, but this place takes the fucking piss.'

The voice belonged to Andy Tyrell, a sprog with the thickest Scouse accent he'd ever heard. He was driving the

Viking, which was always the sprog's job. A more experienced Royal, Denison, was on top cover.

'First tour for you, Royal?' Coldrain shouted up above the
engine roar.

'First and last, mate. After I'm done, there won't be any
Taliban left for you to fight.'

'Sure, mate. I suppose we should just pack you off to
Waziristan with a pistol and wait for the good news to come
through about Bin Laden's death.'

'Where's Waziristan?'

'Forget it. How are your teeth?'

'What the fuck. Everyone's asking me that. Have I got some
shit on them or something?'

'Nah, you're just paranoid, mate.'

It was Tyrell's first tour with Charlie but the new Bootneck
had taken like a duck to water. Tyrell could be a bit hot-
headed and was always the victim of C company pranks. The
previous week a few of the other Bootnecks had taken Tyrell's
toothbrush and given it to one of the dogs on camp trained to
look for explosives. They emailed Tyrell the camera snap the
next morning – after he'd given his teeth a good clean with a
dog-licked brush. He wasn't a happy mucker. But for all that
he was a good Bootneck in the making.

The Viking came to a halt at the edge of the village and
Coldrain debussed along with the rest of 5 Troop. Tyrell
stayed on the .50 cal ready to unleash some serious firepower.
He shouted something to the driver once the last man was
unloaded and the Viking roared into life and started to flank
around the village. Coldrain led the way into Ghorak.

Ghorak was laid out exactly as Coldrain remembered it.
Shaped like a quadrangle, the western edge of the village
presented a wide courtyard the size of half a football pitch
with a clump of naked trees in the middle of it and a few
hedges and thin strips of grass. To the left and right of the

courtyard was a waist-high wall and behind that ran a strip of small single room buildings. At the far end the yard opened up into a wide, bumpy dirt track that passed for a street and was lined with ancient-looking mudbrick buildings. An Afghan Main Street. There was rubbish all over the place, and ditches ran parallel to the dirt track, carrying raw sewage directly out of the homes. The street ran for two hundred metres and terminated at the footsteps of a mosque. Low walls straddled around the edge of the houses on the northern and southern fringes of Ghorak, insulating the village from the outside world. The one new addition to the location was a series of three piles of rock and mud to the left of the courtyard. They looked like oversized rabbit mounds. A pencil thin tree was planted atop each one with scraps of brightly-coloured rags tethered to them, red, yellow, blue, white. Coldrain knew instantly that they were burial plots. The coloured bits of cloth were martyr's flags. That meant they had probably been killed in a recent airstrike. Like the crucifix planted in the middle of FOB Sangin, it was a stark reminder of the human cost of war.

The villagers stood by silently as 5 Troop flooded through the courtyard. That was the first sign to Coldrain that something wasn't quite right. Usually when they rolled into an area the locals came right up. It was either to greet them or to complain. Maybe someone had warned them in advance of the mop-up job. Or perhaps they'd experienced this so many times it was just as much a part of their daily routine as forced marriage and beheadings.

They split into eight-man teams, equal to a single section, and went from the compound to compounder. Building clearances were stressfull and every Bootneck needed to have his wits about him. Coldrain was looking out for his muckers as much as his bacon.

'Let's fucking do it.'

'Stay calm, Belham.'

Adam Belham was a Lympstone lad born up the road from CTC. He and Coldrain set to the right and approached the first housing unit. Each house was surrounded by an outer perimeter wall. They had to be careful as a Taliban could be lurking just inside the walled area, waiting to ambush them.

'On my count,' Coldrain said.

'Ready.'

'Three . . . two . . . one . . . go!'

Coldrain booted the brightly-coloured wooden door in, his foot crashing into it so hard it collapsed in on itself. Inside he found a typical Afghan dwelling: silk rug on the floor, narrow shelves lined with copies of the Qur'an, old posters of Muslim clerics and Hollywood movies side by side tacked onto the walls and a stove in one corner bearing with five or six large metal bowls. Something was cooking. Coldrain could smell it. The scent reminded him of the awful chick pea stews the locals served up on the hearts-and-minds gatherings. They offered the Royals a taste whenever the village elders fancied a chat, but the lads always refused. Quite rightly, they didn't trust anything that didn't come from a ration pack or Marine camp. The last thing a Bootneck needed in Afghanistan was a bad case of the shits.

The home was empty. Not much sunlight got into these places and Coldrain had to squint to readjust his eyes to the filmy darkness, but it seemed to him that whoever had been in here had upped sticks just a few minutes prior.

'Clear!'

'All clear!'

'Move, move!'

They came to the next home.

And crashed the door in.

Inside there was a group of four young girls sitting around a half-finished rug which they were weaving. They were wearing the salwar and kameez dress of loose pyjamas and a long tunic with a chador blouse wrapped around their faces. The girls looked startled and stopped their craftwork. Coldrain felt sorry for them. They were no older than thirteen or fourteen. Soon these poor young women would have to dock themselves up in the full length burqa, or the black letterbox treatment as some of the lads termed it. All they had to look forward to was a future husband who could rape them whenever they wanted, and slap them about if they resisted. It was a hard knock life and although Coldrain didn't give a toss about the locals as long as his muckers were all safe and sound, the sight of subdued Afghan women always left him with a strong sense of injustice.

The room was boiling hot. Coldrain gave a cursory look round but there was nothing to see here.

It was the same for the other homes in Ghorak. Team Alpha turned them over, but there was no sign of a cache anywhere. The locals just stood back and watched. Out of the corner of his eye, Coldrain spied a group of young men lurking in the shadows of the compound. They were wearing the black turbans that marked them out as Talibs.

'What do you reckon their game is, mate?' Belham asked Coldrain as they passed by a group of bearded old men who looked on ominously.

'No idea. But I don't like it one bit.'

It took an hour for 5 Troop to complete the village search. The temperature was forty in the shade. If there had been any. As it was they were redders and they were hanging out of their arses with all the kit they were having to patrol round in. Body armour, knee pads, elbow pads plus the SA-80s they were packing and their back up Browning Hi-Power pistols, the lot. Coldrain carried his spare ammo, 66 mm LAW, trauma kit, 51 mm mortar rounds PMG link and spare rations. It was a shit ton of gear to carry around in such unrelenting heat. He took a stop and necked some water from his camelback. He squeezed the droplets into his mouth. They were warm.

And where the fuck was the cache? D Company were damned if they were going to sod off out of Ghorak empty handed. The wary looks they were getting from the locals told Coldrain they were definitely hiding something. He just couldn't figure out what it was.

Coldrain saw Jamie and another Royal, a stick-thin Bristol lad called Phil Hardman, standing in the courtyard.

'Perimeter's clear,' Jamie said. 'No sign of dickers.'

'Yeah, and not a gun in sight here either.'

Jamie looked up at the sun and squinted. His younger brother hadn't even broken out in a sweat.

'It doesn't look good,' he replied.

They'd covered every inch of every building. That meant the weapons cache had either been moved uber quick, or that the int guys hadn't done their job properly. Neither was very likely.

Coldrain was bang out of ideas.

'You heard of any air strikes here lately?' Jamie piped up.

'Round these parts? Not a word. Why?'

'You see any buildings damaged?'

Coldrain looked around him.

'Me neither.'

Jamie nodded towards the graves.

'Look at the soil.'

The mounds of earth were coffee coloured and distinctly drabber than the surrounding sandy terrain. That meant the soil was freshly dug up. Given how blazing hot it was Coldrain guessed the mounds were no older two days. And there had definitely been no activity around Ghorak in that time frame.

Jamie was grinning.

'Got to be it,' he said, already on the net calling for the explosives detection dog. Coldrain thinking, *Always wanted to be the man of action.* He had an optimism and go-get-'em attitude that bordered on naiveté. As if he was trying to prove something to his best mate.

Coldrain cast another skeg around the area. In the distance, four hundred metres beyond Ghorak, he spotted two blokes on motorbikes at the top of a hill overlooking the village. The men were shadowed behind the sun, and they were too far away to tell if they were armed or not, whether they had bad intentions, or good. Coldrain kept an eye on them for a moment longer, let them know he was aware of them and that he wouldn't take any crap.

A couple of the village elders had been standing a few metres away watching this shit unfold. Their faces had more folds than a newbie in a game of poker, and they were each wearing the trademark beige pakul so beloved of the old Muhjahideen.

The two village elders turned jittery. They started shouting and gesticulating, first to each other, and then to Coldrain and the rest of the Charlie oppos. Soon others joined in the commotion. Jamie was thirty metres from the graves. Coldrain started to get anxious. Belham had walked over to the two elders and was shouting at them to shut the fuck up.

The other guys in 5 Troop had now gathered in the courtyard. They, too, sensed that they were in the rattle. Without prompting they formed a thin semi-circular cordon in front of the crowd, putting eight metres between themselves and the Afghans. Above the wall that ran around the yard Coldrain could see Dennison's head bobbing along on the .50 cal on top of the Viking. Coldrain shouted to Belham.

'Keep these people back. I don't want this getting out of control.'

Belham nodded.

'Where's that fucking translator? Tell these people to lift up their clothes and prove they're not suicide bombers.'

The explosives detection dog and its handler arived at the courtyard. The lads stayed well clear. Chances were high that the cache was booby-trapped with an IED to ward off coalition soldiers prodding at the mounds. But the Royals were one step ahead of the Taliban dickers. No Bootneck in his right mind would go anywhere near the cache until it had been cleared of explosives.

Coldrain found the situation distressing but he had very good reason to suspect that the weapons cache was buried in the graves. He'd never been so certain of anything in his life. There was no other logical explanation on the location of the stash. The absence of a crater in the ground merely confirmed his thoughts. Just because there might be a weapons cache in the village didn't mean the locals were on the side of the Taliban. In fact the opposite was true. A lot of Afghans couldn't wait for the Taliban to be booted out of their region. But as soon as their patrols left town, the locals were defenceless. That was when the Taliban made their move, threatening violence on anyone who dared talk to the coalition, or refused to let the Taliban use their home to store munitions.

Jamie was now ten metres from the burial site. The thin trees cast a sliver of a shadow over him. The bright cloths flapped in the mild breeze.

Belham returned with the translator, some Pashtun kid from the ANP who looked like he was ready to piss himself. His voice was shaking as he spoke. The kid could barely make himself audible above the hysterical crowd.

Coldrain and the 5 Troops lads pointed their guns at the crowd to get them to simmer down. They quietened. Funny the power an SA80 had over people. A few retreated into their homes. Others stood around but stayed quiet, scratching their elbows and muttering under their breath.

Coldrain thought about all the taxpayers safely tucked away in their semi-detacheds back home. He hoped they were enjoying Ant and Dec and tucking into a nice plate of fish and chips.

He glanced over his shoulder at Jamie. He was patrolling around the edge of a nearby compound. Checking out possible threats and managing the locals. Doing his job.

The next few seconds had become a blur in Coldrain's mind and it was difficult to separate them out. He could remember the dog handler confirming that there was a device around the weapons cache. Meaning they would need to Op Barma the site to clear the IED. Op Barma drills were painstakingly difficult and the guys in the team were among the bravest Coldrain had ever met. He was going to wish the Barma lads luck. But he never managed to finish the sentence. Midway through he felt a sudden belch of hot air behind him, and a fraction of a second later came the deafening sound of the explosion. The ground around Coldrain shook. Rocks and fist-sized clumps of dirt were blown past him like projectiles fired into the crowd.

Spinning around Coldrain dropped his rifle and was rushing towards the explosion. His heart sank when he saw where the smoke was coming from. The compound Reese had been adjacent to was obscured behind an expanding mushroom of debris and smoke billowed into the sky, blocking out the sunlight. It was oozing violently like a blackened thermal spring from the exact spot he had seen Jamie a moment earlier. He couldn't see him anywhere. It was like he'd spontaneously combusted.

Coldrain got to within fifteen metres of the compound before Belham grabbed a hold of him.

'Oh no you don't mate,' Belham said. 'Stay the fuck away!'

He struggled against his oppo's bear hug but deep down he knew his mucker was right. The Taliban used primary and secondary IEDs these days and there was a decent chance that Coldrain could get himself zapped as well if he ventured any closer to the explosion. Two birds, one stone.

As he was wrestled to the ground by Belham, he thought about the promise he'd made to Reese's mum to bring Jamie back home alive. He had let her down.

'Man down! Man down!' he heard Belham scream into his radio. 'Need immediate medevac, T1 casualty.' A T1 was the most critical type of casualty and indicated that the victim had an hour before they were browners. But every lad there knew the call was made out of protocol rather than hope. Jamie was zapped. Coldrain had seen explosions on patrols along the roads of Kandahar and Helmand and he knew the extent of the kill zone on such incendiary devices. There would be nothing left of his best mate.

Coldrain found himself looking back to the hill spot, where the two figures had been watching. He glimpsed their retreat, the two shadows sinking behind the other side of the hill, as the motorbikes sped off into the distance.

Most people's lives gradually get shittier over a prolonged period of time. Coldrain was able to pinpoint the exact moment when his life turned gash.

The effects of the rum began to wear off. Coldrain suddenly didn't feel like drinking any more. He screwed the top back on the bottle and dumped it back in the kitchen cupboard. Headed for the front door.

'Off already?' the old man asked.

Coldrain shrugged.

'Jamie's anniversary next week,' Mrs Reese said.

Other families, regular folk, had anniversaries for marriages or engagements or the birth of a kid. Mr and Mrs Reese had one for the day his best mate was incinerated by an IED hidden in a weapons cache thousands of miles from home, in the middle of a shit hole wadi in some godforsaken corner of Afghanistan.

Coldrain said nothing, slammed the door behind him and hit the road.